Dedication

This overgrown how-to manual is dedicated to my family in thanks for their patience and tolerance for all those evenings I was huddled in the basement tapping on a keyboard.

For Carol, Annika, Liisa, and Kelly; the four people for whom my love is completely unqualified.

IT COMES DOWN TO THIS

LEADERSHIP, MANAGEMENT AND
GETTING THERE FROM HERE

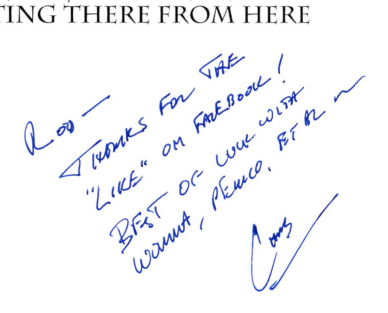

CHRIS KAUFMAN

Outskirts Press, Inc.
Denver, Colorado

Preface: It Comes Down to This

The Pamphlet that Grew

Think of this book as a job-aid that got out of hand. What started as a series of leadership and management concept papers grew to be a sort of general field guide for organizational leaders and managers. It is not exhaustive but it is a reasonably comprehensive set of concepts, instructions, and reminders for people who are in the position of leading and managing others. Managing your organization to success comes down to a few key things: You must understand the identity of your organization, what you are trying to achieve, and where you are starting. Once these are nailed down, a few major themes will help you on your path to success. You will find these themes flow throughout the pages of this book:

1. **Decision to succeed**: The most important element of success is your decision to do what is necessary;
2. **Connection**: You must connect your actions to your Definition of Success;
3. **Results:** You must achieve outcomes and results;
4. **Pay attention:** Listen, watch, and focus.
5. **Stick to the basics**: Most management reading and theory is akin to worrying about lead poisoning when you are shooting yourself in the head. Common sense, discipline, and fundamentals are your most valuable tools;
6. **Accountability:** You, your team, and your organization.

It does not Work Without You

If you are reading this, you are probably a leader or a manager in an organization. In your role, you may have encountered a segment of co-workers who feel what you do is unnecessary or, in some cases (such as Dilbert's pointy-haired manager), pretentious and laughable. Do not believe it and do not let it get you down. Know this: leadership and management are the only functions truly essential to the success of an organization. Without someone to discipline and shape it, the brilliance of technologists, actuaries, engineers, or artists is merely the babble of bright children. Leaders and managers transform potential into achievement.

When a team or organization grows larger than about ten people, the need emerges for management activities and operational structures. We require division of labor, common behavior expectations, and a shared vision. Otherwise, there is no team, just people milling around. The greatest generals, admirals, and rulers in the history of the world were also the great administrators and managers. Amateur historians look at battles; professional historians look at administration and logistics.

It is a plain fact; human organizations cannot succeed without what you do. Take pride and comfort in that.

It is your choice: You are as talented as they are

Beyond being critical to the success of any organization, leadership and management capability lie largely within the control of the individual. Success in this arena depends much more on your desire and decision to do what is necessary than your predetermined genetic makeup. If you choose to succeed you are probably as capable as most other people at achieving success.

There is no magic set of capabilities that differentiate an executive making $25 million a year from one making 99% less. The potential for success and the skills are roughly similar. Major United States corporations, universities, and some charities plead the need to pay ludicrously high salaries based on the competitive market for highly competent executives. Understand this: the excessively high compensation paid to executives in the United States has nothing to do with their competence or their ability to make their organizations successful. It has everything to do with maintaining the perquisites of the club. Those hiring and setting the compensation this week will be looking for jobs next week. The repeated and abject failure of American corporate leadership in the past 25 years, to the point of putting the largest economy in the world at risk of collapse, has had little or no restraining influence on executive compensation. Except in the minds of those receiving the whopper paycheck, there is little relationship between executive capability, performance, and compensation.

The lesson to take away from the foregoing mini-diatribe is simply this: you have every bit as much capability and likelihood of leading an organization to success as those making more than you by a factor of ten or a hundred. Don't be intimidated. Commit to success and you will probably find it.

About this Book

This book is divided into three major sections: *Leadership, Management,* and *Getting There*. The first section focuses on the characteristics, capabilities, and behaviors of successful leaders. The second section discusses the mechanics and imperatives of managing an organization. The third section is about the nuts-and bolts of visioning, planning, and executing the ongoing process of change and growth necessary for healthy, long-lived organizations. In real life there is no bright line between these three facets of a successful organization and there is none in this book. You will find repetition of key items in different areas, usually from a slightly different point of view depending on the topic under discussion. I chose to repeat some items when they became relevant to the topic rather than ask you to flip back to a previous chapter.

Many sections start with a story or an example of the point to be discussed. In earlier readings of this material, the stories were the favorite part of many reviewers. I hope you enjoy them. There are few citations or references. There is opinionated commentary. It is full of my own opinions, prejudices, and experience.

Readers may notice an area that received little focused discussion: managing people. Although it is a subtext throughout the entire book, it does not get its own extensive breakout. It is clearly identified in several sections but as a topic is larger than I felt could be handled in the vignette framework of this work. I hope to deal with it in a comprehensive way in a future work.

There is no need to read this book cover-to-cover. Each section can be read as an individual paper. Very few of the readings are more than eight pages. I have tried to arrange the Table of Contents to help you quickly locate the topic you are looking for or need advice on.

Finally, there is no need to agree with me on anything. Make up your own mind. You are the person on the ground and you are the best judge of the right course of action. Here you will find the results of 25 years of observed behavior and paying attention to what works and what does not. Most of what you will read is tried and true and you will not go wrong if you follow the path I have described.

Thanks for taking the time to read a little of what I have to say.

Chris Kaufman
Seattle, Washington, USA
September, 2011

Contents

Introduction

The researches of many commentators have already thrown much darkness on this subject, and it is probable that if they continue we shall soon know nothing at all about it.

– Mark Twain

Management for the Rest of Us

Managing to Success

THIS BOOK IS about managing to success. Note the use of the words "to success" rather than "for success." The change of this single tiny preposition is the basis of much of the discussion to follow. In these pages I take the position that, in order to succeed in a deliberate and intentional way, you will need to not only do the right thing (often called "managing for success"), you will also need to be sure you have tied those actions to the success you want to achieve. You will need to create line-of-sight from your activities to your desired outcomes.

There are three elements required if you want to achieve success in a deliberate fashion rather than by luck or happenstance:

- Leadership
- Management
- Getting it Done (Operations and Change)

Understanding and mastering these three elements gives you the ability to control your present and achieve your desired future.

Managing to success does not guarantee success. There are no guarantees and there is no magic formula to assure you will succeed. A large number of the variables that can impact your chances of success are outside your control. However, not as many are outside your control as fear or aversion might make you think.

Let's take a moment to give it up to those who need to hear the following statement: There are things you cannot control that can determine your future. You cannot be accountable for items that are outside your control. Agreed! Now that we understand that, we can move on.

This book is about taking control of what you can and managing the elements which increase the odds you will succeed.

Success without Great Management

To be clear, there can be great success without great or even good management. In fact, most organizations which experience a phenomenal growth can attribute this success to something other than good management. The factors that most often cause success in the absence of great management are:

- First to market and timing
- Unique innovation
- Intimidation and ruthlessness
- Lack of competition
- Luck

While the advantage lasts, these companies are the darlings of Wall Street and the business writers. The organizational fat and cash flow generated by the initial bloom are often mistaken for strong management and leadership. Organizations that experience early and logarithmic success will often see a serious dip in performance once the initial advantage peters out. At that point it becomes a question of whether they have the management chops to create a sustainable business. Examples of companies that fall into the fast-growth-masters-of-the-universe category include:

- **AOL**: No recovery
- **Netscape**: Who?
- **Ford:** Surprised? Hubris over the Model T caused Henry to lose half his market share between 1920 and 1926. Partially recovered with the Model A
- **Microsoft** – Great run with dominant major OS, brilliant distribution strategy, and an anal-retentive primary competitor. Still trying to figure out who they are. We will see

- **Starbucks** – We will see

Success is success, however, and no one should degrade the accomplishments of an innovation-driven or even a luck-driven win. The trick is to not succumb to the temptation to believe the cheerleaders who bestow corporate industry awards (often little more than recipient purchased designations) and the stock market. The halo of innovation or luck-driven success can be easily internalized as brilliant management.

Success through Great Management

Organizations with great management can usually be spotted by a track record of success interlaced with dips in results as they hit and work their way through periodic challenges. Some of them have a period of phenomenal growth in their history and they manage to become solid, value-driven companies as they emerge from their ingénue phase. Winning over real challenges and threats are the strengthening exercises that build the depth and knowledge required to grow and thrive when you are no longer the darling of Wall Street.

Examples of organizations that have grown and thrived through solid management practices and consistently doing what needs to be done include:

- General Electric
- Comcast
- Honda Motor Company
- Toyota Motor Corporation
- Nike
- McDonalds

Most of us will not be blessed with a growth curve shaped like a hockey stick at any time in our organization's history. If we are to be successful, we will make it happen through consciously deciding to do what is necessary. We will manage all of the elements required to achieve a successful outcome. We all live at the crossing point of proactive and reactive activity. We handle all of the things we can and connect today's actions with tomorrow's results. We take one step at a time and we keep moving. That is what great management is all about.

The Elements of Success

The Keys to Success

MANAGING AN ORGANIZATION to success is holistic. It requires organizational focus and awareness to assemble all the pieces of the puzzle to create, not only a successful operational entity, but one that can move predictably into the future. It is complex and there is no cook book available to give you the answers. There will be competing demands for resources and priorities. You will never have enough money or skilled people to do everything you need to do. Your native intelligence and skills will be your primary weapons as you fight the good fight.

There is a popular bumper-sticker that says: "Think Globally. Act Locally." In many ways your success depends on adopting a similar mind set. You must think strategically and act tactically. You must plan and govern to connect strategy and tactics. But be clear on this; all the elements of the picture are necessary:

- Without strategy, you can't design your tactics
- Without tactics you will can't achieve your strategy
- Without operational execution, neither strategy or tactics matter because the life of your enterprise will be short and unpleasant

Or, to put it another way:

- If you do not have a good product, it can kill you.
- If you have a good product but cannot sell it, it can kill you.
- If you can sell it but cannot make it effectively, it can kill you.

- If you can make it and sell it but cannot collect the money, it can kill you.
- If you can do all the above but cannot retain your staff, it can kill you.

Enterprises must be competent, not only in the core elements of their mission, they must also have the ability to create and maintain the management infrastructure that surrounds and supports that mission.

Failure in business (whether for-profit or non-profit) almost never occurs in the core and essence of the enterprise. Most businesses have a reasonable degree of core competence. They are pretty good at what they do, whether it is making bread, issuing insurance policies, or manufacturing computers. Most failures occur in the management structures surrounding the core business.

There is, however, good news.

The Good News

The first piece of good news for you is this: the vast majority of the things that impact your ability to succeed or will cause you to fail are identifiable, controllable, and related to common sense more than esoteric domain knowledge. Inevitably, it is not the core subject of an organization that goes bad. It is the surrounding management infrastructure that fails. In other words, the concepts covered in this book are the areas in which you see most organizations challenged. Just to carry the point a bit further, the concepts found in this book, the concepts which will determine your ability to succeed, are industry-neutral; they are the common points of excellence and failure across all industries.

The Rest of the Good News
A Simple Framework for Perspective and Focus

Although above we said managing to success is a complex puzzle, the concepts are not complicated. Everything you need to do can be reduced to a single picture on a single page. If, as a leader, you can keep this picture in your mind's eye, you will be able to anchor yourself in the context of your entire enterprise. When dealing with opportunities, challenges, disappointments, victories, and catastrophes, you will have the ability to stand above the vortex of churning activities and emotions and see the full picture. You will give today's urgent challenge its proper weight and, more importantly, you will have a method to keep an eye on all of the things that must be executed in order to achieve success.

And it is not that hard

You will form a habit of thinking of your organization as an integrated entity. An effective organization is like an orchestra rather than a convergence of competing priorities. When good management habits become ingrained, you will find you think like a conductor or a coach rather than a traffic cop. You will perceive and guide the activities of your team members in such a way they are not simply parallel but cooperative and interlaced. Although you will delve into details with your team, you will do it with a continual awareness of the bird's eye view of the organization. You will develop a gut-level need to complete the equation that balances operations with product with technology with expense management.

Working within the framework of an integrated organization and focusing on results is not that difficult and will improve both your life and the lives of the people in your organization. You will discover as you approach your organization in this way, it becomes dramatically simpler to manage and keep focused on where you are going. Your approach to your staff and to problem solving takes on the discipline of thinking in context of outcomes rather than activities. Much of the fog of day-to-day decision-making melts away as the culture of your organization consistently treats activities as a means to an end and everything you do is seen in light of the way it impacts the line-of-sight to your Definition of Success. Expectations of performance become normal and measured in terms of results. Your team and the rest of the organization become culturalized to perceive and discuss activities in those terms. Marketing results are discussed in terms of prospects attracted and brought to a purchase moment rather than CLIO Awards or cuteness. Branding moves beyond name recognition to become facilitator of call-to-action. Products are discussed in terms of purchase and repeat purchase rather than features and benefits.

Stripping away the chaff to lay bare activities in terms of their contribution organizational outcome, has the dual advantage of being reasonably straight forward and making management simpler.

Managed Success Framework

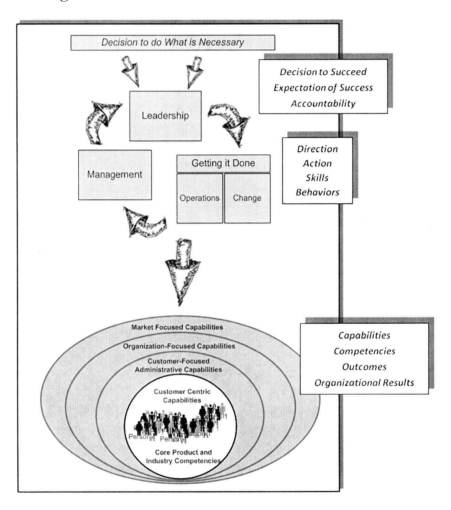

Reduction to Simplicity

You can adopt a simple management framework that allows you to lead, manage, and govern the interdependent elements of your business. The pieces of a Managed Success Framework are pretty basic and track to the above diagram. In a nutshell:

- **Decision to Succeed**
  - ○ **What is it?** This is the individual and corporate commitment to doing what is necessary to succeed.
  - ○ **What does it do?** Sets the expectations for you and your team. You will succeed and you have accepted accountability for making that happen. It places accountability squarely in terms of achievement of results. It clearly delineates between activities and outcomes. It clarifies discussions with your staff and your teams.
  - ○ **What characteristics does it have?** It must be public and visible. It must apply across the board. It is fairly unforgiving in terms of allowing back-sliding or inconsistencies. Once you have made and publicized a commitment, you better hold yourself and your team accountable as your account of trust and integrity will not tolerate many withdrawals.
- **Direction**
  - ○ **What is it?** These are the skills and behaviors which shepherd the organization and provide the firm hand on the tiller. There are three primary elements in the direction tier:
    - ▪ **Leadership:** It is about leading. It means, when you look over your shoulder people are following you. It means, through some method other than coercion or outright bribery, you have managed to get people to do what you want them to do. It means you have in some way established confidence and trust that allows people to believe you will take them where they need to go.
    - ▪ **Management:** The mechanics of effectively running a group of people, whether an informal gathering, a team, or a corporation.
    - ▪ **Getting it Done:** The management and governance capabilities around controlling and directing

- □ Current operational results (it must run effectively in the here and now)
- □ Organizational change (planning and execution)
  - ○ **What does it do?** It is simple really. It's all the stuff that makes sure, as an organization, we are performing today and preparing for tomorrow. It isn't the team; it is the *leadership and direction guiding the team* which enables it to deliver the best performance it can. It's the coach on the sidelines. It's the principal of a school. It is the CEO committed to performance.
  - ○ **What characteristics does it have?** It is usually neutral in regard to the industry or product. The lion's share of the work and capabilities at this tier are not related to the enterprise core ideas and subject.
- **Organizational Results, Outcomes, Capabilities, and Competencies:**
  - ○ **What is it?** These are the things your organization must be able to do and achieve in order to survive and thrive. These organizational characteristics encompass the full spectrum of things an enterprise must balance to be a complete and healthy entity with repeatable and predictable success. They run from internal to external, from skills to results:
    - ▪ **Customer-Centric Capabilities**. These are the things you went into business to do. They are the core capabilities of your mission; the ability to imagine, produce, and deliver our product. Examples:
      - □ If you are in the restaurant business, it is having an eatery open on a regular, predictable schedule and providing your customers the food they want in the way they find desirable.
      - □ If you are in the clothing business, it is the ability to deliver attractive and desirable goods consumers will want to purchase and wear.
    - ▪ **Customer-Focused Administrative Capabilities**. These are the administrative activities that directly touch the customer and are necessary but do not fall in the realm of

end product or service. These are things you do because they support the use of your product or otherwise support your primary customers. They are things you would not do if they were not required to support your core business. Examples:

- □ Creating and sending bills.
- □ Medical providers and pharmacies directly interacting with insurance companies to submit and process claims

- **Organizational-Focused Capabilities**. These are all the things which do not have a direct impact on the customer but which are nonetheless necessary. They are the skills and abilities that are usually neutral in respect to your core mission. This category has the widest spectrum of capabilities. Examples include:
  - □ Financial management & budgeting
  - □ Expense control
  - □ Hiring and personnel practices
  - □ Information technology management
  - □ Maintaining a facility and providing work space

- **Market-Focused Capabilities**. This is the ability to tell your story and attract customers. It is the mechanism which facilitates the recognition of your product and its value by potential customers. It results in their crossing your threshold in a frame of mind that gives you the opportunity to sell your product. Branding and marketing efforts that do not result in the arrival of potential customers with the willingness to listen and buy should be abandoned. Examples include:
  - □ Marketing
  - □ Advertising
  - □ Brand development
  - □ Public relations
  - □ Corporate communications

A Really Important Reminder: The world isn't tidy

If you are hoping for a recipe for success, you will not find it here or anywhere else. Leadership, management, planning, and the spectrum of capabilities discussed in this book are all connected parts of a single functioning and effective entity. They are interdependent and their integration is what makes an organization work. A car needs an engine and tires, as well as a transmission to connect them. If one is missing, the car will not move. If they are not seamlessly working together, it will be a very rough ride.

Leadership is not discrete or separated from management by a bright line. Both disciplines are part of planning, execution, and operations. As you read, you will find management concepts in the leadership section and vice versa. Do not wig out. In fact, if they are not part of one another, they may be intellectually interesting, but they will not be very effective. That is why books on leadership often leave you feeling good but unsure what to do next. Leadership without execution may be inspiring but is more about adrenaline than effectiveness. To make progress, you need both inspiration and the ability to carry water. Accept the fact that the lessons discussed here will not be stand alone morsels but will blend into one another.

Finally; In Just a Few Lines

The framework described above is simple enough to understand though often difficult to manage. It can, however, be recapped in a very few lines:

Do what you need to do:
- Make the decision to succeed
- Lead and manage your organization conscientiously
- Find the key organizational outcomes, skills, and capabilities and make sure they are covered.

Once you have made the decision to do what is necessary, you are ready to use the concepts that follow, to deliberately manage your organization to success.

Leadership

The only proof of successful leadership is the behavior of those the leader presumes to lead. Without followers, a leader is simply a person standing at the front of the crowd.

Leaders Lead

Leadership Looks Like. . .

LEADERSHIP IS A quality that is both elusive and hard to define. If you ask a strong leader to explain leadership, they will usually become frustrated as they try to put it into words. They will, more often than not, scratch their head and then list a few items specifically important to them. It seldom tells the story. The problem is leadership has many faces and forms. It can be handsome or homely, good or bad. However, leadership always displays two characteristics: leaders and followers.

When I was a kid, we were members of a parish in a small Virginia town. Our pastor was responsible for three churches and every Sunday he drove his battleship Plymouth to three services before noon. Those old German Lutherans wanted value for their dollar. But Pastor knew them inside out and he could play them like a piano. They hated being in debt. When we needed a new Sunday school building, he sweet talked them into borrowing the money. Then he rode them about the debt and they paid it off in a few years. The old church building is falling apart? Dig a debt hole for the remodel then ask the congregation why the hole is so deep. Through thirty years he led them though the cycle of debt and payment. But, he undeniably led them. Leadership takes many forms. His methods were not everyone's cup of tea but he left a vibrant, healthy parish for the next generation.

If you are a Leader you must Lead

Leaders lead. Leadership is about leading. It means, when you look over your shoulder people are following you. It means, through some method other than coercion or outright bribery, you have managed to get people to do what you want them to do.

Be careful! We often tend to imbue "Leadership" with goodness. Do not confuse leadership with values, integrity, honesty, or even doing the right thing. Great leaders may or may not listen to other people. They may or may not be leading in a morally right direction. They may or may not be inspirational. They may or may not develop those around them. They may be heroic or despicable. The one thing they can do, however, is take a group of people and, through a mysterious mix of logic, fear, pride, rhetoric, and playing on emotions, make them move in the direction the leader wants and accomplish what is desired.

Leaders create the stress necessary for an organization to avoid becoming flabby. All human enterprises need stress in order to survive. Stress and discomfort are the agents of progress and achievement. Without the stress created by change, bureaucratic operational machinery will spin along in a comfortable groove until it wears a hole in the carpet and gives up from sheer boredom. Spinning, however, is loaded with inertia. It resists change. In an organization not in crisis, a leader creates the path to the future that walks a balance between the limits of tolerance for change and the vision of a new place worth stretching for.

In a crisis, a leader makes the choices necessary to mold the organization into a team able to confront challenges to survival.

Being the president of a company does not make you a leader any more than calling yourself a comedian makes you funny. The audience defines the comedian. Followers define the leader.

The most effective leadership is seen when institutional authority is combined with individual leadership ability. In fact, if a person is given institutional authority but cannot bring to bear individual leadership capability, the organization tends to suffer inordinately. Not only are the tough decisions unlikely to be made nor the difficult actions taken, the suit that fills the chair blocks others from taking necessary actions. It becomes a slow and sad spiral into mediocrity.

Like nearly everything else, being a good leader is dependent on a decision. You must decide if you will do what is necessary to put your team on the track to your chosen future. In the coming articles, we talk about the elements of effective leadership. Understand, however, leadership is a mysterious mix. The key to success is your native intelligence, commitment, and desire to lead.

At any rate, remember this: leaders lead. Let's get on with it.

The Leader and the Led

Responsible Leadership and the Contract

The Joy and Burden of Leadership

LEADERSHIP IS A value-neutral skill. Self-seeking scoundrels can be dandy leaders. They are probably not the sort of people you want to hang out with, but they can be great leaders. Most people who aspire to leadership are driven to be responsible and positive as well as effective. This leadership concept is about the responsibility and accountability of leaders and is particularly aimed at those who want to lead.

For those who enjoy leadership, there is nothing like it in the human experience. Being an effective leader is a feeling unlike any other. Whether it is command of a squadron or a department store, it provides a glorious and heady sense of control and, if you are truly a dedicated leader, involves some loss of self. You and your organization become in a sense, one entity. Herman Wouk said it well in his book, *The Caine Mutiny*:

> . . . *Willie experienced the strange sensations of the first days of a new captain: a shrinking of his personal identity and a stretching out of his nerve ends to all the spaces of the ship. He was less free than before. He developed the apprehensive listening ears of a young mother; the ears listened in his sleep; he never quite slept, not the way he had before.*

Leadership is a joy, a burden, and a responsibility. Read on.

The Leader, the Led, and the Value Exchange

Leadership comes in many shapes and sizes. However, the most admired and effective leadership in our humanistic age of instant communications, world-class successes, and spectacular failures is built around responsibility, constructive positive actions, *and* is results-driven. It is also characterized by a relationship between the leader and the led that can be imagined in the terms of a contract. Like all contracts, it is based on a value exchange. Each party is required to provide certain things and each party is provided with certain benefits. The effectiveness of the contract is grounded on the integrity of the promise and the ability to deliver. Those who are led must believe in those who presume to lead.

The Leader

It is the responsibility of the leader to:

- **Understand the Role**: A leader is not a bystander. The leader is visible and, especially in tough times, cannot be on vacation or otherwise missing in action. If it works or doesn't work, the leader is the lion or the turkey. Either way, the leader must stand up and take responsibility. If you win you get respect. If you lose with accountability – you still get respect (shocker).

- **Cause Success**: It is that simple. If the organization does not succeed while the leader is at the helm, that person must step aside and they should do it before someone else tells them to. If you are the leader your organization must succeed or you must give someone else a chance.

- **Cut through the Tangled Knot:** You must be able to distill muddy issues down to their essence. An effective leader looks for and deals with root causes, even if it is painful. A leader knows small victories can be the biggest enemy. Focusing on a tangential win at the expense of fundamental issues can leave you with shiny brass on a sinking ship.

- **Control and guide their Organization and their Staff**: Repeat after me, "We are an accountable team. We are an accountable team. We are an accountable TEAM. We are. . ." Your team needs to be at work, be visible, know the current business state of their function, and be accountable for results. At 2:30 on any given Friday afternoon in August can you shoot a cannonball through the executive suite without hurting anyone? If the executives are all on their way to lake homes while the hoi polloi remain at their desks, they are taking advantage of their position rather than being leaders.

- **Model Behavior**: The behavior of the leader is the primary guiding example for the rest of the organization. The leader's behavior and results set the standard. If the leader makes commitments and does not meet them, the rest of the team will do likewise. If the leader displays little concern for performance, poor performance will become the standard. If the leader is not worried about expense management, no one else will be either. This topic is discussed at greater length in the section titled, "Culture Never Sleeps."

- **Achieve the Leadership Bottom Line:** It is the job of the leader to do what is necessary to ensure the success of the organization. It is a pretty simple concept.

In return the leader gets:

- Freedom of action
- Lots of control
- Usually the best pay check
- The gratification of succeeding
- The support of their staff and organization
- To be the boss

The Led

It is the responsibility of the led to:

- **Support**: The leader and the organization
- **Accommodate**: Relinquish some freedom of action
- **Be a team player**: The team members are not the leaders of the team although they may display leadership characteristics and they may lead teams of their own. Team members understand they are subordinate to team leaders.

In return the Led get:

- **Success**: The team has the right to expect success. The leader, on accepting or assuming the role has an obligation to craft the team's success.
- **A Job**: AKA: Not laid-off if they are performing and providing value.
- **Survival**: An organization that survives and thrives.

The value exchange is complete. The leader has flexibility, power, and freedom of action. In exchange, he or she is required to lead us to success.

Quis custodiet ipsos custodes?

What happens when things go wrong? Plato asked that question to Socrates. Juvenal crafted it into a poem in his *Satires*. Lisa Simpson asked Homer Simpson:

Who will protect us against the protectors?

We invest power and discretion in our leaders. We trust them to use it in a professional and ethical way to achieve the goals with which they have been chartered. It is a responsibility similar to that of police officers, who have the option of using force to protect the public and themselves. It is similar to the trust you give your auto mechanic to fix only the things that need fixing. We cannot watch everything. We know it is necessary to have this trust in order to do the job. We therefore trust that actions taken out of our sight will be done correctly.

If the leader is not performing or abuses the trust of an orgnization, who is guarding us against the guardian? If an executive is selling stock while cooking the books. If an executive is taking home bonuses while his company is shrinking or losing money. If a President is abusing the power of his office. Who steps in?

In our corporate system, our justice system, and our political system, we have tools and mechanisms designed specifically to both allow effective autonomous leadership as well as provide oversight. Corporations are required to have a Board of Directors. The Board is legally mandated with assuring responsible management of the company. If the Board of Directors is doing its job, it will hold the management team accountable for the success of the company and will act to change management if a company is in trouble and being mismanaged. Politically, we have the separation of powers and the universal franchise. We, the citizens, can vote the rascals out of office. In the end, however, the guardians who watch the guardians must understand their roles, take them seriously, and be willing to do their duty. The toolkit exists if we are willing to use it.

Characteristics of Leaders

And other traits that are often confused with those characteristics

WHEN PEOPLE TALK about leaders and leadership, they often feel compelled to document distinguishing leadership traits. It's *Cosmo* sort of a thing. Make a list of key characteristics or, better yet, create a quiz. Beyond the obvious entertainment value of comparing yourself to the "ideal," there are good reasons to understand the traits and capabilities of a good leader. You may need to hire someone for a leadership role. You may be challenged in a leadership role yourself. You may have a boss struggling with his role and you are trying to understand why. Awareness of effective leadership characteristics and the reasons leaders may stumble can come in handy.

One of the problems we frequently see is the tendency to mix up leadership characteristics with leadership techniques and skills and, in turn, these with general effectiveness capabilities. Characteristics are part of the make-up of the individual. These are usually born in the person although they can be developed and refined. Techniques and skills define a thing you are able to do. Integrity is a characteristic. Defining a vision is a skill.

In this section, we discuss leadership characteristics. In the next section, we will discuss leadership skills.

Leadership is defined by the led

Not to sound like a broken record, but leadership is about your impact on others. As we said before, it means when you look over your shoulder, people are following you. It means you have managed to get people to do what you want them to do. In terms of effective leadership, your feelings and behaviors are meaningless except in the context of the team you are leading. You cannot be a leader without followers.

An important concept to remember: Those you propose to lead have nothing on which to base their decision to follow or not beyond what they can observe. The concept of the "real you" is irrelevant to your leadership effectiveness. Your team cannot read your mind. If your organization is in a grave situation and you take an extended vacation to Hawaii because you have done everything you can do for the moment, you had better make darn sure your team understands what is going on. Leadership is perception.

Successful leadership is dependent upon seeing leadership characteristics, as opposed to you knowing they are buried deep inside. Consistently displaying these traits is like depositing money in the bank. It gives you an account of dependable credibility to draw upon when you need to make tough and unpopular decisions, or decisions for which the value is not immediately apparent.

Leadership Characteristics

Excellent leaders will display a majority of the following traits:

Confidence: Leaders have confidence in their ability to make things happen. They display confidence in themselves and their organization. They rely on their abilities and the abilities of their staff to do what needs to be done. It really does not matter if they know at this moment *how* it will happen; they are simply comfortable they *can* make it happen.

Strength: Good leaders display strength and backbone in their dealings. They are accountable for tough decisions and they do not shy away from dealing with root causes or necessary confrontations. They are visible when times are tough. They do not disappear into their offices, to board meetings, industry conferences, or community events when they should be with their team.

Need to Succeed: Leaders are driven to succeed. They understand failure, they know it is sometimes unavoidable, but they hate it. They display an internal drive for success that is palpable. It can be felt by those around them.

Trust and Believability: Those around and dependent on the leader must be able to trust in what the leader says and know he or she will live up to commitments. They must trust and believe their leader can get them where they need to be. A leader cannot be perceived as dissembling. They cannot parse words in order to present a limited picture as a convincing argument. Not to put too fine a point on it, but using a partial truth as cover is *lying*. Obfuscation is lying. Lying is a leadership killer. Very important note: Trust and believability should not to be confused with honesty or moral integrity.

Purpose: Leaders cannot waffle. They must be perceived as consistently driving to a clear and desirable outcome. Do your actions match your words? If a leader allows a disconnection between actions and words, it creates distrust and worse, ridicule.

Pride in Competence: If people are going to follow you, they must feel like you know what you are doing and are capable of pulling it off. They also need to perceive you understand the business you are in.

Other Characteristics Often Confused with Leadership Traits

There are some characteristics that are desirable but not part and parcel of a leader's essence. Leaders can get by quite effectively without one or more of the following. In general, they tend to help, but they are not required:

Listens: Leaders can be self-absorbed, ego-driven maniacs and still be pretty effective. You need go no further than your local political arena to find sterling examples. Again, do not confuse listening with awareness and use of pertinent information. The characteristic and skill of listening to others and getting advice may or may not be part of a leader's personal inventory.

Honesty: Nope. Not necessary as long as those needing to follow you can depend on your follow-through.

Intelligence: High intelligence is a nice thing to have. Thinking too much or too deeply, however, can actually get in the way of being an effective leader. Purposeful behavior can actually be undermined by too many qualifications:

We will be the number one provider of widgets in 2010. Unless of course there is an earthquake. Or, a power outage. Or. . .

It waters down the impact a bit, doesn't it?

Leadership Capabilities

The Skills of Successful Leaders

Leadership, Raymond Spruance, and Midway – A Story

EARLY IN JUNE of 1942, one of the most important battles in the history of the world was fought and won by a beleaguered United States Navy at Midway Atoll in the Pacific. Raymond Spruance, a junior flag officer, was in command of the battle though he had no experience commanding aviators and he was outclassed by the commanders of his Japanese opponent. The man who should have been in command, Bill Halsey, flamboyant and aggressive, was hospitalized with a skin disease.

Spruance displayed the skills of a great leader that day. He also had great good luck. But luck without decisive action is just cosmic vibration.

Spruance was dealing with a Halsey staff that had little respect for the quiet man from surface ships. He had to countermand Miles Browning, Halsey's opinionated and truculent Chief of Staff, several times during the day.

The launch of a coordinated attack was botched by green flight crews and Spruance had to make a command decision it was better to hit quickly, even if it was not coordinated. He took a shot from the hip.

Through luck or divine intervention, the U.S. attack waves arrived in exactly the opposite order intended. By plan, dive-bombers distract the ships and the defensive air cover to allow the slow-moving torpedo planes to approach and deliver a punch to the gut. Torpedoes are deadly but their launch required a slow, low, vulnerable approach. The torpedo squadrons stumbled on the Japanese Fleet first. Displaying nerve and courage that still evokes hushed awe; the kids in the lumbering TBD-1s knowingly flew into a hopeless attack and were almost totally slaughtered by the best fighter planes then on the planet: the Mitsubishi Zero. Not a single torpedo hit its target or if it did, it did not detonate. They did, however, draw the Japanese Zeros providing air cover down to the wave-tops. At that moment, with precise timing that was completely accidental, Dauntless dive-bombers from the *Enterprise* and the *Yorktown* found the fleet and heeled over into their dive formation. In six minutes the balance of world history changed. Four days later the Japanese had lost four carriers. They never recovered.

Finally, after inflicting a severe blow to the Japanese navy, Spruance backed off and posted his task force in a position to protect Midway rather than chase a wounded enemy. He was roundly criticized for timidity. But it turned out to be a really good idea. Had Spruance taken the bait, Admiral Yamamoto was waiting to ambush the American task force with the most powerful battleships on the planet.

One more example of leadership happened the night after the initial attack. Spruance's planes were flying back after dark and they had no experience with night carrier operations. They were desperately low on fuel and the kids flying them were exhausted. Despite blackout conditions and the danger from submarines and surface ships, Spruance turned on the blazing carrier deck lights until the last plane was hooked. It was a courageous decision in a balance of competing needs.

Raymond Spruance showed himself to be a great leader. To this day, we live in a world shaped and impacted by his leadership.

Go through the above and see how many leadership skills you can identify.

The Leadership Toolkit

In order to be an effective leader, there are certain things you will need to be able to do; certain capabilities you must have in your toolkit. These capabilities and skills, along with the characteristics we discussed before, are the raw materials that build the bond of confidence and trust your team needs. Your personal traits and capabilities inspire people to follow and support you. That support and the desire to achieve will generate success. Success reinforces the behavior of your team and validates their faith in you. In turn, they are willing to give you even more support. You can inspire your team to the next level of achievement. Without depth of character and capability, your likelihood of delivering as a leader becomes less and less likely. When that happens, a leader dwindles to a title.

There's good news, though. These are things you can learn and develop. These are things you control. What are these magical capabilities? What must you be able to do? Read on.

Leadership Skills and Capabilities

Good leaders will develop a majority of the following skills. You need to be able to:

- **Read the Signs.** You must pay attention and make connections. As the leader, you will not be intimate with the details of all situations within your span of accountability. You need to watch for flags that trigger questions. In a conversation, is someone choosing their words too carefully? Are disparate events or comments intersecting which might be connected (Tom said something – plus – a project delay – plus – customer complaint – equals: freight train coming down the tracks directly at your nose). Note anomalies and patterns. Ask questions.
- **Get to the Root Cause.** Leaders find the root cause. They may be forced initially to mitigate symptoms to buy time or stop bleeding, but they will root out the underlying cause and deal with it. In their discovery process, they seek to close the logical loop. If there are holes in explanations or reasoning, they challenge the team and persevere until they have filled them.
- **Deal with Unpleasant Things**. No one likes to deal with unpleasant situations. However, if the leader does not display the courage

to take on the hard stuff, the culture will adopt the same behavior. You will sometimes need to confront others; sometimes even your friends. You can be sure, at some point as a leader, you will be required to make a decision between friendship and doing the right thing. You will discipline and probably fire people. You will sometimes be the bad guy and take the blame. A leader who cannot deal with the unpleasant parts of his or her job rapidly moves from supportive to enabling and from enabling to irrelevant.

- **Make Decisions with Inadequate Information**. You will not always have the luxury of having all the facts and data you would like to make an informed decision. Too bad; figure it out. That is why you get the leather chair. Here is some advice: Reduce and screen. Eliminate as much extraneous noise as you can. Find the key points (less than ten) and see how many you can nail down. Based on the facts you have, your experience, and your intuition, just make the call. Then stop flapping your hands and get a good night's sleep. Remember *Occam's Razor*: *All things being equal, the simplest solution is probably the right one.* (Note: this topic is discussed at length in a later chapter)

- **Create a Vision**. A leader, by definition, is taking people somewhere. You must create a vision your team can rally around. There must be a worthwhile destination.

- **Stay at the Right Level**. Leaders must focus on their mission and achieving their objectives. They must be able to drive their organization. If they become bogged down in a mechanism (such as Six-Sigma, ITIL, Process Engineering, or even expense control) they can lose the connection to the end-game. Remind yourself and your staff: it is the achievement of our Definition of Success that matters. Our actions and decisions must be connected and contribute to that end.

- **Display Comfort with Ambiguity**. Leaders cannot let ambiguity get under their skin. You are the leader. Often there will be nothing in front of you but wide-open ocean and no obvious path to follow. You must know you will be able to figure it out. Notice the word, "Display." The observation of calm behavior is more important than how you feel inside. Your team will pick up on your behavior and remain calm as well. Number one rule in a typhoon: Stay calm. It is panic not hurricanes that sink ships.

- **Recover from Setbacks**. Like Mom said: when you fall down, stand up, brush yourself off, and try again. Persistence is the engine of inspiration. Leaders know that initial setbacks are common and often precede great victories.
- **Enforce Accountability**. If you do not do it, no one else will. Your organization will become dull and flaccid.

Skill not Genetics

The skills and capabilities listed here can be learned. They are disciplines and techniques you can develop and improve. With repetition and practice your brain develops "muscle memory" and they become increasingly natural and effective. Having them in your leadership toolkit is a function of desire and willingness rather than genetics. Make the decision to use them and then work at it.

Decision Making and Triage

Cutting your Losses – A Story

IN THE LATE 1980s, I worked for a company during and after a critical system implementation and data conversion. To put a finer point on it: I was the manager in charge of the project. It did not go well. Those were the pioneering days of large software system conversions. Many of the business systems in place, across all industries, were the original applications created for the early mainframes. The idea of a "personal computer" was still not a widely understood concept. The Intel 386 chip was the newest and fastest gizmo on the block. The very first Commodore Amiga and the IBM PS/2 were state of the art. Businesses requiring robust computing used mainframes. Portable storage was tape or big floppy disks. Our conversion was from a first-generation IBM application which had been around so long it had passed out of copyright.

After the conversion, we took a major hit in our ability to service business. For nearly a year, our daily production output was lower than the incoming. As any service manager will tell you, that is a recipe for disaster. We fell further and further behind the power curve. We continued to work in the only way we knew how; we persisted in operating on a First-In-First-Out basis. The flaw in our reasoning becomes rapidly obvious. Even after we increased our production to the level needed to support our ongoing operations, we continued to create new service issues every day because the incoming requests entered the queue at the end.

What to do?

In the end, we decided to accept the fact several thousand of our customers had received unacceptable service, but the deed was done. We were unwilling to continue to initiate bad service to more customers so we cut our losses. We picked up the backlog of several thousand service requests and physically removed them from the departments. We told the department supervisors they were starting with a clean slate and, under penalty of flogging, they better stay current.

The backlog was placed in a small conference room. We put a focused team on the clean-up job with instructions to pay special attention to abject apologies and accommodation for problems we had caused.

The decision made in this case was to run the risk already disgruntled customers would become more disgruntled in order to cap the problem and allow us to dig out. Additionally, it created the opportunity for mental recovery for our service teams, to remove the most obvious symbol of the nightmarish conversion, and give us the chance to move on.

It was not a great solution but it was the best we could devise given the circumstances. It was a difficult call among bad choices. But, it created a plan of action and put a stake in the ground as a starting point for our next phase.

The Fiber of Leadership

There are a relative few things that define the essence of a leader. The ability to make decisions is one of them.

Turn Right? Turn Left? Decisions Every Second

We make decisions nearly every moment of every day. We make tiny decisions: whether to use a pen or a pencil; whether to turn on the light or walk though the kitchen in the dark to get a glass of water. We decide what to eat, what to wear, and what route to take to work. Our days are filled with decisions. We make most of them nearly instantaneously, usually without being aware of what we are doing. Lest we take this for granted, however, it is this ability to evaluate opportunities and the relative merits of various courses of action that allow us to move through our days and lives with a reasonable degree of progress. Without this ability (it can be lost to certain types of dementia or brain damage) we can become paralyzed and unable to decide to turn right or left. It is a sophisticated autopilot mechanism that most of us have.

The Breakout Skill of Leadership Decisions

The types of decisions that demand leadership fall into a few basic categories. It is these types of decisions that make the leader different from the follower. The major decision types are:

- Decisions that are difficult but obvious
- Decisions with inadequate information
- Decisions with no good choices
- Decisions under pressure

Difficult but Obvious Decisions

Most often, these decisions require a leader to do something un-popular. They are usually necessary when things are not going well. Examples include: expense control, reductions in force, discipline or replacement of non-performing personnel, updating of much-loved but outdated products.

Difficult but obvious decisions carry the double weight of being nec-essary for success as well as having the potential to reinforce or undermine your ability to lead. If a decision is required and the answer is obvious to you, it is also obvious to everyone else. If the executive is not willing to make the tough call, his or her integrity and courage are brought into question and the willingness of the team to believe that person's ability to take them where they need to go is compromised. In other words, if people can't trust you to do what is necessary, they will stop following you. Ridicule is the next step in the spiral and it is nearly impossible to recover from being laughed about.

These are the decisions leaders are most likely to stumble on. Steel yourself and make the hard call.

Decisions with Inadequate Information

The requirement to make decisions or choices when you do not have enough information is something a leader must tolerate. This situation comes in two primary flavors:

There really is enough information to make a decision (but we are so jumpy that our underwear is in a knot and we do not recognize it)

In most situations, there is enough information available to make a reasonably good decision. The trick is to recognize that fact and not let your emotions and prejudices carry the day. The key is to stay calm and objective enough to recognize the pertinent factors. Three things will help you figure this out:

- **Stay calm:** Take a deep breath
- **Reduce the argument to its simplest terms:** Decisions can almost always be reduced to ten or fewer decision points. Most can be reduced to four or less. Find them. Structure a mental exercise that will reduce your decision criteria to as few points as possible. Hold your subordinates accountable for giving you the information in terms that will allow you to make a decision. Ask pertinent questions and require answers to the questions you ask.
  - ○ **Hint:** A common and consistent human trait is the tendency to answer the question we want to answer rather than the question that was asked:
    > *Question to teenage daughter: What time will you be home from the Mall?*
    > *Answer from teenage daughter: Jennifer hasn't found a dress yet.*
    > *Notice:* The question was asked in terms of outcomes. The answer was given in terms of activities.

  Require answers to the questions you ask. Make every effort to avoid getting drawn into discussions of activities to exclusion of significant points related to results. The more time you spend delving into the details of their actions and validating the connection to the results for which your subordinate is accountable, the greater the burden for results shifts from their shoulders to yours. This behavior also trains your team to turn to you for their answers rather than figuring it out for themselves. Examples:

- ○ **Marketing**. You need to know one thing: the value of the marketing dollar spent in terms of touches with interested prospects in our target market. All the demographics and actuarial hocus-pocus, and niche discussions may be necessary for background and understanding. But a good marketing guy understands this: from their nebulous and artistic discipline, they must achieve hard results. Marketing is a support activity and must produce business results in terms of sales or placement. Cute marketing campaigns that get awards may feel good. However, if they do not produce results, they are simply resume items for the people in the Marketing Department.

- ○ **Risk Management / Disaster Recovery / Business Continuity**. When decisions are required in the arena of risk management, do not accept a wad of facts, possibilities, and Chicken Little maybes. Require quantified recommendations in terms of exposure, likelihood, and acceptable practice.

- **Challenge underlying assumptions.** It is amazing how many tortured and tangled decisions are made based on faulty underlying assumptions. In particular arbitrary delivery dates. Rigidly adhered to dates and schedules are probably the most common and damaging underlying assumption you will encounter. Commitments to schedules are often made at remote management levels, cheerfully unburdened by facts or knowledge and by those who will not be accountable for making them happen. Sales cycles are particularly fertile ground for ludicrous schedule commitments. Once made, the underlying assumptions become foundational and are incorporated in the ego and career path of those who made them. A high level of testosterone release is seen from these individuals when threatened by a challenge to their personal commitments. Depending on the level of the individual, there is often little appetite to challenge the person who made the commitment. This is a bad recipe: Commitments made in ignorance plus prideful rigidity result in premature release, poor performance, and a quagmire of mitigation.

A word to the wise: A 90-day delay on a project is rapidly forgotten in the glow of success. Two-year dig-outs and hits to the business are not so easily forgotten or forgiven and can be career-ending events.

We truly do not know enough to make an informed decision

It does happen occasionally. You are faced with a decision for which you simply don't have enough information. A critical factor at this point is to not dither. As a leader, you must maintain an awareness this will happen and be ready to deal with it. Here are some ideas:

- **Get more information**. This is a judgment call. You need to weigh the tradeoff of the likelihood of finding additional pertinent data against the damage caused by delay. Remember: a reputation for indecisiveness may be part of that damage.
- **Make the call.** Just do it. As my good friend Larry informs me, when you are refereeing a game and do not know who last touched the ball before it went out of bounds, it is better to be fast than right. The analogy is not completely true but there is a great deal of wisdom in it. If the stakes are low to moderate, go for it. If the stakes are high, action is needed, and you stand little chance of getting more information, go for it. Decisive action and confidence often make up for starting in the wrong direction.
- **Make the call and mitigate**. Approach the decision in a way that manages the risk. Create decision-gates which will provide more information along the way and provide options as you move forward. As time goes by, get feedback on the impacts and outcomes of your decision.
- **Verify the decision is the problem**. Often the inability to get enough information to make a decision is a symptom of another problem. You could be unable to come to a decision point be-

cause you did not clarify the scope and objectives you are trying
to achieve. It is terribly difficult to decide what road to take if you
do not know where you are going.

Decisions under Pressure

Panic is your enemy. If you can keep your head, you will probably
make the right call. As a leader, it is part of your job to keep the big picture
in mind. Listen:

*A modern warship, functioning properly and handled with wisdom,
can probably ride out any typhoon. The storm's best recourse in the
contest for the ship's life is old-fashioned bogeyman terror. It makes
ghastly noises and horrible faces and shakes up the captain to distract
him from doing the sensible thing in tight moments.*

> *Herman Wouk on captaining in a typhoon*
> **The Caine Mutiny**

Here are some approaches that can help:

- **Outcome/Outcome/Outcome**. Keep your outcome in mind.
  Know where you are going. It helps.
- **Current state**. Get as good a picture as you possibly can of where
  you are right now and the situation at hand.
- **Talk to someone**. Find a calm voice that is not under pressure.
  Get advice from a cool head.
- **Look at the cause of the urgency**. Make sure the pressure you are
  feeling is not mostly in your head. Is it more apparent than real?
- **Shed your doubts**. Once you have made your decision, embrace
  it and move forward. There is a chance you are wrong but, really
  it is not likely. You are pretty smart, if you have thought it through
  there is a pretty good chance you are right. Beyond that, feeble
  support for a decision will probably do more harm than plowing
  ahead at full steam.

The key to decisions under pressure is to eliminate the pressure to
the extent you can. As much as possible, through preparation and stay-
ing calm, you transform a pressure decision to a regular decision. FYI:

Regardless of how big or small, it is just a regular decision. The concept of a pressure decision is about the person making the decision, not the decision itself. Reduce the emotions and you reduce the pressure.

Triage

Triage is the ability in any given situation to prioritize and attack the most urgent and important needs. Triage is often necessary during crises and emergencies. We are in circumstances of high stress and we find we must make decisions quickly and accurately. Inherent in the concept of triage is insufficient resource to do everything we would like to do. Triage is usually not subtle or nuanced. The factors that go into the triage decision are brightly colored and applied with a broad brush. You are looking for the thing that will kill you first if you do not take care of it.

Medical practice provides a conceptual understanding of triage. If a patient has a blocked airway and is also bleeding profusely from a ripped artery, which is handled first? The brain cannot store oxygen and dies quickly once breathing stops. Within ten minutes the patient will suffer severe brain damage and will die shortly after that. Loss of blood usually takes a bit longer to cause irreparable damage. Get them breathing first. Then take care of the rest. That is triage.

In any given business crisis, look for the thing that will bring you down first. The two factors you want to understand are: exposure and likelihood. This usually becomes reasonably obvious if you can screen out the noise and make a list of your needs and your ability to respond to them. If your primary computer system is down, is it more important to get it back up or to find a way to service your customers? If your expenses are out of control and will force you below the threshold of an "ongoing concern" within a year but you also have multiple product and service issues, what should you take care of first to allow you the time to fix the others?

Triage: First put out the fire then start fixing the other stuff. Remember, once the fire is out you may still be living in a damaged building. Next week your shaky infrastructure could be the thing that will kill you. Do not delay but find the killer first.

Study the responses of Tylenol to poisoned capsules, Jack in the Box to the E coli disaster, and the Federal Government to Hurricane Katrina. They are instructive from the point of view of what to do and what not to do.

Stop the bleeding, make a plan, execute, and get on top of it.

LEADERSHIP CONCEPT #6

The Seduction of Victory

AOL and the Arrogance of Victory – A Story

IN MID-2002 AMERICA Online (AOL) had a U.S. subscription base of about 27 million. In mid 2009 it had about 6 million. If you do the math, that is over 77% decline in business. In 2002, AOL was the big boy on the block; the guy with all the muscle and the sex appeal. It was successful and powerful in an incredibly volatile and rapidly changing industry space. It was also highly arrogant, extremely difficult to work with as a customer, and clunky to use. AOL rode a wave of first-to-market and climbed a crest of glory that allowed an upstart, just ten years old to take over venerable Time-Warner. But for some reason, it failed to notice, the very thing that had made it successful, locking up the position of "Internet Kindergarten" laid the foundation of its own demise. If you are painful to work with, you have clunky proprietary tools, and you are arrogant about your position, you can count on your decline being rapid and embarrassing. They were seduced.

The Doolittle Raid and Strategy in the Pacific – A Story

On April 18, 1942, Colonel Jimmy Doolittle rumbled off the flight deck of the USS Hornet leading 16 B-25B Mitchell Bombers on a bomb-ing run over Tokyo. It was the first time the United States had attacked the Japanese homeland since the bombing of Pearl Harbor. It was incredibly brave though it did little damage to Tokyo and none to the Japanese war machine. However, it accomplished exactly what it was supposed to. U.S. and allied morale got a shot in the arm. There was consternation amongst the Japanese military hierarchy. Japan extended its defensive lines to include the Midway Archipelago, which laid the groundwork for the Battle of Midway where the U.S. destroyed enough of the Japanese Fleet to change the course of the war. Ernest King (Commander in Chief, United States Fleet) and Chester Nimitz (Commander in Chief, United States Pacific Fleet) were both aware of the value and context of the Doolittle Raid. They kept their distance, their perspective, and they looked at their strategic and tactical maps more than headlines. They were not seduced.

Operation Mincemeat and the Invasion of Sicily – A Story

On April 19, 1943, the body of a British Royal Marine courier with a briefcase chained to his belt washed ashore near the Spanish town of Huelva. The case contained personal letters between high ranking British officers which included enough oblique references to coming actions to allow a careful reader to connect the dots and figure out the Allied plans for the Mediterranean assault on Europe. Huelva was brimming with careful readers. Before neutral Spain returned the documents to the British, they were given to the German spy network for one hour to be photographed. The copies were sent to Berlin where they were accepted as valid with little more than cursory investigation. The documents were accepted all the way up to Hitler. It was all a fake. The documents had been created and planted on a corpse which was set adrift by a submarine crew just off the shore of Spain in the hopes it would wash up and be discovered by the right people. It was. As a result, German forces were concentrated in the Balkans and Greece when the Allies invaded Sicily. The Germans thought they had scored an historic coup over the Brits and displayed a willingness to believe which prevented them from conducting even the most basic validation protocols. Unforgivable sloppiness and towering desire for the information to be true probably saved the lives of thousands of British and American troops. The Nazis were seduced.

Information Sources:

- The Man Who Never Was by Ewen Montagu
- Operation Mincemeat by Ben Macintyre

In the Aftermath of Victory

Victory is a fleeting moment in time. The real value of a victory is in the effort that secures its achievement, not in the moment it is declared. In many ways it is like being a little kid waiting for Christmas. At some point in our lives we come to realize the joy of Christmas is the month leading up to it. The day itself comes and goes pretty quickly. As John Lennon supposedly said: "Life is what happens while you are busy making other plans." Success is what happens when you straining to achieve the victory, not when they hand you the medal.

We get seduced by victories in a number of ways. The seduction of victory happens when we begin to think of victory as a state of being, not something we are in the process of reaching.

Big Victory

The seduction of a big victory is most often seen in an arrogance that does not recognize the fleeting nature of a win. We have a tendency to translate past success into the expectation of a future success. In ancient Rome, a small number of generals were granted the highest honor in recognition of a victory, the Triumph. Only for a Triumph was a general allowed to set foot in Rome as a military commander. Otherwise he lost his command the moment he passed through a city gate. For a Triumph the general was painted red to resemble statues of Jupiter and rode in a chariot at the head of his army. Wagons carrying the spoils of his victory went before and behind him. Defeated leaders walked in chains. The procession travelled from the gates of Rome to the center of the city, the Forum. At Capitoline Hill he climbed the steps to the Temple of Jupiter on his knees and sacrificed to the god. It was the epitome of achievement for any general and was seldom granted by the Senate. But even in the moment of supreme recognition and triumph, the general was reminded of the fleeting nature of his accomplishment. A slave stood behind him and held a golden crown over his head. Every few minutes the slave would whisper into the general's ear: "Remember, you are only mortal." It was a warning against arrogance and complacency.

If the expectation of future success is turned inward and results in a mindset that drives you to do what is necessary to achieve ongoing success, you are crossing the threshold to becoming a winning culture with consistent winning dynamics. Victory is a pivot and launching point for the next level of success. It should be a forward looking mindset rather than a time to rest on our laurels.

If, on the other hand, the victory is a point where you stop and relax, you will find you are quickly sliding back down the slope. Teams that play up consistently improve. Teams that are stronger than their opponents tend to lose their edge. There really is something in the old Avis catch phrase: "We're Number Two but We Try Harder."

In the military there is a name for this: *Victory Disease*. Basically it means an outfit has become arrogant and smug due to a history of victory and this leads to a decline in effort and focus combined with an assumption victory will be theirs. Defeat, often disastrous defeat, follows.

Companies in the third generation of management are often victim to the seduction of victory and the assumption of success. The founding generation has the vision and drive to take the organization to success. They understand the level of constant work and discipline required and they behave accordingly. The second generation has often worked with the founding generation and although they may not have the clarity of vision of the founders, they understand the need for hard work, focus, and the continual pressure necessary for success. The third generation has grown up in an environment of success and frequently lacks both the vision and the understanding of what it takes to repeat and assure winning. Success has been a state of life rather than an earned achievement. With notable exceptions, (e.g. Nordstrom, Ford) this is why nepotism is frowned upon in modern business. Birth is seldom a valid qualification for effective leadership or success.

Small Victories

Small victories can be stepping stones and morale boosters. They keep interest and hope alive. If managed well, small victories can highlight accomplishments on the path to major success and they can be the proving ground of an organization's ability to make progress in a consistent and predictable fashion. They can also be your enemy.

The challenge for many executives and managers is keeping small victories in their proper context and perspective. It is tempting to focus on the victory in a battle to the exclusion of winning the war. Interim victories give you something to talk about and focus on. They are often necessary milestones and indicators of progress. They fill empty space in a board meeting. The questions to ask are these:

- Is this victory leading to the greater victory?
- Will this victory misdirect our focus from what really needs to get done?

A great marketing plan that wins awards but does not translate into sales is misdirection. Reducing expenses may slow the bleeding but is only part of your success. Becoming ISO9000 certified tells the world you have consistent quality, not that you have a good product. Great processes are simply predictable motions if they do not produce results.

Small victories can be constructive or destructive depending on how you use them as a manager and a leader.

Misguided Credit

People involved in very successful organizations often imbue themselves with credit for that success. This is especially true if they become beneficiaries of the success. It should be said, there is a legitimate and deserved element of pride in being part of a team that achieved a notable success. Legitimate bragging rights, however, should not be confused with being the architect of the victory. Typically, a small percentage of a successful team is responsible for the vision and design of the success. The rest of the team may have worked very hard in the execution of that design. But they should not confuse hard work with being responsible for the victory. Tech millionaires no doubt worked very hard for their respective organizations. So did bank clerks. Most of the tech millionaires were simply in the right place at the right time.

Remember this as you separate fact from fiction after a victory. Being close to a victory and benefiting from that victory does not mean you made it happen. If you are lucky enough to have a big stock option or exit strategy payday because of a bubbling economy or due to an optimistic stock market; that is great. But do not take credit for building the railroad if you simply hopped on the train.

Most importantly, if your success was outside of the things you control, do not make your plans based on the assumption it will happen again.

The Leader as an Actor

The Earthquake – A Story

IN THE FALL of 1906 in San Francisco, a little girl named Bethel Stripling returned to school after an extended summer vacation. In April of that year an earthquake and fire had devastated the town and left two-thirds of the population homeless. Her school was a single room for all grades; first through twelfth. Beth's family was typical of the time. Her grandfather had served in with the Union Army in the Civil War somewhere in Texas. Her father Hank Stripling was unusual only in that he was over six and a half feet tall. Her people were part-time farmers, gold prospectors, maids, and laborers. They were part of the human migration which populated the western part of North America in the second half of the 19th century. Looking at her in later years, we were pretty sure Native Americans had entered the gene pool somewhere along the line. That, however, was something we never could verify as discussion of it was strictly off limits.

There was only one teacher in the school but she soon had the room organized in a way that made it work. She created clusters for those in the same age range and before long the older kids were teaching the younger ones. But here is the thing my grandmother remembered her entire life. Her teacher tacked a quote from Shakespeare on the wall and every child who could write was required to include it on the top of every paper turned in:

Men at some time are masters of their fates: The fault, dear Brutus, is not in our stars, but in ourselves, that we are underlings.

William Shakespeare
Julius Caesar: Act I, Scene II

The message, obviously, is this: you are in charge. Do not cry about your life and how you have been ill-used by fate. Pluck up, stand up straight, and get on with it. It was an interesting message for children whose world had literally been shaken apart and gone up in flames. Beth Stripling later became Beth Kaufman and went on to become a swimming coach at the Olympic level, working with swimmers like Don Schollander and Mark Spitz (whom she accused of stealing her pancakes at breakfast on more than one occasion). She was inducted into the Swimming Hall of Fame in 1967 for her work with age-group swimming. The story about the Shakespeare quote was important enough to her to put it in a letter to her grandson in college in 1975.

I asked her once if she really believed it. We were talking on the phone and there was a pause at the other end.

"I don't know" she said, "But I act like I do."

I try to act like I do too. The line from Shakespeare can be found somewhere in any office I occupy for more than about a week. My friends have received copies lacquered on pine boards for their walls. I am now an old fud but I also know a teaching opportunity when I see it. Choices about how we behave become the reality of our lives. Sometimes you do not feel like you are in control. When that happens, act like you are.

Leadership and Acting
It's all on the Outside

The success or failure of a leader is defined by the followers not the leader; the impact of the leader on others is the essence of leadership. The behavior of a leader is critical to their ability to convince others to follow. Visible leadership, your behavior, is the only thing people have to create the connection which makes you their leader – as opposed to seeing you as someone who simply happens to be higher on the chart of organization.

This is important, and executives have no end of trouble figuring it out. What goes on in your head does not mean a thing. Unless you are in charge of the Psychic Division of your organization, all your team has to go on is what they can see and hear. The real you does not matter. What is on your face, what you do, what you say, and your tone of voice are all your team has. Therefore, what you are delivering to the visible world is not only critical to your success as a leader; it *is* you as a leader.

The Act

There are probably as many ways to create a leadership persona as there are leaders. Each successful leader has a blend of perceived characteristics unique to them. In most cases, a number of these traits are native behaviors and others are deliberately cultivated. Natural leaders tend to automatically display the traits their team needs to see in order to willingly follow. However, just because they are natural and automatic, it does not mean they are done without awareness. If you ask an effective leader about those traits, they will usually be able to give you a pretty good rundown of the key behaviors.

There is no foolproof prescription for how to act to be a successful leader. George Patton's act was very different from that of Omar Bradley. Patton was bombastic, forceful, and a *prima donna*. Bradley was quiet, forceful, and self-effacing. Both were extremely successful leaders. Each leader will have his or her unique persona and shtick. It tends to work best when a leader plays to their natural strengths. No one can tell you what yours should be. What we can tell you, however, is this: your act must work to convey perceived elements of leadership in order to be effective.

The Purpose of the Act

The Leadership Act has one purpose. It creates a depth of faith, confidence, and trust in you. Imagine, each member of your team, whether there are eight or eighty-thousand, has an account in their heart that represents their faith in you. The greater the balance in that account, the more willing they will be to support and follow you.

There are two ways to make deposits to that account: behavior and positive results. There are two ways to make withdrawals from the account: behavior and failures. That account must always have a positive balance. There will be failures in your tenure as a leader. You will ask for blind faith and support on the occasions you are not able to explain why you are making certain decisions or taking certain actions.On those occasions, it is important to have a cushion of belief for you to draw upon. The consistency of your behavior and the leadership act is important because it establishes a core of dependability and fundamental belief in you.

Critical Elements of the Leadership Act

Confidence: Healthy self-confidence, even to point of conceit about your abilities, is the first and foremost element of the public persona of a leader. Introspection is not high on the hit parade of traits your team needs to see. Confidence in yourself, your team, and the path you have chosen is the foundation the people around you require. It is the visible aura surrounding the leader that says, "I know when I bring my skills, intelligence, and experience to bear, I will do the right thing and make the right decision."

Decisiveness: Sometimes it really is more important to be quick than right. The longer you dither and debate, the greater the doubt of those watching. Do not be feeble. Think about it and make the call. And FYI: usually you know the right thing to do. It is just uncomfortable to make the call. Remember this: there is something worse than making the hard decision today: dwelling and obsessing over night on the hard decision you have to make tomorrow.

Strength and Courage: You will sometimes be called upon to be the core of strength for those around you. Be ready; you may be at odds with the common wisdom. Doing the necessary and unpopular thing will invite bullets and arrows. And since you are usually the guy out front you will be the first to get hit. Develop a thick skin. If you are doing your job correctly you will sometimes face vicious criticism. Get shoes with rubber soles because you will be walking into the wind. You do not have the luxury of going with the flow if you want to be an effective leader. However, that core of strength and courage is something your team will rally around like a bonfire on an icy day.

Purpose: Know where you are going. Have a compass that guides you and frames your actions and decisions in a consistent, dependable, and predictable manner. Your decisions cannot be random or scattered or you will confuse people. It is your job to keep your eye on the objective and periodically drag people back to the right path. Your public discussions and visible actions keep the organizational outcomes front and center. Reinforced and constant purpose gives us context for what we do and reminds us of what we are expected to do.

Steady and Unflappable: You cannot panic. You must steel yourself to keep your head when everyone else is spinning like a top. Panic is virulently infectious. Resolution and a determined demeanor are also infectious. If you do not panic in an emergency, others will believe there is good reason not to panic as well. Then . . . everyone will do the most sensible thing to get back on track.

Acknowledgment and Due Credit: Glory hogs make terrible leaders. Part of your public act should be giving credit where credit is due.

Note: Many executives and managers are masterful at giving credit in a way that makes it obvious they are actually taking the credit while they do the right thing with an "attaboy" in a public setting:

- *Everyone knows I actually made Johnny make this happen but let's give Johnny a pat on the head and a gold star anyway. By the way, aren't I the bees-knees for complementing Johnny?*

As Kipling said:

If

If you can keep your head when all about you
Are losing theirs and blaming it on you;
If you can trust yourself when all men doubt you,
But make allowance for their doubting too;
If you can wait and not be tired by waiting,
Or, being lied about, don't deal in lies,
Or, being hated, don't give way to hating,
And yet don't look too good, nor talk too wise;

If you can dream – and not make dreams your master;
If you can think – and not make thoughts your aim;
If you can meet with triumph and disaster
And treat those two imposters just the same;
If you can bear to hear the truth you've spoken
Twisted by knaves to make a trap for fools,
Or watch the things you gave your life to broken,
And stoop and build 'em up with worn-out tools;

If you can make one heap of all your winnings
And risk it on one turn of pitch-and-toss,
And lose, and start again at your beginnings
And never breath a word about your loss;
If you can force your heart and nerve and sinew
To serve your turn long after they are gone,
And so hold on when there is nothing in you
Except the Will which says to them: "Hold on";

If you can talk with crowds and keep your virtue,
Or walk with kings – nor lose the common touch;
If neither foes nor loving friends can hurt you;
If all men count with you, but none too much;
If you can fill the unforgiving minute
With sixty seconds' worth of distance run -
Yours is the Earth and everything that's in it,
And – which is more – you'll be a Man my son!

Rudyard Kipling

Trust: Strength from a Solid Keystone

The Arch – A Story

THE USE OF the structural arch as an element of construction and architecture dates back over 3,200 years. It took a little over a thousand years, however, for architects and builders to pick-up on the phenomenal potential of the arch, of both the physics and the beauty of the structure. Starting in about 100 BC, Roman designers elevated the arch from its purely practical form, used in building underground structures such as sewers or as framing for city gates. They refined both the technology itself and their understanding of it. The arch became one of the foundational elements that allowed human beings to control and manage their environment. It provided for the structures and buildings which have become the physical indicators of civilization. Before the widespread use of the arch, buildings were sticks, stones, and boards piled on top of one another. Until industrial manufacturing processes of the nineteenth century allowed volume production of high-quality iron and steel I-beams, the arch remained the only architectural device capable of providing for both open floor plans and soaring interior spaces. Without the arch, interior spaces were limited by board strength and required roof support piers at regular intervals.

The structural arch is a miraculous design element. It also has an interesting characteristic known as the keystone. An arch always has an odd number of stones. The sides of the arch are constructed of an equal number of wedgestones. These stones have a slight taper so, when you pile them on one another, the inside is smaller than the outside and the pile curves to the middle. At the very top of the arch is the final stone, the keystone. It sits between the two curved piles of wedgestones and creates a remarkably strong and stable structure. The keystone becomes the final and key point where the strength of the arch is realized. The only weakness of the arch is its dependence on the keystone. A weak or cracked keystone can cause the entire arch to crumble.

Trust in a leader is the keystone of a successful organization.

The Privilege and Responsibility of Blind Trust

In most situations we use experience and observation to decide where we will place our trust. This is true for personal relationships, dry cleaners, and grocery stores. There are some areas, however, in which we must trust without proof. Things in which we place trust without proof are usually those we don't understand or have the capability to handle. There are also situations for which it is simply impractical for us to examine closely before we commit to them. Blind trust situations include trustee relationships, automobile mechanics, and insurance agents. If financial management is involved, the specific name for the arrangement is a fiduciary relationship. We also consent to this type of trust when we feel it is for the good of society. The use of force, including deadly force, by the police is considered to be a necessary part of keeping order and we trust it will be applied appropriately. The consistent characteristic of these unexamined trust relationships is this: one person has power over another person and the person without the power is willing to accept the arrangement because they have a need. There is trust the power will be used appropriately. One person is powerful and the other is vulnerable. In a complex modern society blind-trust relationships are necessary. Abuse of that trust, however, is dealt with severely.

In June of 2009, a jury awarded a Kentucky woman $350,000 in damages due to a botched surgery that left her unable to work. The insurance company had offered $75,000. As the court looked into the business practices of the company, it became clear their processes were geared toward the payment of the minimal possible claim amount rather than to fulfill the purpose of insurance; to make the legitimate claimant whole within the limits of the policy. The company used threats and even ignored its own experts in attempting to settle the case for a small amount. Because of the violation of trust, the jury also awarded $3.47 million in punitive damages, ten times the amount of the actual insurance claim settlement. As a society we rigorously punish those who violate our trust.

Leadership, Faith, and Trust

The Mysterious Nature of Leadership

Leadership, by its nature is a mystery. We do not want our leaders to be too close to us. There is an aura of the leader we want and need in order to be confident we can depend of them. We do not want to know too much about our leaders' frailties, doubts, or their inner dialogues. We don't necessarily want them to share too much in terms of explaining their decisions or justifying themselves to us. Although we sometimes ask for a level of transparency, we do not actually want too much of a backstage view. We want strength, guidance, and the right decision when necessary. Not much to ask for our allegiance. Still, to some extent, we set ourselvesup for disappointment if we forget our leaders are human beings and will probably display human tendencies from time to time.

As discussed above, we give our leaders a high degree of unexamined faith and trust, similar to financial advisors, doctors, and car mechanics. In order to be successful, a leader must have that faith and trust. In a complementary fashion, in order to be a successful team, we have a need to give it. That said, when we give trust in this way, we expect something in return.

We have the expectation and assumption that the things happening out of our sight are happening in an appropriate way. We assume our leaders are behaving with integrity and in the best interest of those who have given their trust.

The Assumption

The foundation of the trust and faith necessary for confidence in our leaders is based on assumed (for want of a better word) goodness. Leaders have a great deal of unsupervised latitude and leeway. Leaders are assumed to be making decisions for the right reasons. There is an expectation the leaders are doing their best for the organization, the customer, and the people who work there. It is assumed they are not abusing our trust to enrich themselves and their families, hide misdeeds, or cover up incompetence. In other words, leaders are given wide freedom of action and those that give it place themselves in a position of vulnerability. This position is only acceptable if they can believe in leadership integrity.

The Stab in the Heart

The nature of unexamined trust makes it hard to know when a breach of the trust occurs. The predisposition of those interacting with the leader (or the financial trustee or the auto mechanic) is to believe what they say. The basis of the relationship is just that: you trust them. As a result of this relationship, the first and most effective way to hide or skirt inappropriate behavior is to simply lie or fudge the truth. And, it works.

The Board of Directors believes the CEO has a plan to get expenses under control because he says so. The staff believes we can turn things around if we can just get this system installed. The analysts and investors believe we are producing a 10% year over year because we say so and the regulators are not looking too closely.

As the obfuscation increases, the leader continues to get away with it by hiding in the area of unexamined trust. Building greater and greater webs of words becomes easier and easier. Like any misdeed, the first time is gut-wrenching, the second time is difficult, and the third time gives us a little twinge. By the fourth time we may not even know we are doing anything wrong – at least until it crashes down around us. When the comeuppance arrives, it comes hard and fast.

The flip side of blind trust is the blinding speed with which it can disappear. A violation of trust goes well beyond erasing all the confidence your team has placed in you. It causes an instinctive flood of anger and rejection. The reason: people willingly followed you and made themselves vulnerable. You made chumps of them. They believed in you and you desecrated that belief and trust. You tried to make suckers of them; people do not easily forgive such behavior. What are behaviors to watch for? Here are a few examples:

Devious Communications: Leaders who parse words with their team or their bosses are on the downhill spiral. If you find leaders using convoluted or technical reasons to explain why failures are actually successes, look out. If a leader talks about strength but expenses are out of control, sales are down, and market share is falling: look very closely at what is going on. If one business measure is trumpeted to the exclusion of a rounded picture, chances are the rounded picture looks grim.

Double Standards: Are the leaders still flying first class while asking others to cut back? Are they taking bonuses due to esoteric financial technicalities while preparing for layoffs? Are they pushing for higher team performance while unable to put in a 40-hour work week between June and August?

Lying: People will tolerate a certain lack of candor if there is a good reason for it. However, if you are discovered lying for a self-serving reason and hiding behind the corporate veil, your ability to continue to lead is limited.

Performance Culture: If there is a demand for a culture of performance and results and the leaders are not held to the same requirement, it is a violation of trust.

Blind Trust Violations in the News

You do not have to look far to find examples of violations of trust that have resulted in spectacular implosions of organizations:

- Enron
- Watergate
- WorldCom Scandal
- Clinton-Lewinsky Scandal
- Bernie Madoff Scandal
- Sex scandals in organized churches

You can find articles on the Internet about the above scandals if you want details. In all these cases, however, the downfall was brought about through a series of actions that violated a trust granted by others. In all cases, the integrity of the organization was harmed. In all cases, effectiveness took a hit and in some cases the organization ceased to exist.

Finally

To state it simply and succinctly: do not violate the trust people have given you. If you do, you will have gutted the substance and strength that makes you an effective leader. You will be living behind a façade of respectability until it catches up to you. Then you will collapse like a *papier mache* doll in a warm rain.

Always Teaching

You only do that once! – A Story

IN 1984 I got my first job as a supervisor. I was working for an insurance company at the time. My department was responsible for policy changes and I had 22 people reporting to me. I had no experience managing people but my boss sat directly behind me and felt he could keep an eye on me and probably manage to keep me out of trouble from fifteen feet away.

About two weeks into the job, we met for our weekly talk. I breezed into the meeting, fresh-faced and eager, with a blank pad of paper in my hand. Fifteen minutes later he had asked me at least five questions I could not answer. Correction: he had asked me at least five questions about which I had no clue how to answer.

Ray was old school; a wash-n-wear white-on-white shirt kind of guy. He wore a Timex watch and was a two-pack-a-day man. By the time I had warmed his side-chair for twenty minutes, I was aware in detail exactly how far I away I was from being a competent supervisor. By the time I slunk back to my desk, sweat stains ran from my arm pits to my belt.

Later that day, over a beer, I was less than kind. I was a 27 year-old adolescent whining against the cruelty of the old guard.

"Yep," said my friend as she put her beer down and flicked a cashew into a spin, "You only go unprepared to a meeting with Ray once."

Continuous Teaching – Continuous Training
Opportunities – Moment by Moment

As a leader, you are constantly teaching. Almost every action you take has an impact on your team and guides their future behavior and choices. You must determine what behaviors and organizational culture you are trying to instill and act accordingly. This is not the kind of teaching or training that can be found in books or classes. It is the gradual process of training people to behave in one way or the other. This type of training comes from real-life experience. It uses action and reaction to mold and alter behavior.

If meetings start late and end whenever they run out of gas, you are training people to be lax rather than behaving with purpose. You are encouraging them to be late and lack the discipline to present consistently forceful case-discussions which can be driven to a decision point. If, however, you start and end meetings on time, every time, people will develop behavior patterns to reflect that. Two or three experiences of breaking into an in-progress meeting, combined with being cut off by the clock will have a motivating effect. People will arrive on time and they will craft their discussions to achieve their goals in the allotted timeframe. The combination of positive results and the desire to avoid negative consequences is a powerful mix.

The Key to Success in Continuous Teaching

Consistency is the key to behavior-based and expectations-based training. Every parent knows consistent behavior is effective in training children. They also know, even if only subconsciously, inconsistent behavior is an even more effective training mechanism but in the opposite direction. If a parent says "No" and sticks with it, children learn quickly to accept it and move on. If, when they test it, they hear "No," and "No," and then "Yes," they are being trained to know that if they push back they will occasionally get their way. To the discomfiture of Mom and Dad, intermittent reinforcement is a much more powerful and fast training method than consistent positive reinforcement. The kids don't know when they might get the reward, so they try again and again.

Inconsistent leaders often get results opposite of those they want. If your team is consistently expected to act in a certain way, they will conform to the requirement. If, however, they discover expectations are malleable, behavior will become malleable as well. A very few lapses in holding people accountable can destroy years of training. It's a pain, isn't it?

Situational Teaching and the Results you can Expect

Decision Making. If you expect the majority of decisions to come through you, you are training people not to make decisions. You are training them to fail if you are not there.

Performance: If you do not require a high level of performance from yourself and your team, you are training your team that it is okay to be okay.

Results and Accountability: If you do not hold people accountable for their actions and for producing results, you are training them to under produce and blame others for their failures.

Business Hours: If you do not keep regular business hours, you are training your customers to view you as undependable and to go elsewhere. If the hours listed on the window say you will be open until 10:00 PM and you actually are welcoming customers until 10:00 PM, you are training the person who drives past every night at 9:45 to spend money in your store rather than the store that gives them the stink-eye when they walk in just before closing time.

Fairness: If you play favorites, create lower performance standards for executives, and do not fairly reward good behavior, you are training people to discount the value of their own investment in the organization. If underperforming executives receive high salaries, bonuses, and free cars, you are training them rewards are tied to position not performance.

Candor: If you get cranky and blame the messenger when you hear difficult or bad news, you are training your people to tell you only the good news. You will be the last to know. You will be sitting fat, dumb, and happy in the corner office or sunning yourself in Hawaii when you read about your business problems in the *Wall Street Journal*. This is also known as "the emperor has no clothes" syndrome.

Training for Leadership

If you encourage the people in your organization to take on the mantle of leadership, to take accountability for results, *and* you then reward that behavior, you teach a very different and positive lesson. You are teaching people to invest themselves, in the organization, and to own responsibility for its continued success. You are training them to be part of the next generation that assures continuity and succession.

You are always teaching, always training.

Culture Never Sleeps

Kerry Killinger and the Complexity of Washington Mutual – A Story

IN APRIL OF 2010, the former CEO of Washington Mutual faced Carl Levin and a pack of Senators at a meeting of the United States Senate Committee on Homeland Security and Governmental Affairs. He was there to answer questions about the largest bank failure in United States history. It was an interesting display of restrained grandstanding by Senators juxtaposed to tap dancing by Killinger and other WAMU executives. From his testimony it became apparent Killinger believed Washington Mutual was brought down by the combined forces of a bad economy and a government that didn't like them and wouldn't invite them to meetings. In his six minute opening statement, Killinger took accountability for the debacle within thirty seconds. He then spent the rest of the time explaining why he had nothing to do with the problem. The word for Kerry's performance would be "disingenuous," if not "strikingly disingenuous." It was kind of sad. More than anything he looked like a high school kid trying to explain misbehavior by talking about everything except what he was being asked to explain. Correction: a high school kid who made $25 million a year.

In the course of the hearing, it became clear the primary line of Killinger's defense was to be, "I didn't know." It seemed he was simply not aware of the fraudulent and shady practices going on in his company for the past several years.

In the days following the hearing, opinion on this characteristic of management practice split into two major factions: One: he should have known and; two: in an organization that big and complex, it is impossible to know everything that is going on. Both opinions are true to some extent. It is simply not possible for a single individual to know everything going on inside a large, complex, and bureaucratic operation. On the flip side, business practices on the scale seen at WAMU and which created movement of funds at the level of subprime mortgages and mortgage-backed securities would seem to have been too big for him to have missed – unless he deliberately chose not to look.

That discussion, however, misses the point. There are very few organizations of any size for which a single person can comprehensively know what is going on. It is tough in any outfit larger than about 10 people for one individual to intimately supervise the activities of all the players.

What Kerry failed to grasp or simply failed to do, was to foster and develop an organizational culture of acceptable behavior and doing the right thing. In a world of laws, regulations, and audits, your best defense against wrong-doing is the organizational expectation everyone will do the right thing when confronted with a decision or a chance to cut corners. If you blindly give "attaboys" for achievement of business goals without regard to the way in which the success was achieved, it trains your people to behave to a standard of ends justifying means.

The culture of Washington Mutual apparently did not have the elements necessary at a critical mass to create a herd assumption of ethical behavior. Success was built on a cheat. One of the grand old companies of the United States collapsed. Kerry and his company lost their grounding and lost everything.

Leading through Culture
Expectations and Normalization

As a leader you cannot be everywhere all the time. At least you cannot *physically* be everywhere all the time. However, one of the most interesting and consistent things about human beings is our affinity for teams and cultural norms. We are capable of being highly trained in specific action-reaction, task-based activities. But we are also social animals who desire to be part of a pack, a team, a society. Our need for acceptance and inclusion makes us extremely adept at understanding and internalizing cultural norms and expectations. Although you cannot physically be present everywhere in your company, you can be there in the pervasive presence and guiding influence of the culture you create.

Part of your job as a leader is to understand and articulate the culture of your organization. There will be powerful and deep rules for behavior and action in your organization whether you choose to influence and mold those societal rules or not. Your organization will create them. It will develop a distinct culture of its own. The question is much like the conversation around sex education in schools. Children will learn about sex while they are at school. It will happen. The question is: do we want them to learn about it on the playground or in the classroom? Will we exercise control over it or not?

As with many aspects of leadership and management, it is more important to have a clear vision for your desired culture as opposed to a "best" culture. There are many different types of organizational personalities and cultures. Successful companies do not necessarily conform to one type or another. Culture is a unique combination of people, time, place, business climate, and other factors. The leader's role is to influence the culture in a way to facilitate the development of a positive and contributing framework of norms and behaviors.

This vs. That

At its simplest level, cultural norms are a deeply embedded framework of expectations. They are understood at a level which draws immediate approval or disapproval for observed actions. They are also understood at a level that allows us to anticipate the reaction before we act. Cultural norms operate at multiple layers to proactively guide behavior as well as respond to witnessed behavior. They help us select between two possible paths.

Doing the Right Thing: If Kerry Killinger had been clear on the expectations of ethical behavior, it is doubtful loan officers would have falsified loan qualification documents. It is also unlikely his team would have tried to stealthily market toxic mortgage-backed securities with the conscious purpose of foisting them on unwary buyers.

Performing vs. Enabling: If no one in the organization is disciplined or fired for bad performance, the culture will adopt behaviors which focus on action and entitlement rather than results.

Collegial vs. Paternal: If critique and healthy discussion are suppressed and value is placed on getting along with your peers, the culture will mold itself to a "go-along-to-get-along" model. A culture of agreement is one of the most lethal models in terms of organizational success and survival. The case history of the Space Shuttle Challenger disaster is instructive to gain an understanding of the influence of culture on open discussion and disagreement and how it impacts critical corporate decisions, processes, and outcomes.

Merit vs. Social vs. Certification: If advancement is based upon merit, you find achievement and capability valued by the culture. If advancement is based upon the ability to grease the boss and the system, social skills will be valued by the culture. If advancement is based upon certifications and letters after the name, the culture will place value on achieving additional designations.

Only what's Due vs. Looking for a Way: Different organizations approach their obligations in very different ways. Two different insurance companies I worked for summarized their claims philosophies in stark contrast. It does not take a genius to understand the different impacts those two philosophies would have on a corporate culture:

- **Company One:** We pay what is due under the contract and that is all.
- **Company Two:** Our job is to make the claimant whole if we possibly can under the terms of the contract. We look hard in the contract to find a way to pay a claim.

Your organization will develop a self-sustaining and continuously operating culture that will perform a monitoring function and will exert pressure to conform. Unacceptable behavior which is outside the norms of the culture will stick out and become easier to identify and resolve. The trick is to proactively align the culture with the behaviors and activities that support your organizational goals and ethics.

Norms vs. Attaboys

In a head-to-head competition between desirable cultural norms and an "attaboy," the "attaboy" will win. Norms are created by what the organization values and rewards. If your words *say* a cultural norm is exemplary customer service but you reward and honor high pressure sales, guess what the culture becomes. The "attaboy" becomes the norm. The things you say are merely wistful words unless supported by actions. To take it a step further, when building an organizational culture, stating the "culture" can be downright counterproductive. Statements beginning with, "We need to create a culture that. . ." are usually viewed with amusement as new-age hot air. The only true and effective culture builders are actions and observed behaviors.

Warning: Cultural Merging

Attempting to combine two different cultures is a rocky road. Not to say it is impossible but it is several levels of difficulty beyond rocket science. If you hire a good physics guy and a good engineer, you have rocket science in the bag. Sir Isaac Newton figured out most of what you need to know to get to the moon three-hundred years ago. The earth and the moon travel in extremely predictable paths year after year. To date, no one has figured out all, or even most, of what you need to know about how people react to threats.

Organizational cultures resist change. They will actively and vigorously resist wholesale change. Behaviors and norms which had previously been foundational to our day-to-day life are suddenly highlighted as they come into conflict with THE OTHER. Values and traditions of the tribe take on disproportionate importance as they are challenged; knowing only one version is likely to survive. People feel threatened and fear the loss of a part of themselves. Understandably, they can revert into backup behaviors that are not productive.

There is no foolproof method for merging cultures. Extremely large corporate mergers struggle with cultural friction, sometimes for years. There are platoons of corporate psychologists and change management experts who can help you with listening, respect, meeting the needs of the tribe, *ad infinitium*. They can help you through the transition. On the cheap, however, there are three major things you should be aware of that can help.

1. **Pay Attention**: Once you have made the physical merge, you must deal with the issues around the culture. Make the decision to manage it rather than ignore it.

2. **Overriding Common Cause**: Find a way to focus the two groups on a common goal, a common need, or a common enemy. Try to engineer a step down on *Maslow's Hierarchy of Needs* (look it up). Bring the two tribes to a point at which they have a common goal closer to the level of assuring a food supply rather than self-actualization. If you are worried about survival, irritation about coffee-break protocol takes on a more reasonable perspective. Keeping the kids fed can generate an amazing amount of common-cause behavior and encourage camaraderie.

3. **Play for Time**: The more time passes, the more likely people are to discover the appeal and value of THE OTHER. They make friends and come to identify with co-workers from the other side of the fence. Threat diminishes as familiarity increases. The monolithic "them" transforms into people with children, mortgages, and familiar problems. Over time, they become us.

Culture is a strong thing and a real factor in your success. Ignore it at your peril.

Making Your Own Decisions. . .

Or Buying a Bill of Goods

British Intelligence in WW2; When Success is Truly Important – A Story

WHEN THE STAKES are truly high and it is critically important, serious people make decisions and choose paths of action based on the facts. They do not depend on comfortable truisms. They do not fall back on titles or strings of letters after peoples' names. When life, death, and property loss are on the line, people find the best way to assure success.

During World War Two, the threat to Great Britain was real and present. After the Dunkirk evacuation, the Germans were in control of the western coast of Europe. Across the Straights of Dover, they could see Calais, just 34 miles away. On the far coast was an enemy whose stated purpose was to invade and occupy England. As a measure of the reality of the possibility of an invasion, the British removed all road signs and place markers so as not to facilitate the ability of an invading army to use maps for navigation.

During this period, some of the best intelligence and counter-intelligence in modern history was planned and executed. Massive listening posts were created to eavesdrop on the radio chatter of the Third Reich. Huge clanking forerunners of computers churned away day after day and month after month at Bletchley Park to decrypt messages in the Enigma Cipher using an original breakthrough from the Poles. Information ranging from army movements to submarine wolf packs was decrypted and then used in a carefully orchestrated way to prevent the Germans from figuring out how much the allies actually knew about their movements.

The MI5 section ran remarkably complex and effective counter intelligence, providing dummy and misleading information to the Germans throughout the war. This section was responsible for saving countless lives through activities such as creating an entirely fictitious network of German agents to feed selected bad information to the enemy in a plausible way.

Both the work at Bletchley Park and MI5 was crucial to winning the war. Instead of taking the more obvious route of staffing the operations with career military men and women, the British opted for a brilliant and common-sense based solution: they got the best people available. They found college professors, lawyers, adventurers, novelists, mathematicians, chess champions. In one memorable move, they had The Daily Telegraph sponsor a crossword puzzle contest, then recruited the winners. Skill, creativity, and the ability work to the end result were the ticket to joining the intelligence community.

True threat and the need for success were too great for England to accept the common wisdom and depend on the form of excellence rather than the substance. They needed and found the reality of true excellence.

Recommended Reading: **Operation Mincemeat**   by Ben Macintyre
                                     Enigma   by Robert Harris

Critical Thinking and Making up your own Mind

Herd Mentality

There is an old saying: "No one ever got fired for choosing IBM." It is true. With all that brilliance and tens of thousands of skilled resources, who could fault you for choosing the brainy guy with the rippling muscles? It is safe and it provides good cover. It takes courage and originality as well as a level of critical thought to act on the reality that IBM (or Cisco, Microsoft, CSC, Harvard, Doctor Spock, etc. – you choose) might not be a good idea or that your best chance for success lies elsewhere. As a leader, however, there will come a time when your will need to make the decision where you want to go: safe harbor or the success of you organization.

People are herd animals. Most of us want to belong and be part of the pack. We especially love to be members of the right pack. As part of our need to be a member of the pack, we are prone to being influenced by the opinions of our peers. Three primary behaviors we see in ourselves are tightly tied to our affinity for being part of a group:

Group Thinking and Action: We will do things as part of a group that we would not do on our own. This behavior shows up in a wide spectrum of activities. At its most innocuous level, we see a willingness to sing with a group because our voice is just one in the choir. At a slightly deeper level, the group can drive action as well as providing cover and safety. In meetings you will see people adjust to the opinion of the crowd before committing themselves to one view or the other. Spurred on by the weight of opinion, they may take a much more adamant and vocal position than they would have otherwise. At its most drastic and controlling level, a crowd-think phenomenon occurs. We see the power of independent thought dwindle and the crowd transforms into a mob with its own dynamics of action. The mob can carry individuals along and spur them into behaviors they would never consider outside the group. Lynching and riots are the most severe examples of this type of behavior.

Totems and Stuff – the Trappings of the Pack: Most of the marketing industry is built on the ability to manufacture a desire to achieve inclusion through display of certain types of goods. These include our perceived need for Nike shoes, UGG boots, iPods, iPads, Rolex watches, etc. We all know the obsolescence cycle in which we buy goods is not based on utility or need. An inventory of items we did not need 10 years ago but now consider necessities would reveal a heavy weighting toward totems and talismans purchased primarily to assure the acceptance and admiration of those around us.

Acceptance of Tribal Wisdom: There is comfort in established frameworks and preconceived notions we can count on. As part of the human herd, we have inherited a wealth of general knowledge that gives us the freedom not to need to discover things over and over again. We know about things that work like aspirin and sunscreen. We know about things that don't, like any American car manufactured between 1970 and 1985. These bits of tribal wisdom are valid and useful and help us live our lives effectively.

Group-Think and Common Wisdom

Common or Generally Accepted Wisdom is the area that combines all of the above herd characteristics and creates a trap for leaders. Common Wisdom often has at its core a valid premise. There is a value or a potential value in the acceptance of the bit of wisdom that makes it plausible and difficult to disagree with. There are three markers you can watch for to help determine if you are being swept into a decision based on Common Wisdom rather than making the best decision in the current circumstances:

1. It makes the decision easier.
2. It is plausible at a gut level but you cannot quite articulate the connection between your current situation and the cloud of plausibility you are hearing.
3. Somebody other than you or your organization stands to gain from you accepting the Common Wisdom (someone selling something)
4. It gives you a feeling of comfort because you are in good company in accepting this bit of wisdom; you are a member of the pack.

Examples of Common Wisdom that Make Managers, Executives, and Decision Makers Lose their Ability to Question and Evaluate

- **Evidence-Based Solutions**. Often, common-sense based solutions will serve you better. Be sure to look into the evidence. It is a must. Remember, evidence-based solutions go only as far as the situation that produced the evidence applies. Look for the simplest common-sense solution you can find and then try it out. Remember, evidence-based solutions brought you Whole Math,

New Math, D'Nealian handwriting, and the idea that drinking lots of coffee helps elderly people have better sex lives. One more little nugget to remember: *Correlation is not causation.*

   ○   **Who Benefits?** There are thousands of university education departments, researchers, and doctoral candidates who only have one goal: find a new hypothesis, prove it, and publish it.

- **Post Graduate Degrees and Certifications**: I have yet to find plausible documentation or anyone in a position responsible for hiring who is willing to say that an MBA or a PhD is a positive differentiator in actual contribution to an organization. Yet, it is a requirement for thousands of positions and the holders of the af-ter-name alphabet are paid significantly more. I have never (ever) seen positive performance differential from holders of these de-grees as opposed to those without them. If there is a need for a post-graduate degree and your organization gets true benefit, by all means go get a guy with an MBA. But are the bragging rights of having a phalanx of degrees worth the cost?

   ○   **Who Benefits?** Let us count the ways. . . Universities, col-leges, and online schools: MBA programs are cheap to run and very profitable. MBA magazines. MBA clubs. MBAs.

- **Management Methodologies and Process Frameworks**: As we have said previously, most of these are similar to worrying about lead poisoning when you are about to be shot. Many management methodologies and process frameworks are valid tools. Use of them by management teams, however, is most often an exercise in misdirection or avoidance of dealing with an uncomfortable situa-tion. Find a simple and consistent way to do things and stick with it. The problem is not the tool, it is the workman. Stay away from the latest management tool as you would the latest plague.

   ○   **Who Benefits?** Consultants, book publishers, magazine pub-lishers, college professors.

Challenge the Common Wisdom

Keep your eyes and your ears fresh and tune them to send up a flag when you encounter a safe or standard solution that has the appearance of sensibility but not the reality. Use the *5 Whys* (look it up) to keep digging. Ask questions until you are convinced the solution is a good fit and will produce results. Otherwise go back to the drawing board.

Change: Don't Manage it. Lead it!

Ellis Island, my Great Grandmother, and the Westward Migration – A Story

IN THE 25 years between 1841 and 1866, half a million people left the eastern seaboard of the United States and migrated westward. They uprooted themselves, packed their belongings, and left; despite the knowledge there was no certainty of a better future wherever they finally settled. They embarked on an unpredictable journey, often putting themselves and their families at significant risk. They traveled into country where weather, disease, bad water, or bushwhackers could get you and possibly kill you. Places where your only defenses were your brains, your gun, and the support of your fellow travelers. The natives whose territory they passed through were often, with good reason, less than friendly. Still, they went.

The migration from Europe to the New World shows a similar pattern. The census of 1900 shows over ten million foreign-born people living in the United States. At that time, ten million people made up about 13% of the total population. To put it another way, one of every eight people in the United States at that time was here because they had decided to be here rather than because of an accident of birth.

My grandfather and his parents were in that crowd. It was a one-way trip. Passage on the ship was expensive, even for a bunk in steerage. The trip itself was usually miserable. Weather in the North Atlantic can be foul at any time of the year and anti-roll technology did not appear in a significant way until well into the twentieth century. Once in the United States, an immigrant faced a gauntlet of the immigration officers and inspections. On November 12, 1912, my great-grandmother, Mary Kaufman, was tapped by immigration because of a rattle in her chest. Reading the smudged pages of the Ellis Island immigration record, your stomach twists. Imagine yourself as a parent with a baby in your arms, standing in front of a table facing an immigration officer. He scratched a large heavy letter in chalk on the lapel of her coat and told her she would be held for two weeks while they observed her to see if she got over it or if she was to be sent back. He gave her directions where to go while her children were ferried to New York. My great-grandfather, Benjamin, was already in Los Angeles waiting for the family to arrive. Mary was alone with her eight children ranging in age from Cissie at six months, to Pauline at 18 years old. Mary walked away as her world spun. When she had put some distance between herself and the immigration officer, she must have decided she was hidden from watchers. She handed baby Cissie to Pauline and without fuss, in one smooth motion, flipped her collar inside her coat. Then she took Cissie back and walked out. Mary Kaufman was not about to be separated from her family.

These examples show change at a life-altering level. They also show change that was embraced, battled, and conquered even though it shook the foundations of their lives. They contain the elements of understanding the real issues around "Change".

Lead Change
The Myths of Change

There is a mythology around the concept of "change." As with many aspects of the industry built around advising and consulting on management matters, it has been developed with a keen awareness of who writes the checks for consulting fees. The basis of much of the literature and many of the techniques for managing change begin with a focus on the general population upon whom change is being inflicted. The most visible, seductive, and salable elements of the Change Management industry are built on an assumption of passive victimization. This is misdirection and crafted to appeal to executives.

The correct focus for managing change within an organization is on leadership and strategy. The very concept of "managing change" makes the assumption change is something that "happens" and which we need to manage. Change is characterized as a force of nature; something with a life of its own. The underlying assumption created is we do not control change. Rather change controls us and thus, the best we can do is soften the blow while everybody gets used to it. Baloney! This presentation of the concept, however, has two things going for it. One: It neatly lets managers and executives off the hook in terms of proactively dealing with change and providing leadership in a dynamic organization. Two: It creates an aura of complexity, fear, and doubt which leads to a desire for a "change management" expert. Note: The same people who created the "change management paradigm" will be happy to provide consulting services to help you identify and resolve your change issues. Consultants need to make a living somehow, you know.

The word "change" is like an A-line skirt or a well-cut suit: it covers a multitude of sins. Change is simply a word used to describe the transition from one state to another. In general, change of any kind creates some level of stress. This is because the physics and emotions of the world in which we live are subject to the effects of inertia. An object at rest will resist being moved; an object in motion will resist changing direction. That said, human beings have the capacity to experience thrilling and motivating excitement due to change. The differentiating factors are around the kind of change they encounter. Can they can harness, drive, and control change or, at a minimum, perceive it is a path to a better future? Or, are they repeatedly hit and knocked around by change for no good reason?

People greet change with open arms all the time. They get married. They buy new cars. They move to new places. They have kids. In fact, human beings who do not change or have an unreasonable fear of change (*cainotophobia*) are not people most of us want to be around. They become recluses or, if they are unusually cynical and witty, curmudgeons. Most people crave and seek change and they hate stagnation.

Purveyors of change management services carefully avoid going to the core issues of the leadership skills and capabilities of the management team. The result: a plethora of techniques for putting out the message:

"Poor you. We really understand what you are going through. And we really, really appreciate it."

The most pervasive and damaging concept to come from change management gurus is the idea "people don't like change" and the corollary subtext: "change is a negative." In reality, most of the issues change management experts help you fix are related to lack of control and the feeling of being victimized. As a leader you can head-off much of this before it becomes a problem.

Kinds of Change

Although change comes in many shapes and sizes, in general the issues around change which cause disruptions and problems fall in one of two categories:

1. **Fear of Change**: This is often seen in the wake of an announcement or a change in an organization which has the potential to impact people but has not yet done so. The retirement of a beloved leader, the hiring of a new senior executive, a merger, a dip in profits or stock value. These are events that create an anticipation of change and can plunge the team into the unknown.
2. **Reaction to Real Change**: This is seen when something impactful happens to change the circumstances or status quo of the team. These can be almost anything but often include: change in benefits or pay, change in work processes, change in performance expectations.

It is important to know this: the perception of a potential change can have as much impact to the performance of an organization as genuine material changes.

The Psychology of Change
Symptoms are not unique

Symptoms that manifest themselves as a negative reaction to change and which get the attention from change gurus include:

- Resistance; active or passive
- Anger
- Resentment
- Decrease in efficiency
- Lack of concern or caring
- Absenteeism

These same symptoms can be seen in other situations as well as those in which "change" plays a factor. Examples of these include:

- Regimented and paternalistic organizations that impose rigid structures perceived as arbitrary and inequitable;
- Marginalized segments of most societies;
- Organizations with ineffective leaders who are rewarded despite poor performance;
- Abusive or enabling families.

Underlying elements are consistent

Although the symptoms of poorly led and managed change can vary significantly, the elements that go into producing them are usually similar and predictable:

Lack of Control: When people find themselves in a dysfunctional organization or are going through a change causing them to act out in a negative way, it is often because they feel they have no control over their lives or the outcome. Changes in policies, pronouncement memos, all-hands meetings, tend to blend into a random generator of arbitrary orders – usually for the worse. If people are being buffeted around at the whim of the suits, if they do not know why, and if they cannot exercise control over their work life, they will become frustrated.

Lack of Investment: If it does not matter very much one way or the other what happens, it is difficult to work up the energy to get excited. In a community, citizens who see the value in following the rules tend to be those people with something to lose or gain. If you do not have an investment in society, where is the gain in following the rules or going out of your way to make it work? If you do not perceive a value or gain in the outcome of the change or in working toward the success of your organization, why would you do more than the minimum? If you have not seen the movie "Office Space," it is worth it if only for the scene below between Peter and the management consultants, the Bobs. Get it, watch it:

Peter : The thing is, Bob, it's not that I'm lazy; it's that I just don't care.

Bob Porter: Don't... don't care?

Peter: It's a problem of motivation, all right? Now if I work my ass off and Initech ships a few extra units, I don't see another dime, so where's the motivation? And here's something else, Bob: I have eight different bosses right now.

Bob Slydell: I beg your pardon?

Peter: Eight bosses.

Bob Slydell: Eight?

Peter: Eight, Bob. So that means that when I make a mistake, I have eight different people coming by to tell me about it. That's my only real motivation: not to be hassled. That and the fear of losing my job. But you know Bob, that will only make someone work just hard enough not to get fired.

Hopelessness: If it is bad and there is nothing on the horizon that suggests it is going to get better, why bother?

Unfairness: We learned about this in kindergarten. If your organization is in trouble, facing disruptive change, and the burden is disproportionally dropping on your shoulders, you will probably react in the natural and expected way. If people are being laid off and the executives are still driving company cars, leaving for their vacation houses Friday morning, and flying first class, angst and anger will bubble to the surface. If executives talk about "betting the farm" then lose the bet and nothing happens to them, you will be able to measure the loss in productivity simply by listening to the hallway chatter out of earshot of Executive Row. Perceived shared sacrifice is a key factor to unity and success when working through tough times or organizational change.

Reciprocity: Loyalty and going the extra mile is a two way street. If there is a desire for individuals in an organization to put in the extra time and cancel vacations to work through crises or implement new systems, the organization will need to reciprocate in some way. You can run your business in a way that does not involve extraordinary loyalty or commitment of the organization to the employees. However, if you choose that model, the business should not expect extra effort in changing and troubled times. You can only go to that well once.

Confidence in Outcome: Are people being led to a place worth going and is it likely the leadership will get them there? No one wants to kill themselves in a losing cause.

Spark in the tinderbox

Given the above, where does change fit in? Change is a triggering event. It can both create the underlying causes of discontent and focus attention on those issues. If an organization already has several of the elements listed above, a change can be the event that pushes people beyond the point of tolerable acceptance and triggers bad behavior. If change equates to loss without a reciprocal benefit, the behaviors we fear are likely to begin. Change is a pivot in the life of an organization that spotlights the underlying issues, whether they were caused by the change itself or were already in existence.

The Veneer and Refuge of "Change Management"

Change management techniques are valid and valuable tools. However, they are primarily reactive in nature and aimed at those impacted in order to help them "cope" with and accept the change. Change management consultants provide a safe harbor for those who want to impose change rather than provide leadership for positive forward movement. The general acceptance of change management as a discipline has created a framework behind which managers and leaders can take shelter with some level of respectability. "People don't like change," is powerful absolution for those who are unable to inspire and lead a forward-looking organization through dynamic and exciting change and must settle for plodding reactivity.

The Real Secrets of Change Management

The real secret to managing change is to be perceived as leading change rather than managing it. The key is effective, driving, and competent leadership which creates a focus for action and achievement. In times of fundamental change you need to make sure you and your team have your heads high, you can feel the breeze in your face, and your eyes are on the horizon. Four rules:

1. Drive change rather than being driven by it or victimized by it.
2. Lead your organization and your team to a worthwhile goal and demonstrate success.
3. Create an environment in which your team has impact on the outcome and has an investment in success.
4. Do not inflict arbitrary decisions and whiplash on your team. Change should fit logically into your strategy and contribute to your Definition of Success

A note on a change in leadership: Do you remember when you were young and broke-up with your boyfriend or girlfriend? Remember the churning stomach, the heartache, and the deep sighs? The one person who could have made it better, the one person you really needed to talk to was . . . the person you just split-up with. Dealing with a leadership change, especially an unexpected leadership change is like that. Succession planning is your first line of defense: be ready. Failing that, new leaders must step into the void if the organization is to avoid descending into confusion. Time is critical. For every day of confusion, you can count on two days of recovery. The people with authority must do their best to find a leader to take the helm and settle things down. An interim leader is fine but it must be clear this individual has the mandate and the authority to keep the organization moving forward.

What this doesn't mean

Be clear: you will not please all the people all of the time. There will be tough decisions which will negatively impact some people. In that case, change can be painful. So is an appendectomy. But without it the patient will usually die. People are very tolerant of pain, hardship, and change if they understand the need and feel they are moving to a better place. If you are leading effectively and taking your team to a successful future, the need for the trappings of "change management" dwindles.

LEADERSHIP CONCEPT #13

Winning through what you Control

Because you are sure not going to win using what you can't control!

The Colonials Change the Rules – A Story

IN 1776 THERE were a handful of superpowers in the world and they were all European. France, England, and Spain along with the Dutch and Portuguese were the major owners of global real estate with colonial possessions circling the earth. The idea a handful of colonies along the eastern seaboard of North America could take on the power of the British and win seemed laughable. The effective fighting forces of the Continental Army probably never exceeded 21,000. The British, by contrast, peaked at a total force of about 37,000 with effective fighting troops of about 27,000. The British had good weaponry and experienced commanders. They were disciplined, had the support of King George III, and they came prepared to straighten out a treasonous insurgency. The problem was they arrived prepared to fight a different war than the one waiting for them.

The Americans began by refusing to engage in stand and fight battles. They used un-gentlemanly guerrilla tactics: firing from the woods and down hills on the packed British columns. They exploited ancient rivalries and engaged the French against their old enemies. They used misdirection and tricks such as Benedict Arnold engineering the "leak" of information to the enemy about the three thousand troops under his command heading to attack Fort Stanwix. He only had a thousand but the British did not know that. They skedaddled and the fort was empty when the colonials arrived.

Primarily, however the colonials held on until the British exceeded their willingness to fight for a distant possession. They were highly invested in the outcome and they fought their own war on their own terms.

Miami Dolphins: 2008 – A Story

As the 2008 NFL Season started, the Miami Dolphins were coming off a humiliating previous year record of 1-15. That was when Head Coach Tony Soprano and Coach David Lee decided to stop playing by other teams' rules. They knew the entire NFL defense is built around reacting to the quarterback. They looked back in time and revived the old single-wing offense created by Pop Warner to take advantage of the talents of his star player, Jim Thorpe. In the single-wing offense, sometimes called the wildcat or wild hog, the backs and ends line up in a lopsided formation and the snap can go to any of the backs. It removes the quarterback as your key point of control as well as you single point of failure.

The inherent value of the single-wing is not that it is intrinsically better than the standard "I" formation. It can be better if the talent on your team can leverage it. The value for the Dolphins, however, was simple: no one was expecting it. No one knew how to adjust quickly to defend against it. Even when they figured it out, opposing teams had to balance the return on investment of preparing to counter a single team in a 16 game schedule.

The Dolphins went 11-5 that season and won the AFC East. As anyone will tell you, that is a big improvement on 1-15. The Dolphins did not go out on the field to play "football." They went out to win football games within the allowable framework of the rules. They did not play someone else's game. They chose instead to play their own game.

Do What You Can . . .

Whose rules?

Human activity takes place within a framework of rules and assumptions. One of the big mistakes we make is confusing the assumptions with the rules. When we do that we are conforming to other peoples' ideas and desires rather than doing all we can to win.

Here is a bit of information you need to know: If you play the game like everyone else and you work very hard and get as good as you possibly can, but the other team has a fundamental underlying advantage, you will usually lose. If the players on the other team are slightly more talented and both teams have the same level training and coaching, you will usually lose. In order to win, therefore, you must do three things:

1. Understand what you can control and what you cannot control;
2. Determine how you can use what you control within the broad framework of rules; and
3. Do what you can when you can.

Using what you Control

Make a list of the things you can control and cannot control. Once you have a handle on them, you can decide how to use the things within your control, either to create to an advantage or to mitigate the things outside your control. Below are some examples of things within your control and outside of your control from the world of sports (basketball) and the world of business.

Basketball

Basketball	
Control	**Don't Control**
Conditioning	Opponent Conditioning
Spirit	Opponent Shot Percentage
Shot Percentage	Opponent Talent
Game Strategy	
Ability to Draw Fouls	
Teamwork	
Game Knowledge	
Knowledge of Your Opponent	
Ability to React to Opponent	

A basketball coach must make the decision on what foundation he or she will choose to win:

Plan A – Teach "Pure" Basketball: If a coach has the luxury of a great talent pool, he can choose to focus on conditioning and fundamentals. He can teach the game of "basketball" and know fundamental execution will likely bring the team success.

If, however, the team does not have the same level of physicality as the opposition, something else must enter the mix or he will lose. If a coach does not have a complete field of capabilities at his disposal, continuing to act as if he does will probably not work. Brain must triumph over brawn.

Plan B – Excellence in Control: Do not ignore the basics but look inward and find areas of control and advantage:

- **Foul Shot Percentage:** For most basketball teams, the area under their control that will bring the highest return is an improvement in their percentage from the foul line. The game of basketball is much more physical now than in the past. It is not unusual for there to be twenty or thirty free-throw points available in a high school or college game. Every ten percent increase in the free-throw percentage will yield between two and three points. If your team makes 25% of their free-throws, raising the average to 45% will yield five points per game. How many games have been lost by less than five points? The effective yield is even greater due to the double pay-off for successful free-throws in the single bonus period. Many teams could win three more games a season and be in the running in the final seconds of several more games. These are free points and are left on the table on a regular basis.
- **Talent Pivot:** Most teams have at least one excellent physical player. Decide the highest use for that player. Can they take the best opposing player out of the game by dogging them all night?
- **Game Strategy:** If you are an underdog, you will need a strategy and you will need plays. Create a disruption squad to spell your mature squad. Drop the immature speedsters into the mix for two minutes to throw off the opponent's game.

- **Overplay:** If something works for a team, they will tend to over-play it. Watch for it and turn it against them. If aggressive traps have worked for them, draw them into placing three of their players away from the basket. If they are draped over your players, teach your kids how to turn into them and draw the foul. If you can exploit overplay, three things happen:
  - **Sucker-punch:** Until they adjust, you beat them by taking advantage of the overplay.
  - **What's our backup?** They have to back off. If overplaying has worked well for them, they often do not have a fall-back game.
  - **Fouls:** They start to get fouls, you start to get points.
- **Conditioning**: If you don't have finesse or the skill, you *can* develop the ability to run opposing teams off the court and put them on their shorts. You will play against a couple of teams every season that are running short of players that night. Wear them down. A tired player is an easily frustrated player.
- **Draw Fouls:** Excellent players and excellent teams accustomed to winning are apt to get frustrated. Watch for it and exploit it. Learn to draw fouls by going up through the crowd. Assign someone to drape themselves over the high scorer. If you dog a player who habitually has their own way, they will start taking swings at your players. When that happens, you have them where you want them. Every foul you draw is a chance for 2 points. Count the players on the other bench. How many subs do they have? Are they cocky and willing to foul? If you can bait them into a high foul count, you may be able to force them to back off.
- **Game Knowledge/Crisp Behavior:** Do not allow confusion on the court. This is simple and unforgivably overlooked on a regular basis. The game is won in the classroom as much as on the floor. Enforce efficient court behavior: Run-on/run-off. Clear player-to-player sub instructions. Loud and clear talking to each other. No blind saves when you are under the opposing basket. Basic discipline: get some.
- **Fundamentals:** To be clear: games cannot be won on razzle-dazzle

alone. Team fundamentals must be at a level to at least slow down a stronger team.

Business

Business	
Control	**Don't Control**
Customer Service	Competitor Products and Pricing
Your Product & Pricing	Economic Cycles
Expense Ratios	Laws & Regulations
Personnel Performance	Competitors' Strength
Productivity	
Teamwork	
Clarity of Niche and Positioning	
Knowledge of Your Competition	
Ability to React to Competition	

Success in sports and success in business have fundamental similarities. In business, as in sports, you can control some things and not others. Also, in business you will find yourself competing against organizations with deeper pockets than you and with capabilities you do not have. Your ability to succeed will depend on your ability to find areas you control that will offset the advantages of your competitors. These areas are then managed in such a way to do one of two things: Either they contribute behind the scenes to the efficiency of your operational model or they are managed to a high profile in order to embed themselves in customer and prospect awareness.

Stop-Loss or Differentiator

Your winning strategy requires a conscious decision about which areas you will select as competitive weapons and which you will use as stop loss. Things allocated to stop-loss are those for which you are willing to concede a competitive edge to others but not to the extent it allows them to create a decisive point of differentiation. If, however, you are willing to concede things as stop-loss, you must bring others to the front as competitive differentiators. In other words, you can concede in some areas but not in all. If you do not have benefits to outweigh your stop-loss concessions, you will move steadily and relentlessly down the food chain. Any aspect of your product, service, or relationship can be a differentiator or a stop-loss. But it must be deliberate and managed positioning. It must not be an accident.

Some Examples:

- **Product as Differentiator:** Leading edge trend setter. Market: Early adopters. Examples: Nike, Apple, Tommy Bahama, North Face. *Note: Products often cost significantly more than equivalent competitive items. The extra cost is the value of owning a branded product.*
- **Product as Stop-Loss:** Followers of proven successes. Market: Mid-to-late adopters. Examples: Emerson Electronics, Sears, Timex
- **Price as Differentiator:** Low-cost leader. Market: Cost-conscious and cost-driven consumers. Examples: Costco, Wal-Mart, Coby Electronics, GEICO.
- **Price as Stop-Loss:** Keeps pricing within market expectations. Market: General product and service oriented consumers who can be driven away by inflated pricing but will not make decisions on small percentages. Examples: VISA, Ford, Nordstrom, Safeway.
- **Relationship as Differentiator**: Relationship can balance other elements through high levels of service and appearance of partnership. Market: Affinity-driven consumers and those for whom personal service has high value. Examples: American Express, Nordstrom, AAA. Caution Flag: The relationship model is often used by executives as a cover for the fact they have little else to offer. Lots of companies talk about relationship and partnership with their customers, few actually have it. Relationship as a differentiator is not an intangible item. It is manageable and quantifiable. If you are counting on relationship with your customer to bring you a competitive advantage, that relationship must provide a benefit to your customer. Relationship does not come from advertising

cute spokespersons. If you have a relationship model, you must ask yourself this question: What is it about this relationship my customer will be willing to pay for? If you cannot answer that question, you are fooling yourself.

The Single Most Important thing to Remember about Competitive Differentiation: If your organization is a Fortune 1,000 company, all stuff they teach in business school about choosing your area of competition is valid. It is critical the management teams at Nike, Nordstrom, Intel, etc. decide in which arena they will compete. Michael Treacy and Fred Wiersema, in their book *The Discipline of Market Leaders*, tell us that our strategic market management should focus in one of three areas:

- Operational Excellence (resulting in excellent pricing)
- Product Leadership (best on the market / latest and greatest)
- Customer Intimacy (service / relationship)

They are absolutely correct . . . if you are Nike, Nordstrom, Intel, or American Express. Michael and Fred, however, make the error of most college professors, consultants, business pundits, etc: they seem to believe their audience is comprised of Warren Buffet, Howard Schultz, Steve Jobs, and similar Grand Poobahs of American industry. For most of us, on the other hand, the read is interesting but not incredibly relevant to the real life decisions we make. On the return trip to real life, we note our organizations operate and survive outside that lofty plateau, and our choices are much simpler. Listen: If you compete without the benefit of being so big you have your own gravity, here are the areas in which you will win:

1. Service (you pay attention to your customer)
2. Relationship (you know your customer)
3. Quality (you do it right)
4. Location (you are convenient)

You will not win a competitive war on price. You will not win a competitive war on product. You will win in the hearts of your customers.

Do What You Can When You Can

He who will not when he can
Often discovers, he cannot when he will.

If you understand what you control and manage it to your best advantage, you will increase your chances of success. If you construct the game to favor your areas of control and excellence, you multiply the leverage available from those areas. If do what you can when you can to grow and hone the areas you control, you will be ready to strike when the opportunity comes. In that way, even the areas you do not control will sometimes slide into your column.

Advantage you.

The Core Trait of the Leader

A Driving Desire to Lead

George Patton and Omar Bradley - A Story

George Patton

WORLD WAR II General George Patton was flamboyant, profane, impatient, impetuous, and driven to lead. Patton was fascinated with the glory and romance of war. He loved the trumpets, the costumes, and the rituals of military campaigning. General Omar Bradley, Patton's colleague and contemporary who, early on, worked for Patton and later became his boss, wrote this about Patton:

> *Why does he use profanity? Certainly he thinks of himself as a destined war leader. Whenever he addressed men he lapsed into violent, obscene language. He always talked down to his troops. When Patton talked to officers and men in the field, his language was studded with profanity and obscenity. I was shocked. He liked to be spectacular; he wanted men to talk about him and to think of him. "I'd rather be looked at than overlooked." . . . He was living a role he had set for himself twenty or thirty years before. An amazing figure!*

> *I would have relieved him instantly (after the incident at the 93rd Evacuation Hospital) and would have had nothing more to do with him. He was colorful but he was impetuous, full of temper, bluster, inclined to treat the troops and subordinates as morons. His whole concept of command was opposite to mine. He was primarily a showman. The show always seemed to come first.*

George Patton was arguably the best tank commander ever produced by the United States. He was an incredibly effective leader despite his nearly Shakespearean flaws. His reason for living was to fight a war and lead men.

Omar Bradley

Omar Bradley was quiet, self-effacing, and respectful of subordinates. According to Ernie Pyle, a journalist during World War II, Bradley seldom gave an order without preceding it with the word "Please." Carlo D'Este points out in his book, *Patton: A Genius for War*, Bradley was uncomfortable with the trappings that accompany senior rank, especially the carnival atmosphere of Patton's movements as "he steamed about with great convoys of cars and great squads of cameramen." George Patton wrote about Bradley:

> *A man of great mediocrity. On the other hand Bradley has many of the attributes which are considered desirable in a general. He wears glasses, has a strong jaw, talks profoundly and says little, and is a shooting companion of the Chief of Staff. Also a loyal man. I consider him among our better generals.*

Omar Bradley was one of the most capable and impactful leaders produced by the United States. After his service in World War II he went on to become the first Chairman of the Joint Chiefs of Staff and was the primary advisor to Harry Truman during the Korean War and the crisis surrounding Douglas MacArthur's insubordination and his eventual firing.

The Essence of Leadership

Omar Bradley and George Patton were almost polar opposites in terms of outlook and leadership style. Both, however, were great leaders. They were great because they shared the one trait common to all leaders: the gut-level, driving need to be an effective leader.

The Core of Leadership

Successful leadership requires a fierce and driving desire to lead. The trait common to all effective leaders is the willingness and commitment to do what must be done to take your team, company, army, or nation to the place it needs to go. The illustration of Patton and Bradley, however, shows the very different ways this trait can show up in human behavior.

At the root of this trait are two different driving mechanisms which tend to intertwine within the psychology of the leader:

- **Ego**: Some people are driven to lead by sense of self and their desire to be out in front. These are people for whom the act of leading is energizing and once tasted, find it very difficult to take on the role of follower. They are the kind of person that would agree with Julius Caesar's comment when he was passing through a tiny and muddy village. One of his officers observed that, even in an obscure backwater such as this, there must be people who scrabble and compete for leadership. Caesar replied he would rather be the first man in this mud-hole than the second man in Rome. Some leaders have an innate need to lead and be the center of attention. People at the extreme end of this type are not the most balanced and secure individuals. They draw their worth and reinforcement from external positive reinforcement. They can, however, be some of the most effective leaders because the need to successfully lead is at the core of their being.
- **Obligation**: Some people are driven to lead by their sense of commitment to getting things done. These people are often those who enjoy leadership but do not fiercely seek it. They rise to fill the need when the tasks of leadership are either given to them or there is a void that needs to be filled.

In most leaders you see a mixture of these elements. A leader who is fully driven by ego will tend to become self-centric to the point their decision making becomes skewed as they judge things and make decisions weighted disproportionately to the impact on them rather than the enterprise. These leaders tend to discount the input and value of others. A leader fully driven by obligation, however, tends to become exhausted because they do not get the vital recharge the act of leadership provides for those who thrive on it.

The Common Judgment

The other element common to all effective leadership is success. The actions and activities of leadership cannot assure success. There are no definable formulas or structures you can employ to guarantee success. There are two factors which go into passing judgment on the success of a leader:

- **Followers**: Your success as a leader is not determined by you. Successful leadership is not about the forms or techniques of leadership. Successful leadership is defined by the reaction of the led. No matter how silly and ineffective a leader seems, if the team is moving and performing, the leadership is successful. No matter how iron-jawed or inspiring the leader seems, if the team is not following and performing, leadership is failing.
- **Team Success**: Even if you have succeeded in creating a loyal team that will follow you into the fire, if you do not achieve the outcomes you desired you cannot be considered a successful leader. You may have done good things. Your team may remember you fondly and tell their grand-children about your charismatic leadership. You may have imparted invaluable life-lessons to your team. But if you do not achieve what you set out to do, it is not success.

Leadership is judged entirely on results.

Caveat: Leaders will have failures. The ability to lead a team through a failure to success is one of the key capabilities of an effective leader.

Innate or Learned?

Can leaders be created and developed or is leadership an innate, inborn skill? This question has been debated since the caveman days of management consulting. The truthful answer is: no one knows. However, since this book is not attempting to solve cosmic riddles about human potential, here is a rough-and-ready answer that will work pretty well for day-to-day thinking:

- Leaders cannot be created if the essential desire or ability to lead is not there.

- Leaders can be discovered even if leadership skills had not previously been in evidence. Leaders can appear where they are least expected. An individual who has shown little interest in leadership can suddenly step into the void and take on the mantle of the leader. Leadership skill can be a deeply buried seed waiting for the right opportunity.
- Leadership skills can be developed
- Overwhelmingly, leaders must be trained, whether passively (observation), actively (formal training), or by the school of hard knocks.

An individual must have the inborn desire or at least the capability and willingness to lead. The willingness to do what is necessary is the key. If these things are not part of the package, the leader will fail.

Just because you think so. . .

Leaders must be developed and matured. Natural leaders often come with a fighter-pilot mentality. They have a high degree of confidence in themselves and their abilities; an opinion often not burdened by a relationship to reality. Life is seen through the lens of their opinions and approach to the world. Having no experience managing people may not seem like a significant deficit in their background when they take on a new position or challenge. Young leaders, as they develop, are often surprised by the limits of their power, especially in terms of their power over the inertia of an organization. Organizations are seldom convinced to follow a leader by his or her words. A logical argument, while necessary, is not sufficient. What seems self-evident to the new leader may not seem so to the team.

Young leaders developing their skills need to observe and learn about politics and organizational dynamics. They need to develop an appreciation for the concepts of buy-in and consensus as well as how to make an unpopular decision or force an issue. Leaders need to learn not only they must hold people accountable but also *how* to hold them accountable. If leadership was easy, the world would be full of people like Omar Bradley and George Patton. At the risk of sounding trite, remember: leaders need both the iron hand and the silk glove.

Management

Management is the essential element for the creation and effective function of human organizations. Without skill and discipline in administration, process, and organizational dynamics, you will simply get the babble of bright children and a lot of people milling around.

Universal Requirements for Managed Success

Count 'em: Two

THERE ARE TWO and only two elements universally required in order to manage an organization to success. Once these are known, everything else can be built upon them. These elements are:

- **Identity**: Who are you? What do you do? What is your mission? What are your values?
- **Definition of Success**: Where are you going? What are you trying to achieve? What is your vision? You will be successful if you do this thing.

If success is achieved by organizations that cannot articulate these elements, it is a result of either luck or someone has them locked in their brain and is driving the organization based upon them. You cannot, however, have deliberate, managed, and sustained positive results without understanding your identity and the way you define success.

Note: A third item, necessary to create a plan is an honest understanding of your current state. We will address that a little further down the road.

Universal Requirements for Managed Success

Identity and the *Definition of Success* provide the foundation upon which all else is built. They are the framework within which the future state can be crafted and decisions can be made. They provide a launch pad for action as well as a restraining influence which prevents willy-nilly, unfocused activities. Their guiding limits, structures and goals, paradoxically, provide the team with freedom of movement and action. They empower focus on achievement rather than process.

Identity and Definition of Success are not sufficient to plan the road to a successful future but without them it is not possible. These concepts are necessary at all levels: enterprise, department, initiative, product, program, and project. Without an understanding of what the "thing" is and what it means to be successful, you will find yourself wrapped around your axel and unable to effectively manage. Many runaway projects reach that state because the project team and the organization's management team did not clarify what they were about and what they were expected to achieve.

Identity

- In 1983 John Martin took over as president of Taco Bell. He asked a simple question: "Are we a maker of food or a feeder of people?" The answer had fundamental impacts on every aspect of the business: distribution, store design, menu, personnel, vendor management, and others.
- Does GEICO sell insurance or money in your pocket?
- Is the iPod an MP3 player or iconogrpahy?
- Are periodical publishers in the newspaper and magazine business or the information business?
- Are the "Yellow Pages" about a book of yellow pulpy paper or about connecting customers with businesses?
- Were railroads in the "railroad" business, or in the transportation business?

Know who you are and what your product is. Know why your organization exists. Know what values are core to your behavior and actions. If you fail to understand your identity, there is a very good chance you will find yourself making plans around something very different than the thing you are in business for.

Hint for success: The name of your company or industry can get you in trouble. Product-based naming is particularly tricky. At some point it will bite you. It is important you know the difference between your product and the business you are in. And it is an area in which you probably cannot get a good opinion from your market base. Your customer is probably perfectly happy to use the name you have provided for the item that fills their need. However, they are remarkably quick to discern an alternative if something attractive is presented to them. The history of automated teller machines is illustrative. The idea of getting cash from a machine in a wall was conclusively rejected by consumers when they were initially asked about it. Nonetheless, a few cash machines were installed and became wildly successful. People figured out very quickly the advantage of getting money when they needed it rather than during banking hours. If your identity is based on what you provide rather than what your customer buys, think about it long and hard. Other examples:

- Insurance = Protection
- Clothing = Image or utility
- Internet = Convenience
- Human Services = Life Success
- Vinyl Records Albums = Media

Definition of Success

In addition to knowing who you are, you must understand where you are headed and at what point you can declare success. In almost all cases, your Definition of Success must be measurable. If it is not quantifiable, it has little meaning and will not be usable for planning and decision making. The Definition of Success can be a quantified version of your identity or it can be something entirely different. As a general rule, the Identity and Definition of Success of nonprofit organizations closely align (e.g. fewer encounters with the juvenile justice system for at-risk children). For-profit enterprises typically use their Identity as a vehicle to achieve their Definition of Success (i.e. increased corporate value). Examples of Definitions of Success:

- Profit
- Stock value
- Achievement of Vision or Mission goals
  - Elimination of homelessness in a city
  - Universally accessible education
- Achievement of program or interim goals
  - Market penetration
  - Expense ratios

Remember, the specific type of success is less important than the agreement on the definition and the unified focus it provides. What is the Definition of Success of a marketing campaign? Branding? Awards? Increased sales? Figure it out.

Examples of Definitions of Success:

- Jack Welch: GE will either be number one or two in any business they are in (ongoing success)
- JFK: Put an man on the moon by the end of the decade (program success)
- Starbucks 1992-1993 Expansion Strategy (interim success): Opening 20 stores in each targeted city in the US in 2 years.

A Final Note on Definition of Success

It is amazing how often people take exception to the concept of Definition of Success. The objection often focuses on the idea of "declaring success." To be clear: the Definition of Success is not, in most cases, a one time achievement or an end point. It is dynamic. Ongoing success takes continued focus and energy. The Definition of Success may include a repeated metric such as ten percent annual growth. It may be an interim achievement; one of many over time. Do not misinterpret the Definition of Success as a single goal or objective which, once achieved allows you to sit back and relax. It simply provides an agreed upon state which the organization is required to reach. It is always beyond where we are now – even if we have just achieved it. Next year we will not be able to achieve ten percent growth the same way we achieved it this year. Celebrate success and keep moving.

Business Competencies Necessary for Success

The Big Four

THERE ARE FOUR major areas in which all businesses must be competent in order to succeed:

1. Customer-centric core capabilities
2. Customer-focused administrative capabilities
3. Organization-focused capabilities
4. Market-focused capabilities

These four areas define the required core capability set of business. Business results come directly from the ability to perform in these four areas. They are not optional; you cannot select just one or two. A successful business (for-profit or nonprofit) must execute well in all four.

Business failures usually do not occur in the heart of the business. The core, customer-centric essence of the business is most often the place where heart and passion are found. It is also usually the place of the greatest competence. Management infrastructure surrounding the core is most often the source of business problems.

Business Competencies Necessary for Success

At the heart of most businesses is a core of domain knowledge, passion, and expertise. It is the essence of the business. It is usually the subject of the mission statement. It can range from gardening services to banking to baking to insurance, or anything else. It is why our customers are attracted to our business and why employees want to work here. It is our *reason d'être*. It is our center and our pivot-point. It is almost never the problem.

Successful businesses understand they must be at least competent in all four full rings of execution. Businesses failures usually occur in the three outer rings of infrastructure surrounding the core business.

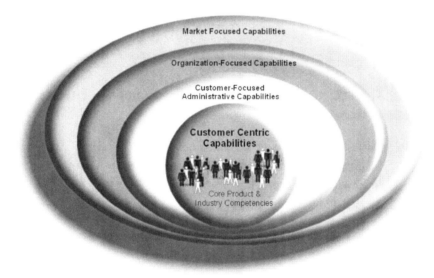

Figure 1. Rings of Capability and Competence

The Four Rings

Ring 1: Customer Centric Capabilities

These are the reasons your customers come to you. They include your product and the immediate delivery. Examples:

- Do you have the item the customer wants? Is it in stock? Can you get it in their hands in an excellent manner?
- Do you treat the customer or member with respect?
- Have you delivered your product or service with high enough

quality and in a way that is accessible enough to encourage a second purchase?

- Are you clear on the nature of the product? Are you meeting the needs of brand, cost, or quality?
- Do you have the trust of your customer?
  - Trust: Customer trust is built on two primary perceived characteristics:
    - Clarity and minimum confusion:
      - Product: What is it?
      - Web site navigation
      - Clean stores with good layout and good lighting
    - Doing what you say you will do:
      - Delivering product as and when promised
      - Being open and available at predictable times
      - Having sufficient inventory to provide the goods today

Ring 2: Customer-Focused Administrative Capabilities

These are the second level customer contact items that can make your relationship with your customer a joy or a nightmare. Examples:

- Can you bill accurately and efficiently?
- Can you handle and resolve problems in a seamless and efficient manner?
- Are you reachable when necessary?
- Are you friendly and service oriented?
- Is customer data handled in a manner that respects privacy?
- Can you manage secondary processing efficiently (e.g. billing other companies or the government on behalf of your customers?)

Ring 3: Organization-Focused Capabilities

These are all those things the customer should not be aware of and will never know about if they are handled well. They occur behind the scenes and range widely. Note: These capabilities are, however, very interesting to and closely watched by investors, competitors, and industry professionals. Examples:

- Information technology infrastructure
- Expense ratios that indicate good stewardship and create the ability to bring a competitive product to the market
- Operational strategy
- Efficient FTE ratios
- Human resources management
- Compliance management
- Risk management
- Disaster recovery and business continuity
- Facilities management
- Business services management
- Corporate communications
- Leadership
- Succession planning

Ring 4: Market-Focused Capabilities

These are the capabilities that allow you to talk to and learn from the market. You must have the ability to tell the market about yourself in an effective and impactful way as well as listen and act upon what the market is saying. Examples:

- Branding
- Marketing
- Call to action
- Market research
- Product development
- Market strategies
- Public relations and communications

Pay Attention

You must make it your business to do what is necessary to succeed. That means you must care, nurture, and manage all the critical elements of your enterprise. You will only be as strong as the one you neglect.

Honesty and the Holy Troika of Planning

Overview

IN ADDITION TO the twin titans of Identity and Definition of Success, a third item is required to a create plan and build your path to organizational success. In many cases, this third item is more difficult to get right than the first two. The three legs of the stool of successful planning are:

1. Identity
2. Definition of Success
3. Honest Current Situation Assessment

With these three, you will know: who you are, where you are going, and where you are starting from.

The Current Situation Assessment, however, is problematic because it is, in many ways, an evaluation of the performance of the organization today and implicit commentary on how well management team has prepared for the future. The ability to be honest about organizational performance, expense ratios, market success, operational efficiencies, etc. is the key to understanding the gap you must cross to achieve success. In turn, it provides the basis for creating the correct initiatives and priorities. Without this knowledge it is almost certain you will misdirect your efforts and resources.

Honesty in describing and embracing the current situation often carries the drag chute of ego, previous decisions, and anticipated career impacts. It can get tangled in sunk cost thinking rather than looking for the best and shortest path to success.

Strong leaders understand and act on the knowledge that, in order to reach a destination, you must know where you are starting. Strong leaders look forward rather than backward. Strong leaders will learn from the past rather than avoiding it or justifying it. By knowing where you are today, you can build a plan to travel to where you want to be.

The Holy Troika of Successful Planning

As mentioned in a previous Management Concept, there are two universal requirements for managing an organization to success:

- **Identity**: Who are you? What is your mission? What are your values?
- **Definition of Success**: Where are you going? What are you trying to achieve? What is your vision? You will be successful when you achieve this.

Identity and Definition of Success are creative in nature. They can usually be agreed to with a minimum of disagreement or perceived threat. The third item is more concrete but, paradoxically, more difficult to agree upon. The third item necessary for creating a successful plan is the honest current situation assessment.

Current Situation Assessment

In order to reach your chosen future, you must be able to clearly articulate where you are today. The ability to state your current situation, both qualitatively and quantitatively, gives you the baseline from which you can make effective plans for the future. The lack of ability to do this leads inevitably to holes in your planning and misapplication of resources, money, and focus. Areas of particular interest in this exercise are:

- Operational effectiveness and efficiency
- Expense management

- Customer satisfaction
- Repeat business or retention
- Revenue trends
- Complaints
- Quality of product
- Financial management
- Market position, penetration, and success
- Investment performance (all types of investment: financials, project, product, etc)
- Risk
- Information technology results and performance
- Market threats and opportunities
- Regulatory compliance and anticipated changes in laws and regulations
- The current state of our old friends: "Identity" and "Definition of Success"
- Locked-in plans and commitments

As we look at the above and any other areas key to your organization it is important to recognize both the current state of performance and the underlying root causes of excellence or need for improvement.

There are many tools available for the discovering and articulating your current situation. These include facilitated discovery sessions, SWOT, and others. The key factor in this exercise, however, is the commitment to honesty, openness, and listening. You must be strong, up-front, and must be paying attention. When gathering information about your current state, it should not be expected that executives and senior managers will have intimate and detailed knowledge at their finger tips. They will, however, be expected to have a pretty good picture of the current state and a strong awareness of major indicators around operations, product, and finances.

The Honesty Thing

When creating a valid current situation assessment, you should anticipate the following truism: the higher in the organization an individual resides and the longer they have been there, the more difficult it will be for them to honestly evaluate the situation. The current state of the organization is a result of their management and they are now in the awkward position of being asked to pass judgment on their own performance.

If the organization is wildly successful, it is reasonably easy to be self-critical. There is even a certain cachet in humble self-deprecation. On the other hand, if the organization is experiencing mixed results and senior managers are required to bring their performance into the sunlight, you may see reactive behaviors. Team members may start to focus on perceived threats as they consider the reaction of the bosses. In this situation, you may see misdirection in regard to results and root causes. If an organization is failing, executives and managers may be galvanized into brutal honesty or they may look for reasons they are not to blame for the situation. Remember, these individuals, regardless of how senior they are or how much money they make, are human. They will more than likely have a human reaction to things that could negatively impact their careers and compensation.

The Fix Threshold

Once individuals have reached a point at which they are heavily invested in the past, it is difficult for them reorient themselves to the future. In general, the longer a manager or executive has been responsible for a problem area, the less likely it is they will be able to accurately report on it or fix it. There are several reasons for this:

- **Lack of Understanding**: The situation may have been in existence long enough to have entered the realm of standard operations and the manager does not see the problem.
- **Gone Native:** The manager may not be willing to undertake the difficulties associated with fixing it. If he or she has personal relationships with those likely to be impacted, the trade-off of fixing the situation may not be worth the perceived disloyalty to the group.
- **Loss of Face:** If the manager currently responsible is the same person who sold the investment or has been in charge while the problem existed, the potential embarrassment of having not fixed

it grows greater. There is an increasing self-awareness that he or she will look foolish if they make an about-face.

- **Career Impact:** Big mistakes can impact the overall trajectory of a career. Beyond that, the sad reality is, at some point in a career, one large mistake is the end. If a threat is perceived to the standing or career of a manager or executive, you should expect the natural fight-or-flight response.

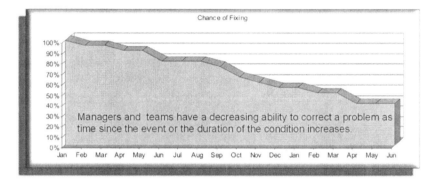

The Fix Threshold is one of the main reasons Boards of Directors replaces executive teams and CEOs if an organization is unable to turn itself around or make progress. Being caught in the inertia of the Fix Threshold makes it difficult for managers and executives to provide an honest current situation assessment. Be aware: you may need extra effort to get the real picture of sensitive areas.

That Sounds Pretty Negative

Maybe, but understanding is the basis of opportunity. The way to get through the challenges of compiling a good situation assessment lies in leadership and culture. The leaders of the organization must be clear about their orientation. Are they leaving sunk cost thinking at the door? Are they looking for the best road to the future? Are they looking for answers or pointing fingers? Honesty in self-assessing a current situation lies in the knowledge (from the boss) that inappropriate justification of the past is not compatible with a sincere forward-looking approach. Safety without enablement is the key. People are usually receptive to accountability combined with disciplined hope for the future. They react almost uniformly negatively to the prospect of getting their heads chopped off.

A Note about the Fix Threshold

The Fix Threshold is an indicator. It helps us watch for the point beyond which recovery is unlikely. Before the point of no return, encouragement and support should be provided to assist in rectifying problems. The concept helps facilitate thinking in terms of the potential for success. It helps leaders identify when it is time to take drastic remedial action and when it is acceptable to work the current situation. Being alert to crossing the Fix Threshold helps spot when it is time for executives and managers to move on or be replaced. It is a concept to remember whether you are dealing with an individual who has reached a threshold point or you are in danger of reaching it yourself.

If you are the supervisor of an individual who is unable to fix a persistent problem, you may need to cut your losses and replace that individual. By far the best predictor of future behavior is past behavior. If you have seen behaviors repeated multiple times, you will probably continue to see them. Hoping for a change in results in the face of persistent poor performance will almost always result in disappointment. When that happens, the failure is no longer the responsibility of the directly involved individual. Rather, it becomes the failure of the higher-levels in the organization, whether manager, executive, or Board of Directors. If the president of an organization is persistently unable to create a winning company, the Board's responsibility is clear. If a company's product and price model cannot penetrate the market consistently, the product officer probably needs to be replaced. Allowing ongoing churn after it is clear the Fix Threshold has been passed indicates poor judgment and poor leadership. Accountability travels up the ladder.

If you are the leader in a persistent trouble spot, you need to be aware your organizational superiors will eventually lose confidence in you. You must proactively find the way to solve the problem or get clarity on the factors causing trouble. If you can solve the problem, do it. If it is unsolvable, communicate fast and get clarity on expectations versus the potential for success. Remember, your removal is the most likely change. If your bosses are doing their job, they will not tolerate persistent chronic problems without a predictable solution. A change will be made. If your leadership is the problem, fix it. If the problem is elsewhere, make it your job to help the organization figure it out and take care of it.

The Nature of Resistance

RESISTANCE IS A natural and normal part of management. It comes in various forms and disguises. It can be good, bad, or neutral. It cannot, however, be ignored.

If you are not getting resistance and disagreement, either you or your staff is not doing their job. Perhaps you are not being bold enough in your ideas or your team is not strong enough to confront you. You need resistance and disagreement. They are the keys to creating, vetting, and finally implementing the best solution possible. Resistance and challenge tests ideas and provides the heat to temper them and give them strength. If you do not encounter resistance and actively work through it, it will fester interminably in underground caucuses that undermine your ability to act as a team and move forward.

Try to understand the nature of resistance you encounter. There are four major categories:

- **Legitimate and Correct Resistance**
- **Adjustment Resistance**
- **Fear-Based Resistance**
- **Belief-Based Resistance**

Misdirection: In all of the above, watch for misdirection and hidden agendas. Fear-based resistance will almost always try to dress itself as something else. You will need to probe, listen, and talk to be sure you understand the nature of the resistance you are encountering.

The Nature of Resistance

In most phases of your management career, you will encounter resistance of various kinds. Resistance and disagreement are two close siblings. As a leader and a manager, you should understand you will deal with resistance. Additionally, you should encourage and embrace disagreement.

- **Disagreement**: Disagreement and discussion are at the heart of getting it right. You are perfectly capable of saying "Yes" to yourself. You do not need your staff and co-workers to do it as well. Disagreement, discussion, and rigorous debate allow the brilliance of the team to create the best solution and outcome. If more often than not you find yourself getting support and agreement, you might want to do a little snooping around. Eventually the truth will out. Get copies of "The Emperor's New Clothes" by Hans Christian Andersen and give it to your staff. Let them know you will not be caught wearing imaginary clothes.

- **Resistance**: Resistance is inevitable. It is a form of static inertia and is usually a reaction to proposed or implemented changes. It is important to face resistance and work it through. In order to do that, you should try to understand the basis of the resistance:

  - **Legitimate and Correct Resistance:** You could be wrong. You may be encountering resistance because you are about to do something really dumb. Be open to that possibility. Make sure you can explain clearly and succinctly, without holes in your logic, why you are asking people to pursue the course causing the resistance.

  - **Adjustment Resistance**: You are actually getting agreement but the ideas are in need of tuning or overhauling. Do not be paranoid; treat this behavior as support and embrace the offer.

  - **Fear-Based Resistance**: Fear-based resistance is, surprisingly, something you can work through in a fairly straightforward manner. There is fear or concern about what is happening, either the process or the outcome. Some causes of fear-based resistance include:

- I will be personally affected negatively.
- It will be detrimental to a group I care about.
- It will fail.
- We don't know how to do it.

Fear-based resistance can usually be mitigated or defused. Look for the items triggering the reaction and try to find the action or assurances that can defuse the concerns. The answer may be as simple as opening your ears and listening. It may be a risk-taking and safety issue. It may be training and support. Within the cost-benefit structure of the item(s) being resisted, take the mitigation steps to deal with the fears.

> *Hint: A good place to start when dealing with fear-based resistance is this: Find the high-level outcome to which all parties can agree. Then work your way down, from the general to the specific, until you find the wall. In that way, you can peel back the onion until you find the true locus of the issues.*

- **Belief-Based Resistance:** This is the hard one. If a fundamental belief is in play, it is often extremely difficult to overcome. Leadership, listening, and decision-making become critical to working through belief-based concerns. Again, look for common ground. But be aware: the true believer is hard to convince and change.

Resistance and the Team

Disagreement should be embraced and leveraged to assure a more rigorous and effective outcome. Resistance should be handled, as often as possible, within the context of the ongoing team. However, it may come to the point the leader must make the hard decision to assure continued forward movement. The team deserves, and success depends upon, strong leadership that can manage through disagreement as well as mitigate and defuse resistance when possible. In the end, however, you must make sure everyone on the team is in the same boat pulling in the same direction. It may be uncomfortable, but it needs to happen.

*A **final note**: If the people resisting change are within your span of* *control, you can to manage and control the process. If the resistance and disagreement comes from areas beyond your control, you must try to determine if discretion is the better part of valor and redirect your efforts rather than beating your head against a wall.*

Stop Reading. Start Leading!

MUCH OF THE time spent reading management literature is a misdirection of energy and effort. There is not much new under the sun and if it is new, it is probably so esoteric that most organizations should not worry about it until they have mastered basic blocking and tackling. As mentioned before, most management reading is akin to worrying about lead poisoning as you are shooting yourself in the head.

This is not to say the concepts you find in the books at the thrift store are not valid. They are! They work. It is almost always good stuff. But it is also endlessly recycled and repackaged in order to extract money from your pocket and put it in the pocket of the author and publisher.

Pick a relevant methodology or framework and stick with it. Choose a relevant toolset and focus on the discipline of making it effective. TQM, MBO, BPR, ITIL, and other alphabet methodologies work just fine. Your job is to make sure they are used as effective *tools* to help you get where you want to be. They must not become an end in themselves and they must not be used for cookbook management.

Use your native abilities as a manager and leader to be sure any work done using any method is firmly connected, line-of-sight, to your Definition of Success.

Finally, remember, many times you do not need a "methodology" at all. A simple sheet of paper with ten metrics on it may be just fine. You will find if you enforce discipline around the obvious and controllable items, they become operational; the mythical well-oiled machine. You can stop fighting the alligators and actually drain the swamp.

When you are about to buy a new book about the world being flat or guerrilla marketing or ways to keep your workers happy without actually doing anything substantial for them, ask yourself a question: *Am I about to do something that will result in a positive change for my organization or am I avoiding the ten things I already know need to be done?*

Then, act accordingly.

Stop Reading – Start Leading

Walk into any managers' office (including mine) and you will certainly find a common decorator accent: the shelf of management books. Ask almost any management person what management methodologies or frameworks they have used and you will likely get a capsule run-down of the management, planning, and technology flavors of the month from the last 20 years. The usual suspects:

- Business Process Reengineering
- Total Quality Management
- Management by Objective
- Information Technology Infrastructure Library
- Value Analysis
- Kaizen
- The Learning Organization
- Performance Prism
- Balanced Scorecard
- ISO (too many variants to mention)
- Etc.
- *ad nauseum*
- *and then some. . .*

Note: *For an interesting listing, see Value Based Management web site (valuebasedmanagement.net). It takes your breath away!*

As a visual aid, here is one of my shelves (almost all bought at Goodwill):

Test: Ask the manager or executive on whose shelf you find the mini-MBA reading list:

- How many of the management methods or books are still being used?
- How much effect the tools had? Better yet: ask the people that work for them
- Why or why not?

They actually do work. . .

Each of the methods listed and the books shown above actually do work. Each one is a gem. They are the result of experience and discipline and have proved successful for the authors and usually others as well. If used properly, they give you an extremely high return on the amount you spent to acquire them. For a minimal investment, you can avoid the trial and error of developing your own unique methods. But remember:

We have met the enemy and he is us. – Pogo by Art Kelly

You only need to buy the idea once. After that you need to use it with discipline and rigor. Continual repurchasing and restarting with different flavored management methodologies translates to avoidance. Worse, spending major ducats on consultants to bring in new concepts for basic management jobs of control, operational people management, and accountability for results will inevitably lead to "speed bump" management and flaccid leadership.

Note on consulting support: Consultants should be used like Tabasco or saffron: to bring something different to the mix: a little spice – a little POW! They should not take the place of the meat and potatoes or even the salt and pepper.

Choose one and go

In order to achieve stability, predictability, and success, settle on a set of tools:

1. Use with consistency, accountability, and rigor:
    a. The methodology used will have an opportunity to build on itself
    b. You will come to understand it better over time and will be able to optimize the tool rather than learning a new one every year or so
    c. Your organization will learn to speak the same language and develop a culture of shorthand knowledge which is a foundation for effective communication and collaboration.
2. Connect use to outcomes and achievement of your Definition of Success:
    a. Any toolset should be part of a cause/effect dynamic leading to results.
    b. If you budget, it should be used as part of a planning system that results in the optimal amount spent to achieve optimal outcomes. If, however, budgeting goals are just cost-control or creation of an "allowance", budget adherence will be achieved, not organizational success.
    c. If you use a balanced scorecard and it is the accepted measure

of performance, you will likely get a good balanced scorecard as opposed to results.

Do not spend too much time polishing your tools; they should be dog-earred and well-worn if they are to help you achieve success.

A note on overkill: Use the simplest toolset you can get away with. If a simple report with expenses, holdover, sales, customer retention, etc. will fill the bill, go for it. Keep an eye out for methodologies, frameworks, etc. that take on a life of their own and cease providing value to match the effort they require.

Thinking Right to Left; Starting at the Beginning

DOROTHY KNEW SHE wanted to go back to Kansas. That was the right-hand side of her page. Everything she did was based on that objective. Along the way she learned, changed, and grew. She was heroic in her determination and focus. Glinda, the good witch, advised her that the best place to start is at the beginning.

Right-to-Left Thinking. Left-to-Right Action

We have discussed the universal requirements for managing to success: Identity and Definition of Success. This management concept places these components in a larger framework and reminds us there are no shortcuts. If you want to reach your destination, you will take the first step, and then the second, and then the third. You will keep putting one foot in front of the other and the very best place to start is at the beginning.

Job 1: Right-to-Left Thinking

Thinking should always be in a right-to-left context. Once you understand the right-hand side of the page, the Definition of Success, all that remains is nuts and bolts.

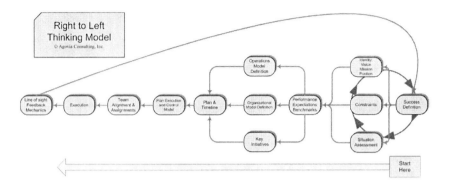

When used effectively, the processes of planning and execution have consistent characteristics. At the highest level, a few indicators will tell us if our planning is likely to result in success for our organization:

- Do we have an understanding of the Definition of Success?
- Do we know who we are? Can we clearly articulate our identity and our mission?
- Does the strategic plan drive us to manage to result? Does it drive our activities in a line of sight to our Definition of Success?

In order to succeed, we will need to begin our journey by thinking about where we want to go. The concept of right-to-left thinking is used to illustrate this. The illustration above provides a visual representation of this concept. It shows the need to understand where we are going before we begin to design and deploy projects or initiatives.

Note: Strategy, tactics, and operational effectiveness are equally necessary for an effective planning and execution process. They are interdependent. Attempting to plan or move on one without the other two will cause imbalance and place you at risk. Without a strategic objective you cannot design your tactical approach. Without tactical action you will not achieve your strategy. Without the ability to oper-ate effectively in the here-and-now, it is all moot because you will not be in business very long. Strategy, tactics, and operations: all are required to survive and thrive.

Job 2: Left-to-Right Action

The achievement of organizational success is driven by the discipline of using Right-to-Left thinking and executing in a predictable and logical manner. Below are the high points of a rough-and-ready "get there" process. The third section of this book, "Getting There," provides more detail on the planning framework.

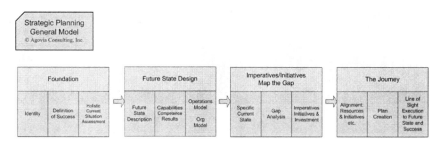

It is tempting to take shortcuts on the framework. Do not do it. There is no need to spend excessive time on any given step but eliminating a step from the process will haunt you later. The most common inclination is to jump directly to the selection of initiatives ("We need a new CRM application!"). Just don't. Move swiftly and deliberately through an effective process. Do not let yourself get stuck in planning paralysis, neither should you create a new organizational structure nor implement a new multi-million dollar piece of software to solve a simple operational people management issue. If you need to improve sales, make sure your sales team is not spending their time playing Solitaire. You may not need a new CRM application. Figure out the real problem and act with deliberate speed.

The items in the framework above are executed in order of importance and create a process of major phases or steps. These phases are:

- Foundation
- Future State Design
- Map the Gap: Imperatives and Initiatives
- The Journey

Foundation

The foundational items provide the context within which we build the plan and achieve success.

- **Identity and Definition of Success:** These are both leadership issues. They tell us who we are, what we are trying to be and how we will know whether we succeed or not.
- **Current Situation Assessment:** This is the environment in which we exist. It is largely factual in nature, though not entirely. Perception can be as valid an element of our current state as anything else. We must understand where we are as an organization, what we are capable of, and what factors impact, constrain, or facilitate our success.

Future State Design

In this phase we describe the state our organization must achieve in order to fulfill the requirements of our identity as well as achieve our Definition of Success. The primary components are:

Description of Future State: This is a general description, almost an elevator speech of what we will be and how we will look.

Capabilities/Competencies/Results: This is a much more detailed description of the things we must have in our inventory of capabilities or, if a differentiator, execute with excellence. We should be able to clearly state the results we will achieve in our future state. At this point we determine and prioritize critical success factors and imperatives.

Operations Model: How do we operationally achieve this? Do we manufacture our product or do we acquire, consolidate, and distribute? As a manufacturer, we need certain operational capabilities. As a consolidator, we need very different operational capabilities and structures.

Organizational Model: Based on the operations model, what is the optimal organizational structure to achieve our goals? Do we need carpenters and programmers or do we need contract specialists, lawyers, and vendor managers? What organizational structure best supports our operations model?

Map the Gap

In this phase we clarify the gap between our current state and where we have chosen to go. We identify what will need to happen to bridge that gap.

Specific Current State: In terms of our future state capabilities, competencies, and results, where are we now? This is a more specific and detailed look at the current state and will allow us to define and quantify our required initiatives and change activities.

Gap Analysis: We determine how big a bridge we need to build and how much effort it will take to cross over.

Imperatives, Initiatives, Investments: We come to understand the things we will need to do in terms of specific goals and objectives and the programs, projects, etc. necessary to bridge the gap. We also discover and prioritize the critical threshold level for success.

The Journey

In this phase we get down to the nuts and bolts of how to make it happen.

Alignment of Resources: We will probably not have enough money or people to do everything at once. In this phase we make decisions regarding resource-based execution. We align our available resources to the work we must get done. The standard triad of time, cost, and quality will be utilized heavily in this step combined with dependencies and urgency. Hard decisions may be required in this step.

Plan Creation: We develop the actual mechanics of the plan. We create program and project artifacts and nuts and bolts of execution. We use the techniques of timelines, dependencies, work breakdown structures, project management, and others.

Line of Sight Execution: We implement the plan with necessary metrics and monitoring tools to assure continual and active steering as well as connection to our desired end state. Success depends on robust but easy-to-use governance practices, commitment to results, and organization-wide accountability.

And there you go. . .

It is actually a fairly straight forward process. It is not, however, easy. The key ingredient of success is your organization's decision to make it happen, your commitment to follow-through, and the accountability of your leadership team.

The Perils of Soundbite Management

Don't Get Bitten

We all Love a Good Turn of Phrase

Here are some classics:

- *Money doesn't motivate people*
- *Don't create strategic plans – think strategically*
- *Titles don't matter*
- *The budget evolved from a management tool into an obstacle to management (Carlucci)*
- *Don't automate, obliterate (Michael Hammer)*
- *Don't pave the cow path*
- *People resist change*
- *Leadership is irrespective of position*

We have all heard them. They come from a vast store of management lore and tribal knowledge. They put in appearances at planning sessions and conferences. They are often heard when something needs to be justified or refuted. If, at any given moment in a business discussion you are at a loss for words, pick one of the above and let it fly. Don't worry if it is completely off-topic and non sequitur, there is better than a 50% chance of getting away with it. There is an excellent likelihood those with you will assume they are missing some nuance you are commenting about. It works like a charm and they can be whipped out quicker than a jackrabbit on a date (Jean Shepherd).

Management sound bites have the additional advantage of implying there is depth of wisdom beneath them; possibly the result of experience or research. Because of this implication, the soundbite often wins the day. Disagreement implies a lack of enlightenment and, in any event, requires a subtlety of discussion that is frequently not suited to the venue. The combination of baloney and chutzpah can take you a long way.

In reality, each of the sound bites listed above does contain some element of truth. Sadly, however, management in a hurry tends to grab a simplistic concept and combine it with a point we would like to prove at the moment. From there it is a short step to acting as if we had read the whole book when we create plans and actions. It is like trying to take an exam after having read only the table of contents and looked at the pictures. Although this may get by in a college class room, the impact of having a dilettante in charge of an organization can be more damaging. When tempted by management pearls of wisdom, remember this sound bite: a little knowledge is a dangerous thing.

If you plan to use these nuggets, you should commit to finding the true depth that lives under the sound bite. These are titles, not wisdom. They have some value as guide posts that point you in the right direction, not as maps.

To paraphrase Albert Einstein: *Everything should be made as simple as possible but no simpler.*

Proverbs and Soundbites

We all do it. We latch onto shorthand versions of wisdom to help us remember things. These come in many shapes and sizes and go by many names: Proverbs, sayings, truisms, etc. We learn them early and use them for the rest of our lives. There are thousands of them. Here are a few:

- Blood is thicker than water
- A stitch in time saves nine
- Still waters run deep
- Silence is golden
- The best things in life are free
- Don't cut off your nose to spite your face

In some cases, these proverbs are concise and useful distillations of wisdom that can help us understand peoples' motivation or can provide useful counsel in choosing a path of action.

Management by Soundbite

The concept of the management soundbite is a natural extension of the ancient human tendency to shorten concepts to a memorable phrase. The problem occurs when soundbites are actually the beginning of an idea as opposed to a distilled version of it. Through a desire for convenience, lack of understanding, or simply laziness, we use them as if they were capsule versions of deeper truth. In doing so, we can lose critical pieces of the core concept, to the point we are able to justify misguided actions which may not even be consistent with the idea we are citing.

Here is the tricky part: there is often an element of truth in the sound-bites. Here are some examples:

Money doesn't motivate people: Often opined by people who make a lot of money. In any event, it can certainly *de-motivate* people. I also suspect money had something to do with the motivation behind the 2009-2010 mortgage crisis which almost caused the world economy to implode. I would also suspect the potential for raises, bonuses, keeping the kids fed and the bills paid can provide a modicum of motivation. Is money the sole motivator? No. Still, do not discount its importance in motivating your people to action. Stop talking about 365 ways to motivate your staff without spending money. It shows a profound lack of respect for your staff to assume they cannot decipher that code. Reality: Money is important and for many people is the primary motivator or de-motivator. Get over it.

Don't create strategic plans – think strategically: This one is a doozy! I am reminded of Professor Harold Hill in movie *The Music Man* touting his *Thinkology Method* for learning to play musical instrument. (He was a con man, by the way, trying to fleece the town of River City) Yes, you need to think strategically. But you need to make that thinking real through a disciplined planning, execution, and governance. I believe the concept here was to avoid making static plans and to keep moving strategically. Good idea. However, the ideas are not mutually exclusive. The unfortunate internalization of the concept has evolved to thoughts of grandeur and minimal action. Here is another bite of wisdom: Do not throw the baby out with the bath water.

Titles don't matter: Actually, they do. They matter to people who are building a career. They matter to those outside the organization who are trying to do business with you. They matter to resumes. They matter to the government (an officer must be on all bank floors during all working hours). I can count on one hand the number of times I have heard this from non-executives. This statement is made, almost exclusively by those already seated on officers' row. The nugget of value here is the attempt to avoid the counterproductive effects of an overly hierarchical organization (i.e. managers get 100 square feet of floor space and an arm chair but supervisors on get 85 square feet and a steno chair).

The budget evolved from a management tool to an obstacle to management (Carlucci): Grow up. The budget is a planning tool like any other. If you let it control the enterprise, the plow just started running the farm. A budget simply helps you find the best and most efficient allocation of resources to achieve your objectives and success. It is not the blob from outer space; it is just a set of spreadsheets and processes.

Don't pave the cow path; don't automate, obliterate (Hammer): Sometimes the very best thing to do is to pave the cow path. More organizational transformations and system installations have failed because they tried to fix everything at once and pushed the organization beyond its ability to absorb change than because the ideas or the technology were bad. You need to approach transformation and change strategically and tactically, not explosively. Granted, we do not want to simply do the same things we do today faster if we can do it better. However, sometimes paving the cow path is the first best step toward a super highway.

People resist change: This is true to a degree. People are subject to inertia – just like everything else in the universe. However, people really resist dumb change or change on a whim. People can be pretty supportive of change if it meets four conditions:

- They understand it
- They perceive it is change to take them to a better place
- They perceive they are being told the truth (not lies or semi-truths)
- They think there is a likelihood of success

Leadership is irrespective of position: Some elements of leadership come from personal characteristics and some from organizational authority or position. The truth is, the most effective leadership happens when these two are joined. In order to have the most effective leadership and to have the greatest organizational impact, an individual must have both organizational authority of position and internal personal leadership capability. One without the other can be admirable or tragic but it will not be terribly effective.

As a leader and a manager, you must work to avoid the pitfalls of sound bites. Use the concepts but understand them before you let yourself be carried away.

Operations vs. Change: Survival and Growth

ALL PLANNING REQUIRES objectives for the future *and* operational requirements for the present. Executive planning frequently focuses only the future. You must live both in the future and the present. Lack of planning for tomorrow can lead to irrelevancy and failure. Lack of solid operations today can eliminate the need to plan for tomorrow. You must understand and account for operational performance today as well as achievement and growth for tomorrow.

Organizations do two primary things. Everything a business does, whether for-profit, nonprofit, or school, falls into one of two categories:

1. **Operations**: Your organization lives and breathes on a day-to-day basis. It produces goods, products, or services and serves its customers within a currently defined state. You have certain required levels of productivity, quality, responsiveness, sales, etc. based upon your current state of existence.

2. **Change**: Successful organizations continually prepare for the future. Planning and executing for the next life phase of the enterprise is the key to ongoing and repeatable success. Static organizations have a limited life span. Products, services, or operational capabilities, if unchanged, experience a bell curve of:

   • Introduction
   • Acceptance and growth

- Peak performance
- Decline
- Expiration

Plan for effective operations as well as ongoing growth and change. Be accountable for both. Today and tomorrow are not separate tracks. They are two points on the same track.

Note: Organizationally, some areas are dedicated to operations and some areas are dedicated to change. Some must perform both. When we make change it must eventually be operationalized. Production departments' acceptance of change (new systems, products, processes) can generate tension and strain within the organization. When the introduction of a change does not go as planned, production departments will claim inadequate testing and preparation. Change departments will claim lax management and inability to follow procedures. Integration of changes into day-to-day operations requires team work, hard work, leadership, and sometimes the wisdom of Solomon. Keep your eyes open.

Planning for the Future and the Present

All too often, "planning" is exclusively about the future. Executives disappear from the building for several days to attend a facilitated retreat in a comfortable resort and return with *The PLAN. The PLAN* is usually a set of objectives or goals for the future. It is handed to someone else upon return, signed receipt requested. At that point, the executives return to their day-to-day activities while they await word on the progress toward the goals of *The PLAN. The PLAN*, however, is seldom based upon the current operational picture. *The PLAN* often drives a model in which today and tomorrow are treated as divergent and unrelated concepts

Do not misunderstand: facilitated retreats are fine. Objectives and plans for the future are essential to the success of organizations. If you do not change and grow you will die. The point is this: you must live in two worlds simultaneously. You must perform today and change for tomorrow. Your strategic and tactical plans must have a parallel operational track that is just as important and fits hand-in-glove with change activities.

After returning from the retreat, plan in hand, a cursory look around your organization will remind you: the vast majority of what you do is operational in nature. Without results in terms of production and operations, there may be no need to plan for the future.

The challenge of balancing the competing dynamics of change and operations can be visualized as having three elements. These are shown in the visual below:

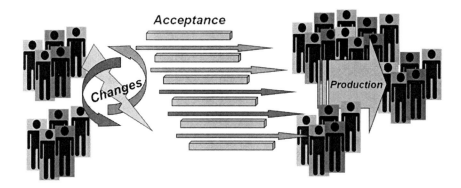

Stability and a strong organizational heartbeat depend on solid production and operations. Growth and future success depends on the ability to make changes. The interface of change and operations is the acceptance process and it is as important as the other two. If your organization does not have a good understanding of the interface zone between change and operations, you will be well served to get familiar with it. Production acceptance is the key to successful change control and avoiding disastrous transitions.

Make improvements and changes. Implement them well. Stabilize and internalize them for ongoing repeatable and predictable operations.

The Chart Room

Keeping Your Finger on the Pulse

Do it Now!

EVERY SUPERVISOR, MANAGER, director, executive, etc. must have a way to maintain a bird's-eye view of their operation. If you do not have one in your possession that provides you with an accurate picture of your sphere of responsibility and it is less than seven days old, stop whatever you are doing and get one. No, really: stop. Do it right now. Do not go to another meeting; do not go to lunch. If you need to go to the bathroom, do it as soon as you get back. This is important!

You are in luck, however. As with many of the most important management practices, it is pretty easy to do. Just keep it simple.

You need a high-level report that provides the key operational indicators for your organization. Focus on creating a way to gauge the effectiveness of your operation *today*. It should inform you of successful results and let you know *now* if problems are developing. It should *not* diagnose a problem or craft a solution. Do not try to assemble the *Super-Duper Master Operations Report and Vegetable Chopper*. You simply need flags to tell you where to look. I call it a "Chart Room" after an old friend who created posters to track his important metrics. You can call it a dashboard, snapshot or whatever you like.

You need a Chart Room. Kudos if you have one. Get one now if you don't.

The Chart Room

Keeping your finger on the pulse

In the old days, I had a friend whose job it was to maintain the Chart Room at a company I worked for. The CEO had about ten key indicators which provided a good picture of the operational state of his company. Every week, Pat gathered various statistics and updated the charts in the executive break room. Every week, the CEO wandered in shortly after the update and scanned the results. If something caught his eye, he picked up the phone and got more information.

Notice what this did:

- It kept the executive management team current on the operational state of the business. The entire executive team had a view and was educated on how things were going.
- It was simple and provided only flags of underlying situations. The genius of the tool was in the simplicity. It allowed identification and action on items needing attention quickly, before they became entrenched and hard to fix. Simple, quick, and dirty.
- The entire organization quickly learned that the things they did were important to the executives. Their activities and results were impactful to the company. What is watched is done. What is important to the boss is important to everybody.
- The operational staff knew the expectations of performance were not theoretical. Rather, they would be asked to explain their results within a fairly short period of time. The directors, managers, and supervisors were always up to date on the operational state of their departments.
- It clarified the levels of performance considered exemplary, adequate, and unacceptable. It led the company to management for outcomes and results.

Life Among the Flags!

One result of this type of activity was the creation of a service committee of supervisors which met every Monday to discuss service in general and production holdover in particular.

The graphic below shows a simple file flagging system used to document service cycle times and to highlight customer requests taking too long. In this service unit, all requests were flagged according to the week they were received. There were three colors: blue, yellow, and red. Each week had a specific flag color assigned and all files received that week were coded according to color. At the end of three weeks it was time to cycle back to the first color. On Friday afternoon, any files remaining with the color to be assigned the next week (aka: three weeks old) were changed to green. Green was not good! Green meant we had spent too long fulfilling a customer request.

On Tuesday morning, we were asked to explain each green flag during the Service Committee Meeting. You better believe we knew what each Green Flag was and what was being done about it. We also could gauge our service levels by watching the diminishing counts on the other color flags. We had a mechanism, not only to highlight bad service; we also had a trending and management tool. The flag counts went all the way up to the vice president of customer service.

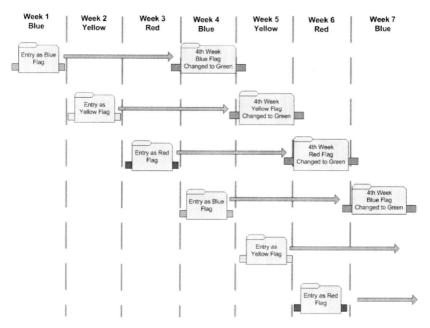

Figure 2. File Flagging System - Holdover Monitoring

You Need a Chart Room or a Dashboard!

You should have a Chart Room or a dashboard or some equivalent tool keep you informed in a concise and simple way if you are operating effectively or not. You will find you become much more attuned to the nuances of your organization and business if you are tracking results on a regular basis. Soon after a Chart Room is in place you will find you are able to predict the lag-time between the moment an event touches your organization and when the operational impact will be felt. You will see patterns emerge and find unintended consequences of your own actions. Spotting these issues early that can generate mitigation actions before, rather than after the fact. If a change in service results in customer cancellations or reduced sales, you will know about it sooner rather than later. If a technology problem leads to increased service requests or cycle times, you will be in a position to see the increasing production holdover and jump on it right away rather than when the hole is so deep you cannot dig out.

You will also see a dramatic shift in the culture of accountability as each area comes to understand both the expectations and the transparency of their results.

Again: find a limited number of key indicators that define the operational success of your organization. Possibilities include:

- Sales (numbers/volumes)
- Second Sales
- Returns or Service Terminations
- Efficiency Ratios (cost/sale, cost/transaction)
- Hold-over
- Service and Customer Satisfaction
- Service cycle times
- Expense and cost ratios
- Systems performance and reliability
- Telecom performance and reliability
- Call wait-time and abandoned rates
- Quality metrics
- Complaints

It should be no more than three pages. Be sure to include required performance levels and trending.

*A **final note**: As you create your "Chart Room," remember the idea is accountability, not finger-pointing. Any time you see an anomaly in a metric, remember this: there is a good chance the underlying cause or trigger of the problem was a management decision or action that changed the status quo as opposed to poor performance. The Chart Room should be a tool to clarify expectations and encourage performance, not a sword hanging over the head of your team.*

Communication: A Lousy Way to Stay in Touch

. . . but it's all we've got

Communication – A Story

SEVERAL YEARS AGO, our family was on a road trip and we were driving over Snoqualmie Pass in Washington State. My daughter leaned forward and asked me if I could drive the car with my shoulders. I was a little confused but after thinking about it, I told her I really didn't think that was something I would try to do. She sighed and leaned back in her car seat, obviously relieved. I looked at her in the rear-view mirror and asked what had brought that up? "Well," she said, "We just passed a sign that said, 'No Shoulder Driving' and I wanted to be sure." So much for clear signage. Nonetheless, communication is important.

"What we have here is a failure to communicate"

When Strother Martin uttered those nine words in *Cool Hand Luke*, he said a cotton-pickin' mouthful. The failure to communicate is at the root of a significant (humongous) portion of management problems and failures.

Examples of Poor Communication

Wonderful examples of communication faux pas are never hard to find. Here are a few samples of particularly elegant miscommunications:

- **Seattle neighborhood lunch restaurant**: "Due to recent law eliminating Styrofoam boxes, we now charge $0.25 for boxed food. Sorry for the incontinence." – *The dangers of spell-check (I hope).*
- **American manufacturing**: A company produced shirts for a Spanish market to promote a visit from the Pope. Instead of "I Saw the Pope" (el Papa), the shirts read "I Saw the Potato" (la papa). – *Not a big seller, I'd guess.*
- **Small town newspaper**: "Miss Dinah Jones sang 'I will not pass this way again,' giving obvious pleasure to the congregation." – *Someone's in the kitchen with Dinah.*
- **Church bulletin**: "Please place your donation in the envelope along with the deceased person you want remembered." – *I can't think of anything to say.*

Is this a "Key Management Concept"?

Communication is the act of transferring thoughts, feelings, ideas, or concepts from one person to another. It sounds easy. In reality it is so very hard. Human beings do not have the ability to interact telepathically. That means everything you do with other people will be done via communication. If you are a manager or coach of any type it is the majority of your job. If you do not get it right, at least part of the time, you will fail.

The Basics

Human communication comes in all shapes and sizes. Here are a few:

Direct Person-to-Person (Direction/Information). You have probably heard these statistics: When communicating face-to-face thoughts are transferred in the following way: 55% body language, 38% tone, and 7% verbal. These numbers came from a UCLA study published in 1971. Although this is probably a misinterpretation of the actual study, you can count on the fact that at least half of what people are taking in about your message is not in the words. Note what this means for non face-to-face human communication: we must infer up to 90% of the meaning we would usually get through non-verbal cues.

Non-Direct Person-to-Person (Direction/Information). This is anything that allows you to communicate without a physical or direct contact. It covers a lot of ground. It ranges from letters to email to instant messaging to voice-mail. Usually it is asynchronous; I send or leave the message and you receive it later. It is very handy.

One-to-Many (Direction/Information). This type of communication is used to get information to a large number of people. It includes memos, directives, web-sites, social networks, advertising, procedure manuals, public address systems, and other methods.

Message-Based (Interpretive). This communication comes through interpretation. It is often unintentional. It happens when you intentionally or inadvertently send a message hidden in the action or as a subtext hidden beneath the words:

- If you involve your staff in planning rather than handing them a completed plan, you have communicated your respect and trust.
- If you consistently advertize your life-style, vacations, and new cars, you have communicated that you make a lot more money than the rest of the team and your focus is somewhere other than the enterprise.
- If you Twitter, email, Facebook, answer phone calls, or clip finger-nails in meetings, you have communicated your belief about your relative position in the corporate hierarchy and your lack of respect for those in the room.

Outcome Based Communication

As a leader, you must manage your communications as actively as you manage your enterprise. Manage to your desired outcome:

- **What are you trying to do?** Figure this out first. What do you want your communication to achieve? Is it intended to:
  - Direct
  - Inform
  - Convince, sell, change minds, create buy-in
  - Mitigate, comfort, apologize

- ○ Encourage
- ○ Interact, converse, exchange ideas
- ○ Send a wordless message or cultural subtext
- **What is the best method?** Remember, it will probably require more than one method of communication and the message must be consistent. Written or spoken communication will need reinforcement via message-based communications. An all-company memo about high performance expectations and dedication to organizational success will be negated quickly by executives and managers with lavish toys and who manage to disappear every Friday by noon to beat the traffic as they head for the lake house. Remember: behavior may lack the precision of words but it is the most effective form of communication if you wish to send a lasting message. On the flip side, inconsistency between your words and your behavior is the fastest way and best way to negate a message.
- **Feedback and re-communication.** Communication is the transfer of concepts, thoughts, etc. It is not a memo, speech or device. These are just the mechanics. If connection or internalization does not occur, you have not communicated. You were just talking. It is likely two or more hearings will be required.

Communication Failures

There are as many ways to fail to communicate effectively as there are ways to communicate. Here are a few of the common ones to avoid:

1. **Failure to communicate at all**. Usually, this is the result of a lack of thinking through how actions will affect others: "Oh, we probably should have said something before we closed the parking lot." *Subtext*: "You are not important enough for me to think to communicate with you ahead of time." *Take-away message*: "I don't respect you enough to think about how this will impact you."

2. **Inadequate or inappropriate communication**. This is usually the result of inadequate feedback and input. Try to use the right medium and approach. When you get it wrong (and we all do) take another run at it with humor and determination.

3. **Parsing words.** If there is an elephant in the room and you are
    not mentioning it, your credibility suffers and people will not take
    what you are saying seriously. Worse, you can become an object
    of ridicule. People, in general, are pretty smart. They have enough
    experience and savvy to figure out the real meaning behind busi-
    ness-speak and word-crafted executive statements. If you think
    you are fooling people by providing a partial truth in order to cam-
    ouflage the true picture, you are probably only fooling yourself.
    Sadly, it is a double-whammy. Not only are you not fooling any-
    one, you are simultaneously diminishing the trust level of your
    team and with it your ability to lead. Effective leaders reach to the
    root of issues, speak about them openly, and solve them. They do
    not dance around problems. They lance the boil and clean out the
    wound so it can heal.

Process and Outcome; don't be Seduced!

Fish are living in Dad's Airplane – A Story

SOMEWHERE AT THE bottom of Lake Washington is the skeleton of an airplane from the 1950s. It belonged to my father and a bunch of his buddies. They thought it would be cool to have their own plane. They pooled their meager funds and bought an old float plane. And it truly was cool. A really nifty feature of this airplane was its ability to land on either water *or* land. By cranking up or down wheels that dropped through the pontoons, you could land at Boeing Field or on one of the many bodies of water in and around Seattle. However, they were such a bunch of guys. They were young and dumb and they blew off the landing checklist. One sunny day, one of the guys decided to land on Lake Washington. Unfortunately, he forgot to crank up the little landing wheels. When an airplane hits the water with about eight inches of wheel sticking through the pontoons, it isn't pretty. Almost instantly it nose-dives into the drink and sinks . . . quickly. Dad's pal climbed out and the plane went down. They really could have used a landing process connected to the outcome of a safe touchdown. Result: part of my inheritance is now doing duty as an artificial reef. C'est la vie!

Words to Send Chills down your Spine

"We have a process for that."
"We're dedicated to Repeatable and Predictable Processes."
"The process works."
"We need to do some process reengineering."

Processes are seductive. But if you hear any of the above statements (or any statement that puts process at the front of the discussion), you should feel beads of sweat popping out on your forehead.

Remember this: processes are only meaningful in context of enabling an outcome. Repeat that over and over until the discussion of a process out of context of an outcome becomes anathema to you. Without that connection, your team is following a cookbook. No matter how good your process framework may be, if the process is the focus, you are likely to fail.

Do not misunderstand me: I am a process zealot. Repeatable operational processes are necessary for most businesses to succeed. This is especially true for businesses that have passed the first inflection point of 50 – 80 people. Strong processes are the foundation of quality, manageability, and predictability. They are the enabler of successful outcomes. Orphan processes, however, those not directly connected to results and outcomes, are just activity generators. Activity requires investment. Do not invest without return.

The Simple Process Test:
- Was it built to achieve a measurable and desired outcome?
- Does it actually achieve a measurable and valuable result?
- Is it repeatable and predictable?
- Is it doable?
- How will it be managed and integrated into operations?
- Is it cost-effective?
- Is it scalable?

Process and Outcome

Processes can be seductive. They provide a warm and comfortable sanctuary and can be highly beneficial to your organization. If not managed well, however, processes can spin on and on under their own power and inertia. Process is the lifeblood of the bureaucracy. Bureaucracies are not necessarily bad. Bureaucracy allows organizations to keep operating through changes in leadership, staff turn-over, and summer vacations. But balancing bureaucratic processes, effective operations, and excellence of results is a requirement of good management.

Other Things to Think About When Creating and Managing Processes

- Enablers of Dull Wits:
  - ○ Processes and procedures become "rules." Rules can harden into concrete.
  - ○ Watch for over dependence on process or procedure manuals. Staff members must have the ability to make logical and, occasionally, illogical leaps. Sometimes people must be required figure out the most sensible thing to do in a given situation without guidance. If the staff cannot figure out what to do in a given situation without a procedure, there is need for remedial creative thinking.
  - ○ Institutionalized processes have static inertia and are difficult to change.
- The Tar Pit:
  - ○ Once you have a set of "Procedures" you are committed to the effort and process of keeping them up to date. Once they become stale, they are, at best, irrelevant and a lost investment or, much worse, dangerous.
  - ○ The process and procedure library cannot be permitted to grow past the point of usability. Weed out, consolidate, and reduce.

To Recap:

- Repeatable processes are necessary for most organizations
- Connect all processes and procedures to outcomes.
- Don't "over-proceduralize." It causes dulling of the senses and is difficult to manage.
- Commit to the care, feeding, and currency of your processes and procedures.

Do What You Can When You Can

It makes a difference!

THIS MANAGEMENT CONCEPT tells you to do what you can when you can; an idea which is fundamental and obvious but overlooked surprisingly often. Taking care of the things you can handle when you have the opportunity generates time, energy, and focus to handle unexpected occurrences. The key to maintaining the proper focus on the correct needs at the correct time but still within the constraining influences of funding and human resources is the ability to make sound business decisions. But be clear: there is a difference between a "bad business decision" and a decision which turns out wrong due to our inability to predict the future. Do not worry too much about the hazy ones. Common sense decisions and reasonable, timely handling of opportunities and challenges will put you ahead of most of your colleagues. Just for fun, look below and you will find a list of some better known "bad" business decisions followed by a comment on whether they were bad or just easy fodder for 20/20 hindsight.

Bad Decision or Bad Luck? – Some stories

- **New Coke:** *Bad Decision*. We own the market. Let's eliminate the product and replace it with something else. In fact, let's replace it with something none of our customers have ever indicated they want. Sounds good!
- **IBM fails to obtain control over MS-DOS:** *20-20 Hindsight*. IBM didn't foresee where things were going. Reality: If IBM had

acquired control over DOS, it probably would not have become the market behemoth operating system.

- **Henry Ford refuses to allow creation of a replacement for the Model T**: *Bad Decision.* Henry was obsessed with the Model "T"; it was his baby. When shown a new model prototype created by his engineers, he physically destroyed it with his bare hands. After 15 years of exclusive focus on the Model T, Ford Motor Company was at grave risk. Its market share was dropping like a stone due to competition from newer and more innovative automobiles. Luckily, Henry's son, Edsel had secretly developed plans for the Model "A", the car which revived and saved the company. But Ford never fully recovered.
- **The Louisiana Purchase**: *Bad decision on the part of Napoleon, et.al.* Even in 1803, three cents per acre was a steal.
- **Decca Records passes on the Beatles in 1962**: *20-20 Hindsight.* Mop-top, skinny kids. Who could know?
- **Variety store W.T. Grant collapses because it forces its employees to give credit to "everything that breathes"**: *Bad Decision.* I mean, really.
- **Western Union passes on the telephone**: *20-20 Hindsight*
- **Schlitz competes with Budweiser in the 1970s by replacing barley malt with corn syrup and speeding up the brewing process from 40 days to 15 days**: *Really bad decision.* It was cheaper and faster but it tasted terrible and the ingredients tended to clump and fall to the bottom and looked like "mucus".
- **Ernst Hardware decides to compete with the big box stores and collapses:** *Bad Decision.* Ernst owned the middle market hardware space in the Northwest. It was locked up. There was nothing between the Mom & Pop hardware stores and the big box mega-stores. They decided to go deep into debt and compete with guys who were already firmly established and owned the super-stores.

Take Advantage of the Opportunity

He who does not when he can often finds he cannot when he will.

Anyone in business, project management, nonprofit management, coaching, or any other form of organized results-driven human activity should take the above advice to heart. In business and in life there are some things over which you have control and other things you do not. Both can hinder achievement of your desired success. However, if you have handled the things you are able to control, it is much more likely, when confronted with the unexpected or uncontrollable, you will be able to deal with it.

Things you can control	Things you cannot control
Operational Effectiveness	Weather
Expense Management	Electrical Grid
Doing the right thing	Economy
Risk Management	Earthquakes
Product	The Market
Succession Management	Illness and Death
Process Controls and Records	Laws
Business Continuity	Future
Informed & Reasonable Business Decisions	

When bad things happen that are outside your control, they can either be annoying or disastrous. Much of what determines the level of impact is driven by how solidly you have nailed down the things within your control when you have the chance. Here are three common scenarios:

1. **Garden variety lack of preparation**: This is seen when the managers of operational units or projects simply are not thinking ahead. When the crunch comes, we spend our time dealing with items that could have been prepared during the quiet times. Example: During catastrophic storms, insurance company claims crews require hotel rooms. If handled ahead, a few minutes on the telephone will take care of it. Hotels are alerted and prearranged reservations are triggered. If done during the crisis, however, several hours are lost to basic administrative tasks, most likely in the middle of chaos and confusion. Additionally, there is no guarantee accommodations will be available at any price, regardless of how much time is spent wheedling hotel managers. Time spent on administrative trivia is

time away from core issues. Additionally, a known requirement for predictable crisis which could have been handled easily if arranged ahead can balloon into a corporate incident and a risk to business continuity.

2. **The sucker punch**: This is the corporate risk two-step. It usually involves an organization placing itself in an exposed position through bad operational practices or over-extension. The management practices of the enterprise have created a situation in which there is little cushion or contingency if things happen to go wrong. The organization becomes dependent upon favorable external factors to survive. Once the ground has been plowed through risky practices, a triggering event occurs such as a turn in the economy, the market entry of a sharp competitor, or the predatory hiring of key personnel and the organization does not have the reserves or depth to recover. Examples include:
   - Unsupportable expense to income ratios
   - Highly leveraged debt
   - Risky product decisions
   - Internally developed software applications
   - Shallow skills inventory in key areas
   - Deferred maintenance in technology or facilities
   - Lax security practices
   - Poor business continuity and disaster recovery planning

3. **Basic bad leadership and decision making:** Usually the result of management inability to confront root causes. For whatever reason, management decision makers choose the wrong path when information to make the right decision is available. We are not referring to impossible decisions which next year may look brilliant or ridiculous. These decisions are fundamental and basic and can be made correctly today. Examples:
   - **Product**: Lack of attention to ongoing product development anticipating future markets;
   - **Accountability**: Inability to hold themselves or others accountable to performance,
   - **Operations**: Failure to address fundamental quality and operational needs

- **Misdirection**: Diversion of energy to grand schemes when the foundational business is unstable or inadequate. This is usually an exercise in avoidance. High risk, capital intensive activities are almost always ill-advised if the fundamental business is not operating well. Major acquisitions or geographic expansion are unlikely to solve business problems if the organization cannot field a product that appeals to its current market, control its expense ratios, or hang onto its current customer base. If a management team cannot execute basic sound business practices, they may believe redirecting focus somewhere else will take the heat off them.

To recap:

Take care of what you can when you can. Then, when things you cannot predict happen, you will be as prepared and solidly grounded as possible to weather the storm. You will have time to concentrate on solving the problem rather than scrambling to deal with the things you could have done before.

It's bigger than me; I'm okay with that

Mission, Vision, Values and the Next Generation

THE MISSION IS: *Bringing the Best to Everyone We Touch.* Who might that be? If you like to smell good you very well could have some of their products in your house. In the hazy territory of mission statements and vision statements, it would probably rank as one of the worst. It is actually a statement of value and quality rather than mission. None the less, this is quite a successful company. A mission statement like the one above flies directly in the face of the premise of this management concept. But it works for Estée Lauder.

There are no hard and fast rules in the world of mission and vision. Still, we believe it is a good thing to state clearly who you are, where you are going, and what is important to you. You can succeed and even thrive without a stated mission, vision or values. But be aware:

- Mission, vision, and values exist in all organizations. They are there somewhere. They may be locked in someone's head but they are there.
- Without clarity around mission, vision, and values, your organization will probably dwindle in the second generation of management and die in the third.

It is a safe bet that more consulting dollars have been spent on mission statements and vision statements than on any other single item with the possible exception of failed technology projects. Mission and vision statements provide the perfect storm for the paid facilitator:

- No one agrees on what a mission or vision really is;
- If we can manage to agree on the purpose of a mission or vision statement, we cannot reach consensus on the content;
- We seem perfectly content to debate them throughout an entire three-day retreat;
- We feel the need to review them every year or two;
- The clock is ticking.

Important? Actually: Yes!

Mission, vision, and values provide the context for the enterprise. They are the basis for everything the organization is now, will become, and the way it operates. They are the foundation documents. Imagine the United States without the Constitution and Declaration of Independence. They are our guideposts. They allow the organization to be self-renewing and larger than the founder. Organizations that successfully move beyond the founding generation have a common trait: the ability to transition power from one generation to the next. Corporate failure between generations is shockingly high with over 80% failing by the third generation. Although there are no guarantees, there are three things that will improve your odds of success both in the short term and the long term:

- Have mission, vision, and values which are organizational rather than tied to the individual at the helm;
- Actively plan for succession at all levels and particularly at the top. Undue concentration of visioning and decision-making at the very top is an invitation to failure;
- Select, retain, and reward on merit and results. Families *can* run businesses through generations. Ford and Nordstrom prove that. In general, however, organizations successfully run by families spend a great deal of time and energy compensating for the narrow talent pool from which they select their leadership. The family members identified for important positions in the organization are rigorously indoctrinated, developed, and trained. Birth is not a qualification. If it is used as a personnel selection tool, the risks it brings should be mitigated.

Mission: Do not get hung up on it. Use a simple definition. A mission statement should say who you are, what you do, and what you are trying to achieve at a basic level. Test: hand your mission statement to a stranger on the street. They should be able to tell you what you do and what your organization is about. If it can pass the "Stranger Test," however, feel free to structure your mission statement any way you like.

Vision: Where are we going? A vision should be a statement of achievement. What state are you trying to attain? It should be measurable.

> *Note: If your mission and vision get intertwined, do not worry about it. Does it provide the things mentioned above? Fine!*

Values: What is at our core in terms of our ethics, values, and integrity? What is important enough from a human perspective to be a factor in our decisions?

What to avoid

A committee-developed mission statement usually sounds like a committee-developed mission statement. Leadership decisions and clear, unambiguous language are necessary for a crisp, usable mission.

Ask yourself why you are in business. If you are a Human Resources Department, you are not in business to develop people. You are not in business to take care of people. You are in business to provide a workforce to support and execute the business of the organization. If you are a stock company, it is unlikely your mission involves employee teamwork and unity. Both of these, however, might be fundamental mechanisms by which you achieve your mission.

Mission Statements – the good and the . . . well, you decide.
The Good:

- **Amazon:**
    - *To build a place where people can come to find and discover anything they might want to buy online.* – Got it!

- **Scandinavian Airlines**:
  - *To become the best airline in the world for the frequent business traveler.* – That makes decisions easy!
- **CVS Pharmacies**:
  - *We will be the easiest pharmacy retailer for customers to use.* – A niche! On every block. Easy parking. I'm not driving to Wal-Mart.

You decide:

- **AOL**:
  - *To inform, entertain and connect the world.* – One of many over the years
- **American Standard**:
  - ***Be the best in the eyes of our customers, employees and shareholders.*** – In case you did not know, American Standard sells toilets. I wish I could have been at the meeting where they came up with this mission.
- **Chevron**:
  - *At the heart of The Chevron Way is our Vision to be the global energy company most admired for its people, partnership and performance.* – Just a guess, but I bet if you timed it, the number of minutes spent on "Admiration" in the CEO's staff meetings is less than you'd expect from it being the key point in the mission.
- **Dollar General Corp**:
  - *Serving Others: For Customers – A Better Life; For Shareholders – A Superior Return; For Employees – Respect and Opportunity.* – Serving is good – I'll take two servings of a better life please!

Fear, Accountability, Focus on the Future *and The Big 25*

HUMAN BEINGS ARE big, complex, resourceful animals. We are motivated to action and progress by a complicated mixture of drives, desires, fears, and opportunities. Positive and negative motivating factors come into play as neurons fire and electrical impulses whiz around in our heads. Beware of single-dimension management and motivation. Feel good motivation is one vector for getting results. But, one dimensional focus on positive drivers and motivators does not work very well for very long and shows a lack of respect for the complexity of the human psyche.

This is controversial and politically incorrect but here it is anyway: absence of fear is a recipe for indolence, sloth, and failure. Guarantees without consequences breed corruption and government bailouts. In general, progress is based on a mix of an optimistic vision of the future and fear of the consequences of failure.

The carrot and the stick is a common concept. Another way to express the same thing: rewards and consequences. Rewards without consequences lead to stagnation and failure. Consequences without rewards lead to any number of bad things including loneliness; nobody wants to hang out with people who beat them up all the time.

Setting and Managing Expectations

The key to balancing this equation is the ability to manage expectations and finding a way get us all on the same page. Here is the mix:

- Clarity of expectations;
- Consistency: Establish predictable and regular patterns of feedback and accountability that support, enable, and enforce expectations;
- Agreement: Get agreement on meeting the expectations. If you blind-side your staff with secret or unknown expectations, it is more counter-productive than not having the expectations in the first place;
- Consequences: A culture of accountability includes consequences for unmet commitments as well as rewards for good performance. Just like dealing with teenagers: if you say you're going to ground the kid if he returns home after midnight, you better do it.

But this isn't high school

Here is the flip side. If you are repeatedly talking to your team about expectations, agreement, and consequences, something else is wrong. You are at risk of becoming an enabler and a crutch. The establishment and management of expectations should, over time, become a subtext and eventually an integral part of your culture. If discussion and reminders about the items listed above are required over and over, your staff is not growing into their responsibilities. This is a team and just because you do not ask a specific question, does not mean it is not important or the team can ignore it. There are some things, like gravity, we expect people at a certain level of seniority to know. The more experience, the higher the pay, the loftier the box on the org chart, the more we expect in the way of proactive behavior and initiative.

Here is the good news; living in a repeating cycle of commitment, expectations, accountability, and reward/consequences quickly creates a performance culture. When that happens, if any of the four are missing it leaves an obvious hole.

The Conversation of Accountability

In all the aspects of your enterprise, whether for-profit, nonprofit, school, or other, you must have an ongoing conversation of accountability. Below is a list of twenty-one questions which can be the foundation of that conversation. The questions shown below are crafted to apply to business, particularly discussions around investments, projects, products, or proposed changes. But with slight modifications they can be applied to any discussion in which a pitch is made, results are predicted, and accountability is expected.

The 25 Questions

Stick to the basics and do not allow yourself to be distracted. These questions give you the script to keep the discussion focused. Require simple answers:

- The new computer system: has it improved our efficiency or not?
- The savings: are they green dollars or a shuffling of personnel?
- The marketing plan: has it produced increased market share and sales?
- Departmental management: is it running efficiently and producing results?

If you focus consistently on a few questions, your team will internalize the expectations and come to provide answers to them before you ask. They will have investment in and ownership of the things they have committed to. They will get the job done.

What just happened?

We have obtained commitment to results and imparted awareness of the fact there are consequences attached to not living up to our commitments as well as rewards for good results. The culture of entitlements is steadily replaced with a culture of solid business thinking and performance.

Post Script:

All of the above is true and, in the vast majority of situations, will serve you well. That said; remember management is both art and science. If you want to do something that violates the above, make an informed choice. Act purposefully and with your eyes open. The hunch is a valid reason for a business choice. However, on whatever basis you choose to make your move, understand the reasoning behind your decision. Inertia, frustration, or the desire to appear decisive does not make a good foundation on which to gamble your future.

The 25 Questions *None of the below are yes/no questions. Each should have quantification and explanation.*		
Topic Area	*Question*	
Background and Problem Statement	What problem are we trying to solve?	1
	Why do we need to solve it?	2
Contribution and Fit	Does it support our mission?	3
	Does it contribute to our Definition of Success?	4
	Does it fit within our strategy?	5
	Is it a good business practice?	6
Justification *At least one must be affirmative*	Does it sell business?	7
	Does it retain business?	8
	Does it increase our profits?	9
	Does it increase the value of the organization?	10
	Is it necessary to our effective operation?	11
	Is it required by law?	12
	What other reasons are there for this?	13
Thinking it through	How much does it cost?	14
	What is the return?	15
	How and when will we harvest benefits?	16
	What is the ongoing support commitment?	17
	Is it a value based on the market?	18
	What are the downsides and the risks?	19
	What is the exit strategy?	20
	What is the confidence of a success?	21
	What is the confidence based on?	22
	Why did you choose this solution?	23
	What are the alternatives?	24
	May I see the numbers?	25

Five Key Concepts in 120 Seconds or Less

It took 25 years to figure these out

(That's a savings of 99.9999. . .%!)

Life Lessons

A UNIQUE THING about human beings is this: we are able to learn, not only from our own experiences, but also learn from the experiences of others. One day in about 1968, I was in the garage with my father on a bitterly cold winter day. At that time we lived on a farm in the Virginia back country. We were working on faucet that had frozen and cracked during the night. My hands were numb and I was working mostly by sight rather than touch. As I tried to thread the faucet onto a pipe, I got frustrated and forced it. Of course the threads were ruined and we had to re-cut the pipe and rethread it by hand. As I looked at the crossed threads, knowing I had just bought another hour of misery, my father leaned over my shoulder and said, "There's never time to do it right the first time but there's always time to do it over." It is a good thing to remember when you are in a hurry.

Want to save 25 years?

Here are five concepts you can put in your hip pocket and use. You do not need to believe me. Try them, keep your eyes open, and pay attention. Let me know if they do not prove out often enough to be helpful. Listen:

What will be. . .

If you are concerned about how long it will take to reach a goal, just get on with it.

- It will take two years to implement and convert to a new computer system.
- It takes 10 years of school and residency before you can start practicing medicine.
- Austerity measures started today will not show up in the financials until a year from now.

Let me tell you a secret. Ten years or two years from now, you will be exactly the same age whether you do those things or not. More programs fail to achieve their goals because they are not started or they are badly managed than if you had accepted a ridiculous timeline in the first place and just done it. If you want to get there, worry less about how long it might require and more about getting starting and doing whatever it takes. Take a look at the "To Be Diamond" below:

To Be Diamond

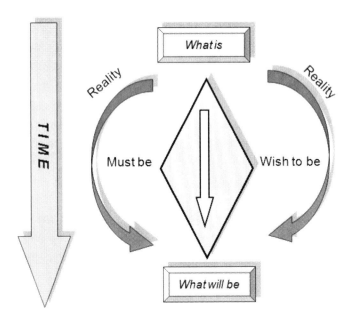

In the future, some state will exist. We will be older; our business will be different.

Wishes and imperatives will not cut the mustard. Our job is to manage to our desired state.

We must craft our actions so that reality is the achievement of our chosen future

Occam's Razor

All things being equal, the simplest explanation or solution is probably the right one.

Try to cut away all the esoteric blah-blah and do the simplest thing that makes the most sense.

- If your expense ratio is too high, you are probably spending too much money and not holding your team accountable.
- If the computer is not working, make sure it is plugged in.
- If your sales are down, look at your operational people management (aka: sales people) and your product before you buy an expensive CRM system.
- You probably do not need expensive consultants to improve customer experience: start by answering the phone, being polite, and efficiently fulfilling the customer's request.

It usually is not too hard to solve a problem if you use common-sense and pay attention. Look for the simplest solution and do not forget to look in the mirror.

X Marks the Spot

This may sound a little cynical but here it is: If you want to make a sale or find an opportunity, look for the intersection of money and one or more of: fear, desire, or frustration. To an experienced sales guy, the combination of fear and the ability to sign a check translates to a prospect begging to buy. "I'm worried about my job and need a victory:" Bingo!

"The system keeps failing and dropping:" Bingo*!* "This project is out of control:" Bingo!

Flip Side: Remember, you can *be the target* of opportunity if you are the person that can write a check and have the need.

Take the Dog

Given the choice of any two situations, one in great shape and one in the pit of despair, take the dog. Take the one that will allow you to have an impact and people will be ready to follow you. Take the failure that can be turned around. If you take over a department, school, company, or project at the top of its game, the challenge is much more difficult. You will be compared to and challenged continually by the ghost of your predecessor. Take the dog.

The Power of "Yes"

"Yes" is a very powerful word, especially if it does not really mean yes. Agreement without action and support is the perfect dodge. It is hard to argue with "yes" and it gets you off my back. If I say yes and then don't do it, I've bought some time. Very likely I now have at least until the next time we meet. Some of us are very good at saying yes and forgetting. Yes does not mean "YES" unless it has muscle and action behind it. In basketball you always follow your shot. If you are good, you may get your own rebound and a put-back. Follow-up on "yes." Validate it with next steps and feedback. Do not be fooled by empty agreement.

They are no smarter than you are

(But they might be doing smarter things)

How to Get a Job in 1921 – A Story

IN 1921, MY grandparents moved from Idaho to Portland, Oregon. My great-aunt Esther had gotten good work as a stenographer for a waterfront shipping company and written home to with the message there were opportunities. On the way, my grandparents ran into a man headed for Seattle who warned them against Portland as having an Earwig infestation and a large number of the population had been affected. After hearing some gruesome descriptions of nasty insects boring into brains, they hesitated but soldiered on anyway.

When they reached Portland they discovered the opportunities were not as abundant as Esther had led them to believe. A new beau had convinced her Portland was the future of the great western empire. Still, my grandfather was a pretty good mechanic and fascinated with cars. After having no luck getting a job, he came up with a strategy that paid off.

He decided the Wentworth & Irwin Garage was the place he wanted to work. Even though they told him there were no jobs, he appeared at the garage door every day and waited, making sure they knew he was available to do anything they wanted. One day, Mr. Wentworth got frustrated, pushed a broom into his hands, and told him to sweep the garage. He worked for Wentworth & Irwin for over fifty years. Ken Mutch was no smarter or better than the other guys tramping around Portland looking for work. But he made the decision he was going to be there and be ready to act when the moment presented itself.

You Can Make it Happen

Look at your hand. You are looking at a marvel of engineering and function. The human hand is an amazing tool. Do you know why? As anti-intuitive as it may seem, it is one of the most fabulously successful pieces of engineering in the known universe precisely because it does not do any single thing spectacularly well. It has no retractable claws for climbing. It has no webs for swimming. It is not armored for protection. It cannot dig holes very well. However, it can do almost anything at some level of proficiency. It can hold and swing a hammer. It can use tools to dismantle the most delicate instruments. It can tap out text messages with blinding speed. It can tell the difference between a dime and a penny in your pocket. It can grip a basketball and gently tip it into a ridiculous metal ring with a net attached. It can throw sizzling fast projectiles, a skill unique to humans. The human hand is amazing because it is a generalized tool that can work with your brain to do almost anything.

You are like your hand. You are capable of thousands of things. The massive pile of neurons inside your skull can figure out a way to do almost anything you choose. You can plan, execute, fill out March Madness brackets, and learn from mistakes. You are capable. You are able to make things happen. With a few exceptions for prodigies, you are every bit as clever and able as anyone else.

If others are doing something well, you can probably do it just as well if you choose to. If others are operating at an efficiency ratio that is double yours, take a look at what they are doing and make the necessary changes. If you are not making sales, look for the reason and fix it. If you are not making the second sale, the one that really matters, look for the reason and fix it.

What is the "management concept" we are talking about? Just this, your success is dependent on:

- Making a sincere *decision* to be successful;
- Your willingness to *honestly figure out what needs to be done*; true root causes even if they are uncomfortable;
- Your willingness to *do what is necessary;*
- The discipline to *execute with consistency and accountability.*

Success is much less dependent on being the smartest guys in the room than on being the most determined. Remember, many of those wildly successful guys were simply in the right place at the right time and, in conjunction with showing up, they probably did the four things above pretty dang well. To quote a phrase:

Success is 10% inspiration and 90% perspiration.

You can do it. Don't be feeble. Buckle down. Get on with it.

Think Globally, Act Socially

Understanding People and the Social Network

A BASIC TRUTH: we work with people. We work for them; they work for us. We sell to them; they buy from us. Even the products we design for animals are really made for people; do a think your dog really wants sunglasses or a cat cares about the rhinestones on its collar? If you want to get something done, you will need to enlist the help of other human beings. It is good to pay attention to what makes them tick.

It's a fact of life. . .

Like it or not, everything you do in your business will be done by, through, and for people. It is a pesky fact of life: in order to succeed in any endeavor, you will need to incorporate the management of human emotions, behaviors, and feelings into your toolkit. Have you ever heard this comment: "That's ridiculous! It was the politics that killed it!" Well, here is a secret: it is all politics. Politics is simply a method by which groups of people make decisions and align themselves for action. If you do not make it your business to understand the politics and social web of your organization, you will be challenged to succeed. You can be the "rightest" person at the table and get no traction at all. If you do not understand and manage political and social relationships, you can come off, minimally, as naïve, and worse, as someone who is offensive and irritating. In either case, you are less likely to get the outcome you are hoping for.

Back to Basics; Back to People

If you ignore this fundamental dynamic of organizations, you are not managing to success. People make decisions and take action based on a complicated jumble of drives and motivations, many of which they are unwilling to speak about out loud. Here are a few:

1. Recommendations of those they trust;
2. Recommendations of those they distrust;
3. Ego;
4. Fear;
5. Inability to admit mistakes;
6. Concern a proposal will be bad for them even if it is good for the organization;
7. Desire to leave the office early and head for the lake;
8. Need for a victory.

In general, motivations that have not been verbalized were not omitted by accident. They are the ones people are unwilling to talk about. The impact of the various motivators of your team on the results of your organization can be good or bad. One thing, however, is almost always true; some of those motivations will be discussed in code. If an argument is both insistent and lacking in logic, look for the hidden motivators. Success may not be possible if these are not addressed. Know this: hidden motivations can be hard to identify because a great deal of energy is being spent to keep them below the surface.

Take the time to understand the social and human side of those you work with. Whom do they trust and distrust? If an executive responsible for making the decision about your program distrusts his peer and this person is also your primary advocate, your chances of success are diminished.

Pay attention to the people factor. Who needs a win? Who is worried about their job? Who is in great shape and willing to take a risk? What coalitions typically win the day? If you are reading this book, you are probably in the management game so, here is a hot flash: Management is all about people.

Note: This concept is not meant to imply you leave your integrity or courage at the door. Do not become a "political weasel." But you must manage human factors as you would anything else in your journey to success. If you distain politics and ignore the social network, you do so at your peril.

Organizational Thresholds

The Enterprise Grows Up

Thresholds of Action

PROBLEMS THAT BUILD slowly can eventually pass a point at which they spiral up and become much more difficult to handle.

Fire in the Attic – A Story

About twenty years ago, my wife's Uncle Norm helped me install some plumbing. Our house at the time was a charming craftsman-style built in 1908. The beams and rafters were almost eighty years old and very dry. One of the more nerve-racking things I had to do was "sweat" pipes in the attic crawl spaces. For those who have never done this, it is a process of joining two copper pipes by sliding one inside the other and soldering them together. It is actually a fascinating thing to watch. The surfaces where the pipes will join are sanded to bare, bright metal. A flux paste is rubbed on the exposed copper. Once the end of one is inside the other, the joint is heated with a torch until it is very hot. The solder is then touched to the seam. Like magic, it melts and is sucked into the joining point of the pipes. It distributes evenly and a little silver drop forms at the bottom. The pipe is sealed and, if you are lucky, there are no "squirters" when you put the system under pressure.

Uncle Norm warned me about one very important thing before I started. Even though I had ceramic tiles between the pipes and the rafters, he told me to fill an old dish soap squirt bottle with water and take it with me into the crawl space. If something does catch on fire, it is easy enough to put out within 30 seconds or so. If you have to run to the bathroom for water, the flames will probably have passed the stage where you can put the fire out.

Without making my wife more nervous than she currently is about my home improvement projects, let's just say Uncle Norm was right. I was glad I had that squirt bottle with me.

Polaroid Corporation – A Story

Polaroid had a lock on instant photography. Despite the disadvantages of exposed toxic chemicals in their product, fading pictures, expensive film, and the hassle of carrying fragile pictures around, Polaroid's brand and penetration was rock solid. They owned the market.

Sadly for them, they got in a series of squabbles with their partners and suppliers at the same time digital cameras were becoming both affordable and easy to use. They missed or simply ignored the challenge of digital photography. In the space of about four years they dropped from a power force in the photographic market to irrelevancy. Polaroid stock was valued in 1997 at $60 per share. In 2001 it had fallen to 28 cents per share. They filed for bankruptcy in October of that year.

Polaroid made the classic error of misunderstanding the business they were in. They thought they were in the instant picture business. They had great technology around cameras, films, and chemical wizardry. Unfortunately for them, they were actually in the image capture business. As others siphoned away the business, they did not come to understand the business they were in until the threshold of recovery had been passed and the death spiral had begun.

The Threshold of Change
What worked yesterday may not work today

Organizational thresholds seldom announce themselves. They sit in the future, quietly waiting to be crossed. They occasionally give hints they are lying in wait but rarely provide you with a bright line to guide your approach. The paradoxical thing is that organizational process and operational thresholds are often brought upon you as a result of your success.

As an organization grows and becomes more complex, the operations model, the organizational structure, and the management team that brought you to this point may not provide you with the capabilities you need to move forward.

Entrepreneurial, hands-on management is usually the key to a successful start-up. The players at the heart of the business have fire in their belly to do whatever the business is about. They are usually in the business because they love the thing at the core. They are passionate chefs, or technologists, or carpenters, or clothing designers. They can be any one of a thousand different things. Their desire is to create a product, make it the best, and provide it to their customers. They are committed to serving their customers and doing it the right way. Their finger is on the pulse, their eye on the operation. They are personally involved in a majority of the decisions and key activities.

These skills and this behavior model, as important as it is to setting an organization on the right path and earning a successful foothold can become counterproductive. As an organization grows, it will pass the point a single individual or a small team can effectively supervise and control it. Managers and leaders who try and retain a high level of control will often find the quality, effectiveness, and results of the organization slipping.

The simple truth is this: organizational dynamics and methods change as an entity passes the point it can be run out of one person's head. The volume of transactions becomes too great for monitoring without standardized counting and cycle time methods. Too many projects and changes are happening to remember and keep track of them. You can no longer holler over the cubicle wall and depend on your team hearing you and executing. Without tools and organizational processes your requests and directives can disappear into the crowd.

Confusion: Process vs. Outcome

Leaders and managers often have a strong aversion to creating a "bureaucracy." In order to avoid this, they try to stay as important and pivotal to the operations as they were when the organization was based in their garage. As they do this, they are creating a fragile and risk-laden operational model. Not only is it likely to become less and less effective, they have also created single points of failure focused in a small number of key personnel. There are a few primary principles that managers should keep in mind as they design their enterprise to successfully transition through organizational growth thresholds:

- **Operations Models and Inertia**: Past a certain level, organizations must be able to operate as entity apart from the day-to-day driving influence of an individual. The enterprise must have an inertia of its own that allows it to keep functioning, even if the founder is unavailable. It needs predictable and repeatable processes, self-governing expectations, and organizationally-driven mechanics to produce results. It needs to be bigger than any individual.
- **Clarity on Process and Outcome**: Leaders of transitional organizations must be clear with themselves on what they are trying to achieve by remaining intimately involved. Originally, the need for personal involvement came from necessity and the desire to get it right. This focus on getting the right outcome is positive and desirable. However, leaders and managers can fall into the trap of thinking their personal daily involvement and getting it right are the same thing. They need to separate these two concepts and understand their intimate involvement was a means to an end, not part of the DNA of success. When the organization passes its threshold point, the leader must find ways to achieve the same success which suit the current needs of the organization.

Common Threshold Points and Indicators

A common threshold for growing organizations is at the point the number of employees or those directly managed reaches between fifty and eighty. Another will often come between three-hundred and five-hundred employees. These thresholds are fairly standard and predictable although they can be hastened or delayed due to the complexity or simplicity of the enterprise.

There are symptoms to be watch for as indicators of approaching or passed thresholds. Some of these include:

- **Increasing Cycle Times**:
  - Delivery of product;
  - Completion of requested service;
  - Vendor payments;
- **Missed Contract Dates**:
  - Renewals;
  - Cancellations;
  - Renegotiations.
- **Individualized Craftsman Approach** Applied to:
  - High volume;
  - Repeatable rote activities;
  - Transactional work.
- **Unanswered Requests**:
  - From you
  - From your staff
- **Procedural Audit Findings**
- **Quality Control Issues**
  - Returns
  - Rework
  - No second purchase
- **Maintenance Delays**
- **Paperwork Delays and Missed Deadlines**
- **Losses:**
  - Due to operational mistakes
  - Inflexibility in decision-making
  - Long processing cycles

The items shown above can, of course, simply be indicators of poor operational management or simple lack of care. When they are combined with growth of employees, higher transaction volumes, or increased revenue, however, you should be on the alert for an approaching tipping point which may require operational and organizational retooling.

Challenges of Crossing the Threshold

When an organization approaches an operational threshold, it is at risk from two perspectives:

- It may not be able to cross the threshold to become a more robust and stronger organization; and
- It may successfully ramp up its operations to meet the more complex requirements of the future and in the process lose its soul.

One of the most difficult conundrums of organizational growth and institutionalization is the challenge of holding on to the heart and soul of the enterprise. The core element that made you successful is the fire in your belly we talked about at the beginning of this discussion. It was your care for your product and the satisfaction of your customers that gave you the ability to grow. It is for that very reason you must relinquish your need to be involved in every aspect of the business.

Your business is probably too big and complicated for you to be everywhere at once. If you persist in the behavior that worked when you were one of ten employees, your business and your customers will suffer. If, on the other hand, you let coldly efficient and impersonal processing rule the day, you will lose the sizzle and join the ranks of the mediocre and adequate. Your customers will become transactions and you will be vulnerable to competitive attack. As the leader of a growing organization it is critical you become the guardian of the heart and culture. Demand operational excellence. Teach, inspire, and expect the continued commitment to the heart of what you do and who you are.

The Choices of the Leadership Team

It comes down to this: the leadership and management team must decide where their joy and the future of the business lie. There is nothing wrong with capping an organization at a size that personal, individual management will work. Boutique and craft businesses can be successful and significant. A choice for growth entails certain actions and requires certain paths be followed. A choice for less complexity and limited growth leads to different paths. It is not nearly as important which direction is chosen as it is the choice is made. As a leader, you must be sure a conscious decision about the nature of the business is made in order to give you and your team the basis for selecting actions and making decisions that will take you to the future.

Risk Management: A Case of Misdirection

Ernst Hardware and the Greatest Risk – A Story

IN 1893, TWO brothers, Fred and Charles Ernst, opened a hardware store in Seattle. Ernst Hardware, later Ernst Home & Nursery, survived the ups and downs of the retail hardware business for a century. By 1992 Ernst was in undisputed control of the hardware retail middle-market in the Pacific Northwest. Five years later, in January of 1997, Ernst closed the last of its stores; the victim of unbridled risk behavior and hubris on the part of its management team.

Ernst Home & Nursery was in an enviable position. In 1991, Pay-&-Pak, their only serious competitor in the mid-market space, filed for Chapter 11. The following year Pay-&-Pak closed the last of its stores. This left Ernst as the only place to shop for hardware and home improvement goods which provided a shopping experience between mom-and-pop corner stores and big-boxes like Eagle, Lowes, and Home Depot. They had good locations, were close to family neighborhoods, and always had parking. They had a reputation for a knowledgeable staff known as the "Fellows-in-Yellow" who were willing to help and give good advice. Both men and women were comfortable shopping at Ernst. The stores were small enough not to be confusing and large enough to have everything contractors needed to build a house. They were staffed locally and developed a strong relationship-based business. Life should have been good.

Ernst owned a market niche. They had positioning. They had penetration. They had loyal, repeat customers. Many of their locations had been owned by the corporation for decades, lowering their overhead. They had economies of scale. And then they turned their back on what they were.

Instead of capitalizing on their unique positioning and value, Ernst decided to play in the big boys sand box. In 1994 Ernst went public and began building superstores in the western states. From the start the effort was clearly and recognizably ill-conceived. Over the years the management team had received advice multiple times from consultants and employees telling them to embrace and build on what they were rather than reinventing themselves in a model defined by others. They were moving into a business space they did not need and did not understand. As icing on the cake, they were entering the big-box market at just the time the space was becoming saturated.

In 1996, Ernst filed for Chapter 11 bankruptcy. In 1997, they closed their last store. Over 8,000 people lost their jobs. The end of a century of good work brought on by high-risk behavior on the part of a few people.

The Ernst executive team was not afraid of the big boys. They should have been afraid of themselves.

Risk Management and Misdirection

The sad truth is this: most organizations spend the lion's share of their risk management effort on things that are never going to happen. They spend little or no time on things which actually create risk and regularly cost billions of dollars. Most risk management activities are centered on preventing or mitigating "events." Most industry definitions center on this as well. Broad-thinking people will understand the word "event" should be read as "occurrence" or just "oops!" "Event," however, is more regularly interpreted as a point-in-time catastrophe or acute situation.

Earthquakes, mudslides, and flu pandemics are easy to get our heads around. They are dramatic and reasonably simple to imagine and devise mitigation strategies for. All of us can visualize swaying skyscrapers and buckling bridges. For this reason, we regularly see companies running drills on their Emergency Operations Committees for 300 year events. We create calling-trees and fail-over sites. We buy emergency rations and stockpile bottled water in the basement. We have identified the corporate spokesman to answer press queries in a disaster or catastrophe.

Now, real quick, how many businesses can you name that have died due to failures of their disaster recovery or business continuity programs? It has happened, of course, but if you set aside businesses impacted by the 9-11 attack, you may scratch your head for a while to think of any.

The real risk to continuity of most businesses occurs in the executive suites, not in the market or the tectonic plates of the earth.

An Example close to the Heart

An absolutely stellar and close to the heart example of the principles of risk management at work can be seen in the case of home ownership and insurance. If a bank holds a mortgage on your home, they will insist you carry fire insurance. If the house burns down, the bank is covered and you are covered. The house is paid off or rebuilt and everyone is happy.

On the other hand, the bank has no requirement you have life insurance. If you die before the house is paid-off and your family cannot make the payments, the bank is protected. They simply take the house, sell it, and get their money. Your family gets anything that happens to be left over. Yet, it is seven times more likely you will die before your house is paid off than your house burn down. The bank is managing its risk, not yours.

Risk Concepts

The definition of "risk" is conceptually easy to understand. It is simply the exposure or amount of a potential loss and the likelihood the loss will occur. In other words, what are the odds the situation will occur and what will it cost us if it does. Risk management is about balancing the exposure, likelihood, and the cost to prevent or manage the event. Here are some examples of simple risk calculations:

- **Head injury while bicycling:**
  - Exposure: High
  - Likelihood: Low
  - Risk Management: Cheap (Wear a helmet and ride defensively)
  - Conclusion: Actively manage risk reduction
- **Frozen outside faucets in winter:**
  - Exposure: Low to Medium
  - Likelihood: Medium
  - Risk Management: Cheap: Faucet covers and weather awareness
  - Conclusion: Actively manage risk reduction
- **Occasional seepage in basement due to heavy rain:**
  - Exposure: Low
  - Likelihood: Medium
  - Risk Management:
    - Prevention: Expensive: French drain and basement seal
    - Mitigation: Cheap: Easily removable throw rugs and weather awareness
  - Conclusion: Mitigate initially and install preventative infrastructure when surplus funds are available
- **Death of family bread winner:**
  - Exposure: High
  - Likelihood: Low
  - Risk Management: Medium: Life insurance
  - Conclusion: Actively manage risk reduction
- **Cat litter box stains hardwood floor:**
  - Exposure: Low
  - Likelihood: Low
  - Risk Management: Cheap: Plastic layer between litter box and floor
  - Conclusion: Actively manage risk reduction

Each of the above is fairly easy to picture and evaluate. Corporate and organizational risk evaluation and management, however, is more complex and difficult. Because it is not easy, risk management in an organizational setting tends to gravitate to more concrete risks. Earthquakes, terrorist attacks, data breaches, corporate espionage are all examples of well-defined risks. There are many risk management methods and standards for concrete and understandable event-based risks. Organizations, frameworks, or standards bodies with useful information include: ISO, ITIL, EMC, IRM, AIRMIC, and others. Any competent risk manager or consultant can guide you through the development of a risk management plan for concrete exposures and eventualities.

Be Clear: you need to manage your concrete, event-driven, and predictable risks. Do not interpret anything said here to imply event-based risk management is unnecessary. It would be irresponsible not to manage and control those risks. The message of this conversation, however, is this: the primary risk your business will face is from executive and management behavior and decision-making. These behaviors must be managed and controlled as well. You may or may not suffer a loss due to exposure to event risks. It is a near certainty you will experience losses due to executive risk behavior.

The Real Risk of Human Behavior and Business Decisions

The risk behaviors most likely to cost money, prevent achievement of success, or bring an organization to its knees, occur in day-to-day management activities. Cast your mind back to the times your organization has been most challenged or experienced a major and unpredicted failure. These can usually be traced to risk behaviors outside the traditional bailiwick of risk management. Here are some examples of risk behavior you may have seen:

- **Date-Driven Releases:** Executive chests tend to swell with macho pride when they talk of holding people accountable to delivery dates. Outcome: products and systems are frequently released before they are ready. The ramifications can be devastating. Potentially good products fail to get a market foothold and new systems do not work. The customer gets the message; we do not know what we are doing. Refunds are mandated, product given away free, and customers leave. Remember this: Although you must drive for expeditious and predictable development and delivery, a year from now no one will remember if a project or product came in three months late. Everyone will remember if you screwed up your reputation, your customer base, or very publically spent millions of dollars to fix a bad delivery.

- **Expense Management:** If you cannot get your cost of goods and operations to a predictable and managed level which will support competitive pricing, you will go out of business.
- **Trade and Industry Conferences (and any trade magazine):** Industry conferences and trade magazines have been responsible for more blockheaded purchases of systems, products, and consulting services than any other single culprit. It is exactly like buying a whistle from a hawker on the State Fair midway. The hawker lit up the night with sounds like a forest of song birds. When you get home and try it, all you get is a wheezy blow. The hawker did not lie exactly; the whistle can make that sound. It takes a year of practice, that's all.
- **Accountability:** If you do not hold yourself and your team accountable to your commitments and for achieving results, you will not succeed and you will not be able to make plans for the future. Your marketing executive must create a call-to-action within potential customers and bring business to your door. Your sales executive must make sales. Your operations executive must consistently and predictably run the operation at a planned level of spending. Your information technology executive must deliver dependable and secure systems support within a supportable cost structure. If you make a commitment to increase your customer base by so-many thousands over twelve months, it cannot just disappear in June or July when it becomes clear you will not make it. Etc.
- **Cronyism and Nepotism:** It is okay to hire your friends and relatives if they produce results. The problem is most of the time they do not. Neither birth nor friendship qualifies an individual to hold a position.

Bottom Line

If your organization is managing for catastrophic risks, technology risks, and physical risks, but not managing business decisions and operations in terms of their potential risk, you are scraping rust on a ship in a typhoon. You should certainly manage for potential disasters. It is the prudent thing to do. However, for every company eliminated by a catastrophe, a thousand are killed by bad decisions on the part of their executives and leaders. Where do you think you should put your energy?

The Perfect can be the Enemy of the Good

Sometimes good enough is good enough

Le mieux est l'ennemi du bien.

(The best is the enemy of the good)

- Voltaire / 1764

Simplicity and the number one killer of children – A Story

DEHYDRATION IS THE biggest single killer of children in the modern world. According to UNICEF and WHO, diarrhea in its various forms, from amebic dysentery to Cholera, kills 1.5 million kids a year and impacts the development of millions more. If you take the total of childhood deaths caused by AIDS, Measles, and Malaria, it is still less than those caused by diarrhea. Diarrhea is the most vicious killer of our time.

Yet, diarrhea is a symptom. When caused by an external trigger, diarrhea is a defense mechanism. Your body is attempting to get rid of the thing that is causing distress. The mechanism by which diarrhea-inducing diseases cause death is your body's reaction to it rather than a toxin or a cellular invasion as with many bacterial or viral infections. Your gut feverishly extracts liquid from your body and uses it to flush out your intestinal tract. You have watery and often violent bowel movements. In the process, the water in your system is depleted and your vital salts and electrolytes are expelled. You become dehydrated. Very rapidly, your body is unable to function due to the lack of liquid and out-of-balance electrolytes. You can die. Every year 3.5 million people travel down this path and do not recover.

How should we deal with this? As you might expect, there are many ways of attacking the problem including:

- Improved clean water supplies
- Clean, well cooked food
- Adequate sewer systems

All of the above go to root causes and systemic solutions. They are undoubtedly the best ways to eliminate chronic and repeated diarrhea outbreaks. They are also expensive, take time, and must be implemented within tricky political frameworks. Fortunately there is also a simple and relatively easy stop-gap made of water, sugar, and salt.

The Miracle of ORS

Cholera and most diarrheas are relatively easy to treat. Your body can handle most antigens which cause diarrhea if your defenses do not kill you in the process. You simply need to help it out by replacing the liquids and salts being flushed away. You do this by making and drinking Oral Rehydration Solutions (ORS). Here is the recipe:

1. Find the cleanest water you can. If it is really murky, filter it through a piece of cloth. If it is clean drinking water (bottled), skip the next step.
2. Boil the water for at least three minutes, then cool
3. In five cups of water dissolve:
   a. 6 teaspoons of sugar
   b. ½ teaspoon of salt
4. Get it into the patient:
   a. Adults and large children: 3 quarts a day
   a. Children under age of two: ¼ - ½ cup per feeding
5. Keep up until the diarrhea stops

Simple Works

Find out where the problem lies and fix it. It is a lesson we all would do well to take to heart. A couple of comments from guys who know what they are talking about:

"The discovery of oral rehydration therapy is as important as the discovery of penicillin."

> *Professor Mamdouh Gabr*
> *Cairo University, Faculty of Medicine*

"Nearly 90% of mortality from diarrhea is due to fluid loss. Accurate and timely replacement of that loss is lifesaving."

> *Dr. Norbert Hirschlorn*
> *Nutrition Reviews Volume 40, page 87, 1982*

Good Enough. . .
What does that mean?

It is simple: Do not let your desire for perfection or even finding a really good solution keep you from getting the job done. It does not mean you should intentionally create shoddy products or let quality slip and impact your customers negatively. It does not mean you should be lazy or slide by at the lowest level of acceptability. It means you understand and are working to the correct outcome.

Repeat that concept: *What is the outcome we are looking for and what is the best way to get there?*

What should we do?

- **Global Deaths from Dehydration**: Should I spend my energy building clean water supplies with a multiple-year lead-time? Or should I start by saving hundreds of thousands of lives with sugar and salt water?
- **Snoring and Lack of Sleep**: Should I try to lose enough weight to stop snoring? Or start by using a $15 dental device to adjust my jaw and prevent 90% of night time snoring.

- **System Implementations**: Should we bring in the new system with the all the new capabilities turned on, also bringing all the new layers of risk? Or, should we just get it installed and stabilized without the all the new efficiencies but at least get it up and running safely and securely?

When is it good enough?

You will have to decide when something is good enough and when striving for perfection will actually impair your ability to achieve your desired outcome. Sometimes, excellence is the desired outcome or is your competitive differentiator. In that case, it is not good enough until it is excellent. However, here are some examples of things that were good enough and worked:

- **Microsoft Windows**: It was pretty crummy when it first came out. But it filled a market need and gave Microsoft their incredible foothold in graphical user interface market.
- **Flip Video:** Low image quality, ultra convenient. Market trade-off met by "good enough."
- **Hulu**: It is blurry and it ties up the computer but I am in control
- **MP3:** Low sound quality but hey, I can get 7,000 songs in my pocket!

That's the ticket!

"Good Enough" may be exactly what you are looking for. Remember, there is no rule that says you cannot improve on a JGE (Just Good Enough) solution. However, if you are late to the table or never arrive because of your quest for elegance or perfection, success becomes much more difficult.

Remember, you are working for solutions and success, not perfection. If perfection happens to align with the other two, that is great. But it is hard to build on success if you do not have one.

Getting There

A successful journey from here to there is mostly a matter of having the discipline to continue putting one foot in front of the other. Even if a trip is a thousand miles, you get there one step at a time.

Ten years from now, you will be ten years older; it is guaranteed. The only way to be someplace other than where you are now is to make the journey. It is amazing how many of us will not take the first step because we fear the journey.

GETTING THERE #1

Getting There; Achieving Success

Nuts and Bolts

NOW WE COME to the most technical and discipline-driven of the elements of success: planning and execution. In this part of our discussion there are fewer stories and concepts and more prescriptions for action. It is laid out step-by-step in order to provide a scaffolding to frame and drive your work. Be aware, however, although in the following pages you will find a series of steps which can be universally applied, it is a framework not a cookbook. As with all you do, you must apply your native intelligence and management skill to what you find here.

A Story: The 1000% Overestimate

Many years ago, I worked for a company that decided to adopt a project management methodology. It was a well known toolset and of course, very expensive. It came with consultants, processes, and many forms and templates. We had scope templates, budget templates, variance templates, TPS Reports, risk templates, hand-off receipts, and a vast array of project paraphernalia and documentation. In short order we had a METHODOLOGY with a life of its own. The process soon became more important than the results.

I was in need of a small modification to one of our systems. My back-of-the-envelope calculations told me it should not have cost more than $10,000. Being a good team player, however, I submitted the request to the project grist mill. In due course, I received an estimate for $84,000. I was surprised. I asked for a meeting with the Project Manager who had estimated the work.

As we reviewed the proposal, it became clear three things had happened. First, the Project Manager had followed the playbook without applying critical thought to what she was doing. She had included every step required for the development of a software application capable of genome mapping. She did not apply the perspective of a reasonable effort to our projected outcome. Second, the overhead of the METHODLOGY was over 50% of the estimated work. Finally, this did not seem unreasonable to the Project Manager.

To wrap up the story: due to the cultural acceptance of the METHODOLOGY, my comments and concerns bounced off the shield of the Project Manager and the Toolkit. I asked for a second meeting with one of the consultants from the company which sold us the methodology. Because he understood how the toolkit was intended to be used, after about fifteen minutes he looked at the Project Manager and said he estimated the project at about $8,000.

Notice what happened here: The methodology was not the problem. The problem was a slavish devotion to a process. The problem was a lack of critical thinking and focus on results.

Follow Up: In the course of the next year, a major customer refused to allow our project managers handle any of their projects and our internal customers developed sophisticated under the table strategies to avoid using the METHODLOLOGY. Our reputation for the ability to execute never recovered.

Pay Attention

In this section you will find a practical components and methods to get from here to there. Using it, however, is up to you.

Most organizations have experience with "Planning" as an exercise. It may happen once a year, usually associated with the budget cycle. An executive retreat is organized (or departmental retreat, or board retreat, or divisional retreat – you choose). A facilitator is hired. Trainer games are played with force fields and circle chats. Participants trudge to break-out sessions and return with armloads of flip-charts for further discussion. A neat binder is duly produced and placed next to previous years' binders; all of them still in their pristine and unused state. There it sits. That is not planning; that is sleepwalking.

In order to be effective, planning and the follow-on work required to transform the plan into reality must be an integral part of organizational life. It cannot be something outside daily life. Planning and execution to-gether should comprise one of the two pivots which anchor all of your organizational activities. Planning and execution are the vehicles for change; the tools that allow you to move deliberately into the future with confidence. The other pivot of organizational success is current operation-al competence: solid, repeatable, and predictable. Note: the operational model itself can be the focus of improvement planning and execution if your current operations are not solid. The lines can blur; management is not an anal-retentive black and white endeavor.

You may hit resistance when you ask for a commitment to deliberate planning. Typically the objections are based on past experience with bad planning. Remember: a bad workman will blame his tools. Earlier in our discussions we mentioned Walt Kelly and Pogo. Pogo's assessment of the problem bears repeating here:

We have met the enemy and he is us.

You may hear

When you ask for a commitment to ongoing planning, here are some of the responses you might encounter:

- We need action, not just a lot of planning:
  - **Absolutely**: But do not confuse action with progress. Planning is part of your action. Not only should it be integrated with your actions, without it the effectiveness of action dwindles. If your organization is making plans without action, that is a leadership and management problem, not a planning problem.
  - **Be aware:** Your strongest push-back may come from the

strongest and most effective leaders in your organization. Why? Because strong and effective leaders are doing much of this already and often doing it in their head without knowing it. It is very frustrating for this type of individual to be asked to deconstruct the intuitive framework in their brain. Think of asking a talented artist to write a page of description instead of creating a painting or sculpture. The problem with this arrangement is: the keys to organizational success live in the head of a single individual. If that individual becomes unavailable, the organization loses its structure and guide. Companies run by small teams or families have an 85% failure rate by the third generation. Great and long-lived companies as well as nations share one characteristic: the ability to effectively pass the reins of power from one generation (or government) to the succeeding generation.

- We don't want to plan strategy. We need to act and think strategically:
  - Baloney.
  - Under that soundbite is a subtle message that is correct. However, most executives and managers will not take the time to tease out the real meaning and it is even harder to use the concept when talking to their team. These things are not mutually exclusive. To the contrary, they are mutually dependent. Thinking without planning and execution is just wishing. And as my former mother-in-law used to say:

    If wishes were horses beggars would ride,
    If cow pies were pancakes we'd eat them 'til we died.

Section Structure

This section is set up as outlined below. Under each topic you will find a discussion of the planning or execution step as well as diagrams illustrating the ideas. In some cases we have included tools and templates to facilitate the step.

- **Introduction to Planning**

- **Universal Planning Process Overview**
- **Planning Step 1: Foundation**
  - Identity
  - Current State
  - Definition of Success
- **Planning Step 2: Future State Design**
  - Future State Description
  - Capabilities/Competencies/Results
  - Operations Model
  - Organizational Model
- **Planning Step 3: Leaping the Gap**
  - Specific Current State
  - Gap Analysis
  - Streams of Activity
  - Initiatives/Investments
- **Planning Step 4: The Journey**
  - Alignment: Requirements and Resources
  - Plan Creation and Approach
  - Execution and Governance

Now, let's get on with it.

The Basics of Planning & Execution

Planning – An Active Part of Organizational Life

DESPITE THE LIBRARY shelves full of books on planning, it is a basic and extremely simple concept. It is the creation of the path by which we will get from here to there. As with many simple things, however, the devil is in the details. In every human endeavor there is a plan. The plan can be as simple as preparing for a walk to the corner café for coffee, or as unimaginably complicated as the Manhattan Project. It may be created almost instantly without conscious thought or it may require reams of paper and hundreds of people to administer it. There will, however, be a plan:

- **Coffee Break**: Planning takes place in a way which is barely noticeable.
    - Time allocated
    - Money in pocket
    - Book in back pack
    - Clothing appropriate to weather
    - Prepared to make menu selection
    - Required return time known
- **Manhattan Project**: Complex, intricate, disciplined.
    - Multi-location workforce
    - Absolute secrecy and containment of information
    - Highly interdependent activities
    - Complicated and scarce resource requirements
    - Massive and unpredictable risk profile

Neither of the above, however, would succeed without planning. Both of them have a clear objective. Both of them have dependencies. Both have tasks.

All organizations have plans. Some are rigorously documented and are part of a repeatable annual management cycle. Some have no documentation at all and everything resides in a single individual's head. Either of these methods or anything between can be highly effective or highly ineffective. There are extremely successful businesses that use no more than a vision and the back of an envelope to manage themselves to the future. There are thousands of failed businesses that created perfectly peachy and detailed plans for the future.

The exercise of "planning" in itself is not a ticket to success. Plans must be created in the context of awareness of where you are and create the path to where you are going. They must be executed in a way that provides the connection to your success. All of this is completely unrelated to the method by which it happens. The planning method most likely to be successful for a given organization depends on the complexity and culture of that organization. I once worked in a company with an annual income of over $200 million that had no budget or planning process and was hugely successful.

All that said, however, the remainder of this discussion assumes there is some organizational need for a reasonably rigorous and repeatable planning and execution method. Please note: Planning and execution. Planning AND execution. Planning without execution has all the value of used copy paper.

To recap: A good plan designs the path to take you from here to there. Execution is the disciplined journey to the destination you have chosen.

Why Create Plans?

Without a plan, you are in the middle of a grove of trees unable to see if you are approaching an open field or heading into a ravine. A plan gives you the map for making forward progress. A written plan gives you many additional advantages, including documentation of organizational commitment and consistency of understanding.

A repeatable and predictable planning process transfers the ownership of the future success to the larger organization. It allows the organization to develop institutional accountability and reduce the risk of dependence on a single individual. Investment in the future is more likely if everyone understands where the company is going and how they intend to get there. If the organizational vision and plans are tightly held by an individual or a small group, there is a much higher risk they will fail in the event the individual leaves or becomes unavailable.

A good planning cycle also provides for continuity from one year to the next and the ability to build next year's goals on last year's accomplishments.

Accountability is more likely when documented plans and goals are retained and reviewed throughout the year.

Three Essential Elements

In order to create a plan, three orientation points are required. These orientation points are needed to understand what needs to be done and to have a context for making decisions as you move forward. The three orientation elements are shown below.

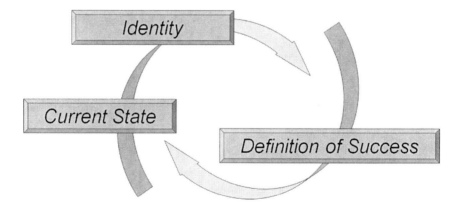

Identity: This tells you who you are as an organization. It defines the kind of business you are in and how you approach that business. The Mission Statement and Values Statement for the organization should provide this information.

- At one time a group of Microsoft employees presented a dynamite business plan for a Microsoft Café. Bill Gates turned it down. Why? It is not the business they were in.
- Taco Bell: Are we a maker of food or a feeder of people? The identity question posed in those eleven words drastically changed how Taco Bell did business.

Current State: This defines your starting point. How good are we at what we do? How much surplus do we have? How sound is our operation? Are our products hot or not hot? What are our strengths and weaknesses? This can be a surprisingly touchy and difficult conversation. Typically this takes place with the people who brought us to our current state. Bringing out too many problems and issues can be understandably threatening.

Definition of Success: This defines where we are going. Once we have our Definition of Success, we can craft a path to achieve it. Depending on the type of organization, it can align precisely with the identity and mission or it can be very different with the identity being only a mechanism of achieving success:

- **Stock Companies**: The Definition of Success will usually be in the realm of increased value. Get the stock value up year over year.
- **Non-Profit Companies**: The Definition of Success will often align closely with the identity or mission. Food banks define success as supplying groceries to people who cannot afford them.

The above three orientation points are discussed in greater detail in a later section about the foundational elements of the planning process.

Two Essential Activity Areas

All organizations that want to survive must have competence in two primary activity areas. It can be argued in fact these two areas are the only things any organization does. These two areas are operations and change.

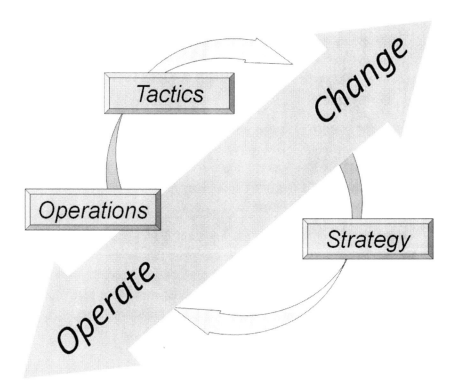

Change: Change is your ability to move forward from where you are *and* to arrive at the place you want to go. You change to get better and more efficient at what you do. You change to create products and services which meet the needs of a changing market or drive new market demand. The organization renews itself consistently to achieve its Definition of Success.

- **Strategy:** This is the high-level path you will take to achieve your Definition of Success. Your strategy may be to win as a product-driven company. From your strategic vision you can develop tactical efforts. Once you know your strategy, you are much more able to make decisions on which tactical initiatives are appropriate.
- **Tactics**: These are the smaller incremental efforts and initiatives that are based on a strategic vision. If your strategy is to win as a product-driven company, it may be more important tactically to have celebrity endorsements than operational efficiencies.

Remember, one of the values of understanding your strategy is the ability to make tactical moves that are not intuitively obvious but achieve a strategic goal. Example: A company that has refined its market niche may intentionally reduce its customer base via a price increase.

Note: Do not get wrapped around your axel on what is a strategy and what is a tactic. The words are not nearly as important as understanding you must have a high-level idea of how you will achieve your success and being able to articulate how your initiatives and incremental efforts fit into it.

Operate: The other half of the equation is an organization's ability to operate effectively and serve its customers in the here-and-now. Reality check: If you do not take care of business today, you will not have the opportunity to execute your tactics or achieve your strategy. If you are out of business the rest loses most of its meaning.

Effective Planning Concepts

Connection to Results: Your plans and activities must have line-of-sight connection to your Definition of Success. If you are making product, pricing, or service changes, do your homework to make sure they will have the end result you are looking for. Marketing must bring in business. Price changes must improve sales or retention. Process changes must improve efficiency or service. These things may sound basic, but often as not there is an assumed connection, sort of a magical line between what we are doing and the results we hope to get. If processes are changed to better serve the customer, those executing them should be aware of the purpose and expectations. Once implemented, measurements and feedback should be used to validate the results. Remember this: Correlation is not causation. Just because a company has funny and catchy marketing does not mean it is the secret of their success. If they have the best price in the industry, the funny ads are making people aware of that fact, they are not the cause of success. Make it your business to know how the things you do connect to your results – good or bad.

Commitment to Results and Accountability: The team must be accountable for the achievement of the planned results or providing an honest explanation of the variance. If there is a commitment to profitable growth within a year, the executive team cannot quietly forget about the profitable part and force growth through extravagant and unsustainable incentive programs. It is completely acceptable to make a conscious and justified business decision to change goals. It is not acceptable to simply let them slip into the ether because the management team was unable to make it happen Leadership, commitment, and accountability are elements that build credibility and acceptance of planning efforts by the culture. If visible, action-based commitment is not seen, planning will be viewed as just one more boilerplate exercise. Enough said.

Watch-Outs

There are certain behaviors and actions which can decrease your odds of transforming your plans into reality. Some of the items listed below are expressions of culture and some show up as code words which cover hidden agendas. Some are things you just do not think about. Keep your eyes open.

Sacred Stuff: It is okay to have a few things off limits, but not many. If you have quiet corners and ineffective employees you are unwilling to deal with, you are agreeing to give away money for nothing. On average, every seven to ten employees represent a million dollars in expenditure. If a department should have fifteen employees and it has forty, you are dropping $2.5 million in the trash bin every year.

Fear and Money: Where fear and money intersect, you will almost always find a problem. If someone is fearful for their job and they can spend money, watch out. Look for new systems, new strategies, geographic expansions. Misdirection of all sorts can materialize. Sellers of software and management methodologies have great radar for nervous directors with checkbooks.

Occam's Razor: All things being equal, the simplest solution is probably the right one. Before buying at a complex and expensive solution to a problem, look for the simple answer first. You usually do not need new technology to solve a problem. You usually do not need a new training toolset or sales system. Check to see if you have simple operational people management issues. Are your people playing Solitaire and waiting for the phone to ring? If your organization spends several million building an e-commerce website only to discover people are not buying due to price, you will feel pretty silly. Keep it simple.

Speed Bumps: Be patient and get real. New solutions, new systems, new methods need a chance to become effective. If you change your approach to a solution before it has a chance to work, it is likely you will pay several times to solve the same problem and have a bumpy ride in the process. When you bring in a new system, toolset, or process it will almost always track to the following steps:

Phase 1: Baseline productivity level prior to making a change
Phase 2: Implementation of new method (Excitement)
Phase 3: Learning phase and decrease in productivity (Beginning of frustration)
Phase 4: Productivity trough (Growing frustration)
Phase 5: Begin improvement in productivity - (Typical point of abandonment)
Phase 6: Improvement to previous level of productivity
Phase 7: Improvement beyond previous level of productivity

A common pattern is giving in to frustration just as results are starting to appear. Research how long you should expect for the entire cycle to achieve improved performance. Then let it happen.

Fix Horizon: As the time since a problem began increases, the ability of the people involved to fix it decreases. If a product is not panning out, the executive who sponsored the product is unlikely to be the right person to correct the problem. If a company is failing, it is unlikely the CEO who got them to that point will be able to lead them out.

Remember

There is nothing magic about planning. You simply need to under-stand who you are, where you are today, and where you are going. After that, it is a case of honesty, focus on results, and commitment to do what needs to be done. It will be uncomfortable from time to time and difficult decisions will be called for. If you keep your eye on the goal; you are as capable of making it happen as anyone.

GETTING THERE #3
Universal Planning Framework

Is a Framework Really Necessary?

STRICTLY SPEAKING? NO. As we mentioned earlier, it is perfectly acceptable to create plans and manage execution from the head of a talented leader. Human brainpower and intuitive action are remarkable things and are capable of accomplishments that stagger the imagination. For hundreds of generations before easily reproduced documents, story-tellers memorized the equivalent of thousands of pages of literature and passed it on verbatim though the centuries. Disciplined brilliance can take you a long way.

For most of us though, it is a good idea to have something to remind us Step 4 comes between Step 3 and Step 5. I'm not saying, I'm just saying; if you know what I mean.

The Fifty-Thousand Foot View

As humans, we are designed to process situations quickly and our brains craft a solution as rapidly as possible. In general, we like to move with an idea as quickly as we can. This ability served our ancestors well. When a tiger is pounding across the veldt in your direction, the ability to spot a grove of trees and know stout clubs are probably available if only we can get there quick, is a good thing. This same behavior, however, can be problematic when used for organizational planning and action. Often we see executives and managers jump to a solution before they have a handle on the problem they are trying to solve.

The Universal Planning Framework is shown below from a bird's-eye view:

Universal Planning Framework

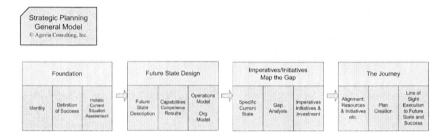

The biggest challenge we observe is the tendency to jump over the foundational work and directly into either the Organizational Model or to make investments and launch initiatives. Creation of a new department, recasting of an existing group, or creating a new position is frequently a gut-level way to bring focus to a problem area. Alternately, new projects such as the implementation of a new customer relationship system or outsourcing business processes can be underway before there is an understanding of what impact they will have on the goals we are trying to achieve. As a final snapper that adds insult to injury, many of these activities come with long tails. A signed contract for something you did not really want is the gift that keeps on taking. Most companies have closets loaded with software purchased and never used. Outsourcing agreements and hot applications can remain on the books for years as a reminder of the rush to buy.

In general, it is better to take the time to clarify what you are trying to achieve and how you intend to achieve it before you make investments or change the structure of your organization. Using a framework such as the one shown above helps you remember to do your homework before you spend your money.

The Foundation

The Foundation is the most important part of the planning process. If, as a team, you can do nothing else, come to an agreement on your foundational elements. Everything that follows the foundational work is nuts and bolts. The Foundation provides you with the knowledge necessary to craft your journey to success. It creates the boundaries within which you live and gives you criteria to make decisions not only about what needs to be done but also what is appropriate for your organization.

Identity: Understanding your identity tells you who you are, what you do, who you do it for and what is important to you. The key elements of identity are:

- Mission
- Vision
- Values
- Philosophy

Current State: Your current state creates your starting point. If you are plotting a route on a map, it is where you begin. Different organizations have varying ways to describe their current state. Some of the key elements might include:

- Market and demographic position and success
- Product and service offerings and life stage of each
- Financial position
- Surplus position
- Operational capability and efficiency
- Customer satisfaction
- Competitive threats and opportunities
- Economic landscape
- Personnel turnover and expected movement
- Regulatory and legislative landscape
- Major known projects and anticipated initiatives
- Organizational and corporate commitments
- Imposed requirements (parent company, Board of Directors, consent agreements, etc.)

The Current State, as mentioned earlier, can be difficult to document honestly due to the challenge of asking the people who created the current state to evaluate it.

Definition of Success: This is the thing which, once articulated, defines what you are trying to achieve as an organization. It may or may not reflect the identity of the organization. For example, the primary obligation of executives of a stock company is to increase the value of the stock for the owners. If your organization is a publically traded provider of photographic chemicals, success at your core business is the mechanism you use to increase the share value. It is not an end in itself. If, however, you are a credit union, you are a cooperative corporation owned by members. In that case, your success may well be the ability to provide excellent service and rates at a low cost of operations. You and your team must be clear on how you define success.

Future State Design

You now know what success means and in what realm of activity you will achieve it. In order to make success happen, you need to understand what future state is necessary. If we can do this or be capable of that, or produce this result, we will be successful. This is the part of the framework in which you describe the strategy you are planning to pursue.

Future State Description: This is the overall, high-level statement of what you need to become in order to achieve your Definition of Success. The time frame of the future is up to you. You can visualize a future state a year from now or five years from now. It is possible to create a long-term picture of the future as well as a medium-term future state. This creates context and allows interim goal-setting which will contribute to achievement of long-term success.

- **General Characteristics and Descriptors:** Think about size, sales, customer base, market penetration, operational characteristics. If the organization is a chain of hardware stores, you may describe your future state in terms of a geographic footprint, number of stores, revenue, and profit. Remember, this is a future state description to support your Definition of Success, not the Definition of Success itself.
- **Winning Characteristics:** The future state will include the items

to differentiate you and make you successful. What are your differentiators? What will set you apart and make you successful? What key factors will give you the win? Always remember: as you describe a differentiator, you must have an understanding of how that differentiation is achieved and how you will convince your customers of its worth. If your differentiator is "relationship," what is it about the relationship your customers will perceive as worth paying for or making a second purchase? What makes you valuable in terms of hard dollars customers are willing to give you? If you cannot answer these questions it will not work.

- **Capabilities/Competencies/Results:** To achieve our future state, we must be good at certain things and achieve certain results. This segment of the framework gives us knowledge in several major areas. We articulate and agree on the areas in which we must achieve excellence and those for which competence will be sufficient. In this segment we also discover ripple-effect competencies; secondary areas in which we must perform in order to support our competitive capabilities. Finally, we agree to the results we must achieve in order to reach our desired future state.
- **Capabilities/Competencies**: What skills and capabilities will we need? These typically fall into two major categories: baseline and competitive:
  - **Baseline Capabilities:** Capabilities judged to be baseline are those you must have the ability to execute but which do not rise to a level to set you apart from the competition. They are important. If you are inept at them, they can kill you, but they will not save you.
  - **Competitive Capabilities:** Those capabilities which are selected as competitive must be better at than your rivals.

The hardware chain mentioned above will need competence in selecting sites and opening new stores. A restaurant will need (among other things) competence in food preparation, providing a specific customer experience, and managing the cost of goods sold. Insurance companies normally compete as a commodity. In that competitive arena, operational excellence and expense control will be critical areas of competence. If a company chooses to compete in the area of relationship, it must be dynamite at building a value-driven relationship. But it must also have competence in opening the thinking of prospective customers to the possibility they might want a "relationship." It is doable but organizations must work and manage deliberately to be good at it.

> **Operations Model / Organizational Model**: Once you understand the capabilities you need and the results they must attain, it is time to set yourself up to make it happen.

> • **Operations Model:** In this discussion, you decide, at a high level, the mechanics of how you will operate. One operational option is the build-and-run model. You own, manage, and run the activities of the various aspects of your operation. In this model, the organization develops and maintains expertise in the various areas required to execute and operate the enterprise. An alternative option is outsourcing part or all of your required operational activities. Should you manage your own custodial staff or hire a company to clean your building? Should you develop software or buy applications? Should you create and run a direct customer service team or contract with an established call-center?

> • **Organizational Model:** Your operations model will determine your organizational model. What skills and abilities do you need to support your operations model? In the examples above, if you choose to own and manage the actual operational activities, the organizational structure must allow for the skills and knowledge to effectively manage a custodial staff or a stable of programmers. If, on the other hand, outsourcing is your selected model, you will need expertise in both contract management and vendor management. The organizational structure can shift from heavy operations to heavy vendor management. Following on your selection, your staffing and departmental structures will need to support the chosen model.

Map the Gap

What is the distance we need to cover and what will it take to do it? That is the focus of the Map the Gap segment of our process. At the end of this step, we should have an understanding of the initiatives, investments, and effort necessary to attain our desired future state.

Specific Current State: The design of our future state from the previous step, gives us the ability to measure our current state against it. A fairly speedy exercise will allow us to find those areas in need of change or improvement. Once found, a specific current state analysis is created. The specific current state is the description of the starting point for the capabilities we must have in our operational inventory if we are to be successful. In this step we look at the specific capabilities and competencies listed above and develop an understanding of how good we currently are at executing them. Remember, a current state analysis is not just a surface statement of where we are, it also must include the underlying factors that drive our current position as well as any known future factors that will impact us. If, for example, we intend to move to a future state in which price is our competitive differentiator, what is today's positioning in terms of price and the underlying drivers of our pricing? Is our price point driven by our operational efficiency or is it driven by a feature-set? What kind of flexibility do we have in our ability to move our price point?

Gap Analysis: Knowledge of our current state and desired future state, give us the ability to calculate how big a task we have in front of us. The Gap Analysis looks at the larger picture in terms of what must change. A change inventory is created. The change inventory should include the end result we are aiming for as well as the underlying items that must improve in order to achieve the result. If it is possible to make an estimate of the effort or costs based on the knowledge at this point, it is included as well.

Initiatives and Investments: Based on the Gap Analysis, we know what must change and how much. In the next segment of the framework we craft the mechanisms by which we will make the changes. If we need an improved level of expertise in our sales force, an initiative might be recruiting, training, and development. If we are opening new locations, an initiative might be a geographical site analysis to discover the best locations with the least build-out costs. If our expenses are out of line, an initiative might be the streamlining of our operational support activities. In this section, we also create estimates of cost, effort, and duration to achieve the changes we require.

The Journey

It is time to face reality. Until this point we ignored the limitations of budget and human resources. This was intentional. As we crafted a picture of the future and what it will take to get there, we wanted to create the best future we could and design the optimal way to achieve it. One of the things we wanted to avoid is the mental editing of ideas before we have had the chance to hear them. If an idea does not make an appearance or is dismissed because "there is no money for that," or "we don't do things that way," or "we don't have the people to do that," it makes evaluating it very difficult. It's easy to take something off a list but it is difficult to evaluate the idea not spoken. An impossible idea may contain the germ of a possible idea. An impossible idea may be possible if we think about it from a different angle. There will be plenty of time to say no later on.

> **Alignment:** We have now discovered many things that need to be accomplished. Unfortunately we seldom have the luxury of unlimited funding or available personnel. In this stage we will compare the needs with our wherewithal. We may discover we can do everything we would like to do when we would like to do it. More likely, however, we will need to stage our journey to the future in a way that accommodates what we can afford. We align our resources and ability to change with the initiatives and tasks we have identified.

> **Plan Creation:** Once we have created a rough alignment of needs and resources, it is time to create a realistic plan. This involves the assignment and acceptance of accountability for the various initiatives and the creation of a portfolio of activities. This is portion of the process involves a high degree of mechanical nuts and bolts. Project and portfolio management tools and techniques are applied to create the formal plan. The level of project management and portfolio management methodology and overhead utilized is based what is appropriate for your organization.

Critical Reminder: From now on it is important to remember that your organization is a single entity. Keep the concept of integrated organizational management in the front of your brain. Manage day-to-day operations and change processes in parallel as two critical and codependent activities. They are different aspects of the same organizational life cycle. If you find yourself managing operational results and project results in two different rooms, find a way to bring them together.

Execution and Governance: You have created a plan and it is time to put it into action. This phase of our framework will see you launching initiatives and making investments. You will build new capabilities and change old ones. You will harvest benefits and results. The most important thing, however, to assure you get what you want is solid and ongoing governance of your portfolio of activities. Governance is the active and regular coordination and management of all the moving parts. You will keep tabs on projects and investments for flags that might indicate they have gone sideways or are becoming runaways. It involves the staging of activities for dependencies as well as monitoring the results of your work in terms of line-of-sight to your Definition of Success.

This is the phase in which your plans are given life and take on substance. The organization must develop the discipline to consistently manage the initiatives and projects. Persistence and team cooperation will develop a smooth inertia of movement and progress rather than fits and starts. When this happens, you increase the chances and predictability of getting the results you need. If this is not done, your plans can become paperweights.

The Cycle

Planning and execution are part of the same continuum of activity. The cycle of plan, act, govern, achieve, and harvest is not a stand-alone sequence of events. These are components of a cycle of organizational life which is continually renewed. As you execute and achieve, your new capabilities are transformed into standard operational activities and embedded in your base organizational competence. The formal term is: operational handoff. You will continually deliver new capabilities into operational standardization. You will continually be striving for improvement and change. Like the shark, if you stop moving forward, you will die.

Keep moving!

Before you start . . .

Frank Lloyd Wright and getting stuck with the Bad Rap; a Caution

YOU ARE ABOUT to embark on a process-based planning effort. There are few things in corporate life that will bring out the Dilbert-esque comments with such ferocity as "planning." Be grateful if the worst thing you hear is muttering about the pointy-haired manager. The types of activities and work you are asking your team to participate in have wasted more valuable corporate management time and resources over the past fifty years than any other boondoggle.

Remember, planning, like any process, is a tool and is only as good as the use to which it is put. It is a fair bet the individuals who have had bad experiences with "planning" were the same ones who did not hold themselves accountable to the commitments they made when crafting their plans. You may hear participants say they were not been able to do the things they planned in the past because more important issues came up during the year and they had no choice. Fair enough. However, that is allowed to happen only once. If this pattern is repeated from year to year, it means "planning" is a corporate checkmark rather than a tool used to achieve organizational success. Plans should include provisions and contingencies for those unknown but predictable surprises that consistently absorb bandwidth.

It is no more reasonable to blame misuse of planning processes for failure than it is to blame Frank Lloyd Wright for the nadir of American architecture of the fifties and sixties. Wright created a moderately interesting diversion from classic American architecture. He used low, flat, planar and cylindrical lines and with little structural adornment. It was minimalist, unexciting, and paradoxically, pretentious. It was inexpensive to build and fabricate due to the preponderance of rectangular surfaces and low level of finish. Low skilled workers instead of skilled craftsmen could be used for construction further adding to its appeal. Additionally, tricks such as wall and ceiling "texturing" added to the speed with which the flat homes covered the American landscape. Sadly, his small and harmless seed grew into ramblers, ranch styles, split-levels, and northwest contemporaries. Frank Lloyd Wright cannot be held accountable for the behavior of thousands of imitative and cheap architects and builders. Similarly, a planning process is not an inherent waste of time. By itself, planning will not make you successful. Planning processes are tools. They simply provide leverage to help you become successful.

Be Prepared; Provide Value

Regardless of how deeply planning and execution cycles become embedded and expected as part of the life of your organization, the planning exercise itself will cause a break in the day-to-day routine of the participants. They will be pulled from their daily activities, including answering emails, dealing with customer service issues, and monitoring the execution of active projects. While they are absorbed in the planning process, they will not be relieved of their operational responsibilities. At the end of each day of planning meetings they will leave your sessions to put in another day of work in order to stay on top of their real jobs.

You must, therefore, be prepared before you kickoff the process. Think of it as a contract. In order for planning to be effective and reasonably ask your team to invest their time, you must be in a position to show you take it seriously. At this stage, there are three primary ways you show it is important and is a commitment of the organization:

1. **Tell Them**: Very simply, the leader must articulate clearly and without question this is an important and supported part of the success of the organization. Tell them it is supported by you and the expectation is they support it as well.

2. **Show Them**: Be visibly supportive. The leaders should attend the appropriate meetings. Pay attention. Keep your commitments to participants and be ready to contribute to the process. If leaders are too busy to arrive on time or if they are answering emails or posting to Twitter during sessions, the observed behavior will quickly be copied by the team. People are adept at figuring out what is important to their boss.

3. **Execute Crisply and Deliberately**: One of the fastest ways to lose the confidence of the team is to flop around and meander through Corporate Planning 101. The leader or an assigned delegate must be ready to run the process from start to finish with confidence, drive, and purpose. This section of our discussion outlines the things to be done in order to be ready to go.

Things you need to do before anyone pulls up a chair

The things you need to prepare fall in a few distinct categories. A description of the requirements in each of these categories is provided below. The main categories are:

- Scope/Commitment/Rules of the road
- Logistics
- Process and Technique
- Behavior
- Kickoff

Scope/Commitment/Rules of the Road

This is crucial to effective planning and execution and it must be supplied by the leadership of the organization. It is common wisdom the three most important things to have when opening a new business are: location, location, and location. In a similar way, the three most important things to have to ensure successful planning and execution are: executive support, executive support, and executive support. Without the support and commitment of the leadership of the organization, a planning exercise is just that: exercise. Before asking anyone to commit their time and energy you must get clarity on the purpose of the exercise, the commitment to achieving results, and the rules of the road.

If you are the leader of the organization, you must make sure your team is aware of the level of commitment you plan to invest in the process. If you are the person tasked with facilitating, you must be intimately familiar with the process drivers, level of corporate support, and expected outcomes. Without knowledge of this underlying depth and substance, you cannot confidently drive the team to a result or in good faith ask them for the extra effort a successful plan requires. At a minimum you must be clear on the following questions:

- **Why are we here?** What is the purpose of the exercise? Are we creating a comprehensive plan for the success of our organization? Is there a specific objective in mind such as an industry accreditation or are there other external requirements? Is there an urgent problem we are trying to address? Has the process been launched in response to an organizational emergency? Are there results we must achieve that are known and can be directed before we even begin? What do we need at the end of the process? Do we need a set of goals? Do we need a plan for achievement? Will the process drive through to establish a functioning project portfolio and governance framework?
- **What is the commitment?** Is the leadership of the organization ready to support and commit to the success of the planning process? Is the level to which the leaders are willing to commit clear to the members of the team? Are they committed to full and active participation in the process? Are they committed to the necessary investment and effort to achieve success defined and designed in the plan? Are they ready to hold themselves and the organization accountable?
- **What is the planning horizon?** How far out are we looking? This is critical as effective planning is built on a defined goal state, after which we back into the effort required take to get there.
- **Are there any taboos?** Is anything off limits? Can we speak openly and honestly in the sessions? Are there untouchable areas we must avoid as we plan to make changes? Items that typically appear on the Taboo List:
  - **Pet products**: " . . .we built this company on top-quality carbon paper"

- ○ **Pet projects:** ". . .but I *want* that new sales application"
- ○ **Senior or long-term employees:** "Let me get this straight: you think $200K is too much to pay for Bob to organize the football pool?"
- ○ **Partners and friends:** "What? Get a competitive bid?"
- ○ **Operational methods:** "That's just how we do it."
- ○ **My staff:** as opposed to say. . . yours
- ○ **Executive perks:** ". . . but I *love* my company car, my bonus, and travelling first-class."

- **There can be off-limits items**: Some; a few. There just cannot be too many. Taboos are a problem: if it is clear to the organization at large a change should be made and it is being shielded by the leadership team, the credibility of that team suffers if others are asked to sacrifice for the common good. It can also be a matter of physics. If the number of items unavailable for change reaches critical mass, it may not be possible to attain the threshold of operational and market excellence to drive your success.

- **Facilitating or driving?** This is important both for the person standing in front of the team leading the exercise and for the participants. Some facilitators are neutral crank-turners. They facilitate rather than drive. This is attractive to consultants for a number of reasons. By remaining neutral and encouraging interaction and heart-felt discussion, they avoid offending anyone. They seldom push people outside their comfort zones. They usually are invited back because everybody feels validated and important at the end of the engagement. Second, a neutral facilitation tends to rely heavily on team exercises thus drawing out the time frame and utilizing more consulting hours. (Charles Dickens was paid by the word. Hence he produced remarkably wordy and discursive works. Most consultants are paid by the hour. The incented behavior is to convince the client they need as many hours as they can afford to buy.)

The exercise sponsor and the participants must be clear on what they expect in terms of behavior from the facilitator. Facilitators that drive the team rather than jolly it along will usually help you produce a better plan in a shorter period of time. They will help you reach conclusions and move on. They will also push the team to create a rigorous plan supported by solid logic. They will help you keep the line-of-sight connection between the here and now and your successful future. They will unearth logic holes and help you be sure your plan does not just feel good, it actually is good.

Either way: be clear. A team expecting a soft-touch facilitator can go into back-up behavior very quickly if they think the facilitator is getting too big for his britches. A team expecting rigor will be frustrated if they find themselves bathing in touchy-feely blather.

Personal Preference Note: *I have very little patience with touchy-feely facilitation. Grow up. If you are serious about success, get the most value out of your facilitator by allowing him or her to drive the team to positive and definitive conclusions.*

Logistics

There are basic nuts-and-bolts items to arrange in order to make the sessions and the exercise successful. Make sure you have bodies to participate and a place for the bodies to get together. You will have to feed them and plan the sessions themselves to assure they run smoothly. The logistics of the sessions will not make them successful. Logistics will not make your organization successful. If not done properly, however, bad logistics can cause the process to fail. If there is confusion about schedules or locations, or if participation is difficult due to poor sound or bad ventilation, people will be focused on irritation rather than the needs of the organization. Keep as many mental switches off as you possibly can. People will have many reasons to daydream and check out. Try not to manufacture additional irritants and check-out moments.

- **The team:** The participants in the exercise will need to be identified and agree to be part of the effort.
- **Team size:** Although exercises and methods can be developed for a wide range of group sizes, the most effective size for a team planning exercise is between four and twelve. You should be able to get them around a single table in an arrangement that allows

them to talk to one another. There will also be exercises which require splitting into breakout groups. There should be at least two groups and no more than five. Enough people must participate in each group to allow effective discussion.

- **Team composition:** Here is a general rule about who should be part of the core planning team: select those accountable for getting things done. This usually will include those with direct divisional operational or staff responsibilities (i.e. Operations, Sales, Marketing, Personnel, Information Technology, Finance, etc.) as well as a selected number of individuals who will contribute in a specific and important way. Examples of this latter group include facilities managers and project portfolio managers.

- **Scheduling:** All participants' schedules must be coordinated and the venue reserved. Again, the support and commitment of the senior-level sponsor is important. Without the influence of the boss' desire for it to happen, lead time for the coordination of multiple busy schedules can be extensive. The venue will need a central meeting area and space for breakouts.

- **Supplies and equipment**: Your equipment and supplies needs should be limited. You will need the items in the "Basic Facilitators' Supply Kit."
  - Pens
  - Pads of paper
  - Marking pens
  - Poster Paper (or butcher paper)
  - Masking tape
  - Post-It pads
  - Sticky dots – multiple colors
  - Laptop computer (optional)
  - Easels (optional)
  - Projector – InFocus type (optional)

- **Facts, figures, and data:** If possible, you should have background information on hand. If you are able to clarify and settle foundational questions quickly, without sending participants away to perform research, sessions will proceed with fewer interruptions. The documentation you should assemble includes:

○   Mission Statement
○   Vision Statement
○   Philosophy Statement
○   Financial results
○   Operational reports
○   Previous plans and results
○   Organizational charts and tables
○   Known required or mandated outcomes

Process and Technique

The techniques and tools used to run sessions and exercises can make or break the outcome. They range from the basic meeting agendas to the management of various types of resistance. It is important you manage the group and the process as well as you can. It is also important to come to an understanding with the team around the joint responsibility for successful sessions and desire for success. There is no planning process or governance structure good enough to succeed if the team wants it to fail. You should be as prepared as you can be and the team should be ready to help make it work.

Planning is an imprecise and very human activity. You run into digressions and unexpected things. Sometimes these will be more illuminating than the formal planned activities. Tolerance and patience is necessary. Both the facilitator and the team should be prepared to see human performances of desire, passion, ego, jealousy, and basic kindergarten petulance. That is okay. It is normal. These moments of unmasked humanity may reveal things which will not come out unless passions are running high. In the final analysis, however, the team must be ready to cooperate and work together in order to get through these moments and manage to success. Below are some process and technique concepts:

Process structure: The individuals participating in the process have the right to know what to expect:

•   **General Structure:** Distribute a general process outline with the projected activities and exercises. This can be done ahead of the first meeting or at the kick-off. Either way, you should review it at the initial meeting along with the outcomes you expect from each session and an explanation of why the process is structured in this way.

- **Agendas:** Each session should have an agenda and stated outcomes.

The Parking Lot: This is a simple and effective technique to keep people on task. A large sheet of paper is taped to the wall with the words "Parking Lot" at the top:

- **Errant thoughts:** The Parking Lot can be used to capture ideas, thoughts, and concerns that, while valuable, are not pertinent at the moment. The human brain fires electrical impulses based on many different types of stimuli. In the middle of a conversation, an idea or a concept may trigger a line of thought in an unexpected direction. It may be important and urgent but not where we are right now. Write it on the wall.
- **Personal Concerns:** A common and consistent behavior in team settings is the quick-jump to solving an individual concern such as a project problem or a product issue. These may be of great importance and necessary to resolve. However, if it is only one of many items under our planning umbrella, using excess time on it can rob the overall planning process of effectiveness. Additionally, while it may be critically interesting to one or two individuals, others are likely to embark on a more interesting daydream if the discussion stretches out too long.

The Parking Lot is a way to give peoples' ideas the respect they deserve while at the same time bringing the individual back into the mainstream of the conversation. By placing the thought in the Parking Lot, we commit to follow-up and dealing with it. It allows them to get the idea off their chest. They know it will be handled. It flips the switch. People will focus on an idea like a shiny toy unless you find a way draw it out and put it in a place everyone can see it. Their idea or concept retains its inherent power but its ability to distract is diminished. Team brainpower returns to the task at hand.

Action Items: Every time a meeting is held, there will be things that require later action. At a minimum, each of these should be noted and marked. It is simple. Using a pen of contrasting color, write the letters "AI" next to the Action Item and circle it. Assign accountability for follow-up and make sure it is in the meeting documentation. Then, make sure it happens! Significant credibility and trust can be gained or lost on the follow through from the Action Items and the Parking Lot items.

Do not be anal: As much as you would like it to be so, people's brains do not necessarily work in the same order as our framework. That does not mean you will not use the conceptual framework, it simply means you may not follow the order in which it is laid it out. That is okay. People may jump away from discussion of the organizational identity and talk about the current state. As long as we are covering the required topics, it is usually fine. As people jump around, capture the information. If they are heading down an inappropriate path or one which will be better served later, you may need to herd them back using the Parking Lot or Action Item notations. Usually, however, you will find it is not wasted time. Rather, it shortens later exercises. Finally: Listen, listen, and listen. If people are irresistibly drawn to talk about a certain topic it nearly always indicates an item that needs attention.

It is a conversation: People are not very good at brain-dumps. If you ask someone to tell us everything they know, you will get a blank look. People are, however, very good at conversations. Ideas, concepts, and concerns develop as other ideas provide the tweaks, reminders, and launching points. Let the conversation flow and repeat. We do not put all of our wisdom in one place or one statement; it comes out over time and discussion.

No bright line: The concepts of Identity, Definition of Success, and Future State are closely related and there is no bright line to divide them. As participants articulate their thoughts in these areas, you will see the same concepts surface from slightly different angles. Part of the function of the framework is to cover the same ground multiple times. The topics and discussions are evolutionary, one leading into the other. They are not clearly demarcated with start and stop points. Each exercise builds on previous exercises and can potentially wander into the subjects of future exercises. In this framework, the repetition is by design with the deliberate purpose of fostering a conversation.

Teasing it out: The facilitator should be able to provide independent insight and observations. As the sessions progress, patterns will emerge and fall into logical groupings. Separate issues may appear which point to a common root cause. Part of the value of the facilitator is the ability to draw several threads together into a unified concept. The future state may be articulated in fifteen statements from the team. The facilitator will work to find the common themes and avenues of progress. This skill may involve upward or downward extrapolation. You may be required to construct a common theme from multiple detailed comments or desires. You may be required to articulate multiple initiatives or details necessary to support a high-level capability of the future. If you are trying to identify the major organizational competencies and capabilities of the future state and the team persists in giving you detailed specific examples, do not beat them over the head to comply with your directions. Get over it and use what they give you. Consolidate the details into a higher level picture. To be successful, you will need to play the hand you are dealt.

Do not make them sew the suit: One of the tricks of consultants and facilitators is to make the team participants draft and author the actual plan. Teams can spend day after day working through document construction and playing the role of wordsmith. This is almost always a waste of the time and talent of the team. Participants should provide knowledge, vision, and support. They should not be required to be writers as well. The person facilitating the exercises can and should document the results of the meetings. They should also write the draft plans. It is much more effective for team members to edit a coherent document than it is for them to create it from whole cloth. The process of crafting a document in a committee environment is like asking ten people to paint a master-quality portrait. They will get in one another's way, get irritated, and the resulting product will probably resemble a patchwork quilt more than a coherent plan. Prepare the draft document for them and let them edit it. It will save time and the overall plan will have more unity and focus than a committee-authored product. The author of the first draft will require a thick skin but it is a better use of time and much more effective.

Decisions by reduction: Reaching a conclusion and making a decision about any given point of discussion can be circular and frustrating in a group setting. There are two major types of decisions you will encounter:

1. **The No-Brainer:** This one is easy for the group although they are not always right. The team is in agreement without much effort. They are comfortable making a decision and supporting it. In this situation, the job of the facilitator can be either much easier or much harder than if the team was in open disagreement. Listen carefully when a no-brainer shows up:

    a. **The good no-brainer:** The decision is logically solid and the consensus appears to be real. Score! Repeat it back to the group, document it, and move on.
    b. **The bad no-brainer:** Consensus is based on something else. Possibly there is fear of disagreement. Perhaps no one has thought it through. The no-brainer may have grown out of inertia or fear of change. Going with the flow of the team while thinking about the lunch menu is a great cause of bad no-brainers. When a bad no-brainer surfaces, the facilitator has the obligation to run it to the ground. Dialogue should be initiated to clarify why the decision or assumption has been made. If there is a gap in the reasoning, it should be held up to the light. It is not the facilitator's job to resolve the decision so much as it is to illuminate it, manage the team to a conscious understanding a decision has been made, and clarify the underlying reasoning. The facilitator's obligation is not to prevent bad decisions. It is to prevent decisions made without awareness. Informed decision-making is the goal.

2. **The Debate:** This happens when there is disagreement within the team. You will be well served to have a decision-making tool ready to go when you embark on a planning exercise. There are many decision-making methods available. It is advisable at the first session, to get agreement on how decisions will be made and if there are any rules for managing disagreement and conflict resolution. Concepts for decision-making:

- State the problem clearly.
    - Important note: Avoid the words "it" and "that" when working to gain a common understanding of an issue or problem. Both are pronouns and are used to substitute for a specific thing. Because of the way they are used, they are subject to interpretation both by speakers and listeners. As dialogue proceeds and the distance from the original problem description increases, clarity around the items referred to by "it" and "that" becomes fuzzier. Pause the conversation periodically and verify the meaning of any pronouns used. When a conclusion is reached, recap the common agreement and avoid their use completely if possible. The final wording may be a bit awkward but that is a reasonable trade-off for positive understanding.
- Agree on the factors to be used for the decision
- Eliminate unacceptable options
- State available options
- Understand the depth of feeling and disagreement around various options
- Utilize the Parking Lot to deflect red-herrings
- Agree on an approach to sunk cost arguments; get sunk cost off the table
- Clarify if trump-cards exist, either organizationally (the boss) or otherwise (i.e. physical or technical constraints)

In any case, the outcome should be documented. At a minimum, a brief discussion should review the ramifications of decisions made by the team and those who will be impacted should be made aware.

Keep it Moving: (agendas, exercises, follow-up, etc.): Be prepared to conduct sessions that are snappy and interesting. Have your agendas and exercises ready to go. Start and end on time. If you commit to an action, get it done.

Behavior: Come to agreement with the team on behavior expectations. Determine what norms the team can expect in terms of participation and interaction. Examples:

- Active participation
- Arrive on time
- Listening to one another
- Texting and emailing
- Interruptions

Ready to Go

Once you are prepared to live up to your end of the bargain, it is time to get the team around a table and have at it.

Top of Mind: The Rocks Below the Surface

Carrots, Lima Beans, and Flipping Switches for Focus

PARENTS KNOW GOOD nutrition is a requirement for healthy children. They also know kids often do not want to eat food that is good for them. Savvy parents and experts in childhood nutrition know how to deal with this. You cannot force your children to eat properly. You can, however, make sure healthy food is in front of them every day. Good food is on the table at dinner, in the fridge, and in the fruit bowl on the counter. Parents can also model good eating habits. The kids observe and, over the course of time, they understand. Make the right stuff available, encourage, educate.

What, you may ask, does that have to do with organizational planning and execution? Do not worry, I am about to tell you.

Planning exercises and the discipline associated with a successful execution effort are much like eating spinach or lima beans as a little kid. It is good for you but you really do not want to do it. In order to make the effort as palatable as possible, you should go out of your way to use techniques and mechanisms designed to encourage success. You must put the hay down where the goats can get it and sometimes help them focus on what is in front of their faces.

Modeling

As discussed previously, visible and consistent executive support is the foremost item that will focus team members on an organizational effort. People are very good at figuring out what the boss thinks is important. There is a common saying in life insurance companies:

No underwriting manager ever got fired for high mortality.
Lots of underwriting managers got fired for high holdover.

The boss is required to explain high holdover and slow service every Monday in the Service Committee Meeting. Very few people die within a couple of years after a life insurance policy is issued. The boss is concerned about Monday, not what happens 24 months from now. Result: get the policies out the door.

Just like the five-year-old at the dinner table, the team will observe the behavior of the boss. If he is in Hawaii during the planning sessions or allows the sessions to be consistently rescheduled to accommodate vacations, conferences, and speaking engagements of the team, the message is clear. However, if he is on time and mentally present in the room, the message is also clear. If he participates and demands rigor, the team will come together like a well-knit sweater. If it is important to the boss it will be important to the team.

We have just flipped switch number one: Clarity on organizational conviction.

The Top of Mind Exercise

Once we have engaged the team by clarifying the importance of the planning process to the boss and the organization, we need to flip the switch of personal focus killers. In other words, we have acquired an understanding of what is important to the boss; we now need to find out what is important to the team. The Top of Mind exercise is designed to do that.

Usually the Top of Mind exercise is used at the very beginning of the planning sessions. A good time is right after the agenda has been reviewed and everyone is clear on the location of the washrooms. By that time they know when lunch will be and what time they can expect to finish for the day.

There are several ways to approach Top of Mind. Regardless of the way it is achieved, however, the goal as we start the process is for everyone to put on the table whatever they are dwelling upon or concerned about.

1. **Explain it:** Tell them what the Top of Mind exercise is and why we do it:
    a. **What:** We want to know what is sitting at the top of their consciousness as they come in the door:
        - What they want to come out of the process
        - What concerns they have
        - What risks they see
        - What they are irritated about
        - Anything preventing them from supporting the effort
        - What they want included in the process
        - Anything else they are thinking about and want to tell us
    b. **Why:** There is an important reason for conducting the Top of Mind. Let them know:
        - We do not want a nagging concern or question festering in the back of someone's mind and preventing them from focusing and actively participating.
        - We want to cover all that needs to be covered. If the things team members are worried about do not fit obviously into a scripted part of the process, we want them called out so we do not miss them.
    c. **How:** Record all the Top of Mind items and revisit them throughout the sessions to be sure they are covered.
        - Tape a poster-sized piece of paper to the wall and write "Top of Mind" at the top.
        - Record every item mentioned.
        - Check-off each item as it is handled.
        - Create action items for those items not covered by the end of the planning sessions.

A Commitment to Answer

A successful Top of Mind exercise will settle down the team. It relaxes them because the tension caused by having nagging silent concerns has been mitigated. The needs and concerns of the participants are brought out in the open and light focused on them. It is similar to the Parking Lot in its psychological effect.

Remember, just because an item appears on the Top of Mind list or on the Parking Lot does not mean it has the support of the team or will be approved for action. The magic of both of these tools is the commitment the items will not be ignored. The answer may not be "yes' but we *will* get an answer.

Another Reason for Top of Mind

The Top of Mind exercise is important for another reason. In most cases you will capture the majority of items important to the team during the hour spent on the Top of Mind. Most of the things you will hear during the course of the entire planning process will surface in an abbreviated form during the Top of Mind. This is the reason good consultants will tell you an honest and fast discussion is more effective than weeks of planning sessions. The truth is this: at any given moment, you could take a well-informed and tuned-in manager into a room with a white board for a couple of hours and get nearly everything you need to make the tactical and strategic plan for that organization. Unless the executive has been spending his time in Hawaii or pontificating at conferences, or hobnobbing on charity boards, they will have a pretty good handle on what needs to happen.

The Top of Mind exercise gets at gut feelings and understandings. It is an unvarnished statement of what the team thinks without the padding of crafted words. It is valuable.

Foundation 1: Identity

How Pacific Iron and Metal became Pacific Fabrics and Crafts – A Story

SOCRATES TOLD HIS students, "Know thyself." Knowing who you are, what you do, and what you stand for creates the foundation of everything else. This is as true for organizations as it is for individuals.

Do not, however, be anal. Your identity is not carved in stone. It can change over time. Many successful organizations are not in the same business they were a generation or two ago. Pacific Iron & Metal was founded in Seattle in 1917 as a reprocessing business. Every day, Jules Glant collected scrap metal, rags, glass, and paper for processing and resale. The rags were cleaned and restored to usable condition and the housewives of Seattle found an economical source of material for sewing. Over the years, the rag business grew and evolved. Today, Pacific Fabrics & Crafts has six stores in the Puget Sound area and a healthy web business. Identity is important; you need to understand who you are. It is not, however, immutable.

A Word on the Process

The following process is provided in (sometimes excruciating) detail to give you a framework for developing and documenting your organizational identity. You can use all of it, part of it, or none of it. The desired outcome is a strong and clearly articulated identity for your enterprise. It must provide a fundamental grounding for your organization. How you achieve this is not as important as that you do achieve it.

Identity Defined

The first thing you must do in order to succeed is understand your identity as an organization. What is it you do and why do you do it? What is important to you? What ethics do you embrace and enforce?

The identity of the organization may or may not define why the organization exists. It may or may not align with the Definition of Success of the organization. It will give you and your team boundaries around the things you do and clarity about kinds of activities you will engage in.

Some organizations have a close alignment of their reason for existence and their identity. They can measure achievement of their Definition of Success with the achievement of the goals tied to their identity. This is seen in nonprofit and cooperative enterprises. Homeless services organizations define their success in terms of successfully provided housing. Credit unions define their success in terms of value provided to their members. Identity and success walk hand-in-glove.

Some organizations do not align their identity with their Definition of Success. In these situations, the identity of the organization defines a set of characteristics that is organized to achieve success unrelated to the form of the entity. This is seen in stock companies and other organizations whose primary success is built around monetary value. The value can take the form of equity or cash distributions. Identity, in this case, is a tool to achieve success.

Typically there are three corporate statements that define organizational identity:

1. Mission Statement
2. Vision Statement
3. Philosophy Statement

Sadly, many organizations with these statements have little idea who they are. Upon examination it becomes clear the statements were drafted by committees without a clear understanding of the organizational purpose. There are, however, two tests for effectiveness of your stated identity as a corporate tool (rather than a logo or a sound-bite):

1. Ask a stranger who has never heard of your organization to read
    your identity statements and tell you about your organization. If
    they can accurately describe what you do and what is important to
    you, you can be pretty comfortable you have managed to articu-
    late your identity.
2. Without warning, ask the executive staff to describe the identity
    of their organization. If they can do it quickly and with reasonable
    consistency, there is a good chance the organization knows who it
    is. The majority of executive teams cannot do this. If the primary
    team responsible for managing an organization cannot articulate
    its identity, there is little chance the rest of the organization can.

Identity should be simple and memorable. It does not need to be memorized. The essence of it should be easily remembered and internalized. It
does not need to be weighted down with philosophical baggage beyond that
which will help make decisions and determine courses of action. It should
reflect the desires of the owners or the group to which the organization is
obligated: stockholders, family, members, or the Board of Directors. If an
identity statement contains words regarding development of employees or
the experience of being an employee, it is probably off target.

Hand your identity statement to a twelve year old. If he or she can tell
you what you are about, you are on the right track.

Why it is Important

In my work with leadership teams, I tell them this: If we can get nothing else accomplished, there are two things we must do. There are two
things crucial to your ability to deliberately manage to success and which
absolutely must be supplied by the leadership team. If we have these, we
can stumble through the rest of the nuts and bolts. Without these, it is impossible to succeed except through blind luck. These two things are our
Identity and our Definition of Success.

Since our Identity defines who we are and what we do, it provides the
basis for all of our actions and decisions. It lets us know if we are actually
in the business named on our business cards or if that is just a vehicle to

succeed in our real business. It tells us where we should focus our energies and how far we are willing to push ethical boundaries.

Beyond giving us the fundamental shape around which we can build our business, our identity provides a valuable tool for management and control. The identity of an organization can drive and guide behavior. Decisions are made daily throughout any enterprise. In dynamic and robust organizations, decision-making is distributed and the overwhelming majority of decisions will not be referred to the executive level. An understanding of what the organization is about and what it is attempting to achieve provides context and direction for decisions. An understanding of the ethical standards of the organization provides boundaries of acceptable behavior. It is much less likely questionable ethical practices will develop if the fundamental tenets of our identity place bad behavior outside the boundaries of acceptability. It also provides an unquestioned reason for action if unacceptable behavior occurs.

Clarity on identity, however, can be a subtle thing. Here are some examples of tricky identity questions. Each one comes from a real-life situation and the choice made fundamentally altered the shape of the organization or industry:

- **Restaurants**: Are we a maker of food or a feeder of people?
- **Insurance:** Are we an insurance company or a technology company that happens to provide insurance?
- **Newspapers:** Are we in the newspaper business or the information business?
- **Railroads:** Is our business railroading or transportation?

Note: Successful organizations have a strong corporate identity. That does not, however, mean it must be written down or articulated to the company. Tightly held companies can get away with a corporate identity in an individual's head. Be clear: the identity is there; it is just not widely shared. There are lots of inherent risks and inefficiencies with this model but it can work. Just do not let the person with the picture in their head step in front of a speeding bus.

Outcome

At the end of a discussion of organizational identity, you should have in hand an articulated definition of what your organization is about, what you do, and what is important to you. Key characteristics of an effective Identity Statement:

1. Definition of the business you are in
2. Identification of your customers
3. Description of your primary product, service, or deliverable
4. Definition of the philosophical and ethical approach
5. High-level future state from a market perspective
6. Detailed and specific enough to provide for creation of plans and effective decisions
7. Clarity and accessibility that make it usable across the organization
8. Actions and behaviors clearly support and can be traced to elements of the identity
9. Generates actions, initiatives, and behaviors which define the organization
10. Agreement and support from team members.

Method

Articulating an organizational identity can be as easy as falling off a log or as hard as the most difficult thing you will ever do. An identity statement is the least scientific and most artistic piece of the organizational foundation. It is the result of a creative process rather than a mechanical process. It is the driver of everything else. At its core it is the most dependent on arbitrary decisions and least subject to logical arguments. It can be difficult to put into words. This part of the process will require the active use of the facilitator's ability to synthesize, interpret, and extrapolate. In other words, the facilitator is likely to be required to listen to what everyone says, stir it in a pot, and create a cohesive statement from disparate thoughts.

When it is easy: Identity is easy in an organization with a strong sense of self and a firmly established culture which mirrors and supports its identity. If organizational leaders are doing their jobs properly, a brief discussion will reveal a deeply embedded identity which can be articulated and discussed easily by the management team. There will be little need for facilitator tricks or exercises to draw it out. An identity discussion with a leadership team of this kind reveals an underlying set of shared assumptions and agreements. The conversation moves quickly past the identity itself to organizational behaviors and activities that support or contradict the identity.

In the case of these organizations, the strength of the identity can be tested by using the characteristics listed above. Examples of corporate choices which are dependent on the organizational identity should be identified and posed to the team. If crisp decisions and determinations can be made based on the identity, you are in good shape.

When it is not easy: More often than not, settling on a solid identity will be difficult. In these circumstances, the team must find a way to clearly articulate and document the organizational identity. There are two situations in which you will often encounter this:

- The leadership of the organization understands their identity but has not been able to communicate it to others: *". . . well, I may not be able to say it, but I know what it is."*
- The leadership of an organization thinks is has a defined identity but it does not; and
- The leadership recognizes it does not have a good definition of its identity.

In each of the above, the process for coming to resolution follows a similar path.

Finding an identity – step-by-step

Just like eating an elephant, the key to extracting ideas from peoples' brains and constructing a usable identity, is to take one bite at a time. Below are a series of steps useful in this effort. Some steps refer to tools or forms. These are provided at the end of the section.

Step 1. Overcoming Denial

This step is necessary only if the organizational identity is not effective and the leadership team is not able to perceive the need for additional work. Depending on how firmly the team believes they have a lock on an identity will determine the difficulty of the task. The three keys to solving this issue are:

1. **Desire to improve:** Just as the primary factor in physical healing is the desire to get better, the most important condition for organizational improvement is a desire to make it happen. In order for this desire to produce results, the leadership team must have the willingness to listen, leave their zone of comfort, and explore ways to improve. If there is not a willingness to do what is necessary, it is unlikely a robust identity can be created.

2. **Permission:** At the beginning of the planning process, the facilitator should ask for permission to initiate and deal with subjects as necessary. The leadership team can reserve the right to terminate conversations if necessary. But if a course of action or decision is grounded in reasoning that cannot be discussed, there should be a commitment to vouch for that reasoning. The leadership team has every right not to discuss their reasons if it is not appropriate to speak of them. However, if blind trust is required they are accountable for the business validity of the decisions as well as the need to maintain silence. It is important the leadership team understands their responsibility in the matter of acting behind closed doors.

3. **Check it out:** Ask each participant to write down an identity statement for the organization. Allow about ten minutes and ask them to work individually. Have them each write it on a large piece of paper. Have each person present their statement to the team and tape it on the wall. Compare them for consistency. Are they easily reconciled? Remember: the object of this exercise is not to embarrass anyone. If you perceive intimidation or fear, collect the statements and combine them anonymously.

4. **Test:** Utilizing the characteristics of an effective Identity Statement pose questions to determine how solid the articulated

identity of the organization actually is. At the end of this section is the *Organizational Identity Effectiveness Test.*

As you work through the above, it will become evident if the organizational identity in its current form is sufficient as a basis for planning and execution. Sufficiency, however, is a judgment call made by the leadership team with the advice of the facilitator. If there is a need to re-craft or clarify the organizational identity, move on to Step 2.

Step 2. Identity Brainstorm

Brainstorming is simple and effective. This is a modified brainstorming session. It brings out the thoughts of the team members and gets them on the wall. Additionally, by observing the behavior of the participants, it provides insight to the level of comfort of each person in speaking to the room as well as the reality of a shared corporate vision.

1. Post on the wall:
    a. What is our identity?
    b. What business are we in?
    c. Who are our customers?
    d. What are our primary products, services or deliverables?
    e. What are our key philosophies and ethics?
2. Explain brainstorming protocol:
    a. No comments
    b. Record everything
3. Spend 15 minutes storming thoughts – write everything down
4. Allow 2-3 minutes of silent review or take a short break
5. Take any final thoughts (5 minutes)
6. End of Identity Brainstorm

Step 3. Process Decision

Now that we have a good idea who our team thinks we are, we need to make a decision on how we will finalize our actual identity statement. There are a couple of options on how to move forward:

1. **Executive Decision:** The senior executive or executives can provide the organization with an articulated identity to be used from

that point forward. In this situation, the Identity Effectiveness Test should be used to flesh out the identity and make sure it has the necessary rigor to be useful. It is perfectly acceptable for owners or executives to dictate the identity. With the occasional exception of cooperative corporations, this is not a democracy.

2. **Identity Construction:** Participants, acting as a team, can articulate the organizational identity. In this situation, the team uses their knowledge of the corporate identity and behaviors to create a foundational statement. The below steps may be used to build this statement. There are two things important to note if you continue down the path of identity construction:

   • The senior executives or owners can, at any time, dictate the results of any step or the final statement.

   • The exercises in this process are intended to reveal the essence of the identity rather than to actually craft the words and phrases. Creating a cohesive statement will be the assignment of an individual or small team as an off-line activity. Editing the statement will be the responsibility of the team.

If the path of identity construction is selected, the below steps will help to bring the concepts together.

Step 4. Identity Breakout Session

In the Identity Brainstorm, we gained insight into the perspective of our teammates regarding the question of whom and what we are. Now we will take the time to create a basic identity statement. For this exercise the participants should split into breakout groups. The groups should be no smaller than two and no larger than five. Each group will need writing materials, markers, and poster sized sheets of paper.

1. **Basic Information:** Provide each group with a copy of the *Identity Effectiveness Test* and the *Identity Worksheet*. Examples of these tools are included at the end of this section. If possible, have any standard and available information previously filled in. The pre-entered information might include the organization mission statement and vision statement. If not previously filled in, this information should be easily accessible for team review.

2. **Instructions**: Tell the groups they have thirty minutes to work. Their assignment is to create two things:
    *   A completed *Identity Worksheet*. They will be working from their own knowledge and opinions.
    *   A bulleted list of descriptive statements which tells us the identity of our organization. Breakout groups should use the *Identity Effectiveness Test* to be sure the necessary elements are included.
3. **Review:** Each group will report back to the rest of the team how the identity statement they have produced would work as a foundation for planning and effective decisions.

Step 5. Initial Consolidation and Ordering

This step provides for a quick and dirty look at what the team came up with. As with much of the development of organizational identity, it is more art than science. Look for patterns and points of emphasis. Allow no more than 35 minutes for this discussion. The below general steps can help provide a framework for the discussion:

1. Post the results of the breakout groups on the wall adjacent to one another.
2. Use colored pens or other indicators to find and join the common threads.
3. Optional dot exercise (emphasis, not voting):
    a. Provide each participant with ten green sticky dots and ten red sticky dots
    b. Have them place them on the various identity threads to show how important they are to the organization:
        i.   Green indicates it is part of the identity
        ii. Red indicates it should not be included in the identity
        iii. Up to three dots may be used on any single item to show importance
4. Ask if anyone is willing to take a shot a recapping the overall identity of the organization based on the information the team has provided so far.
5. If no one is willing to create an overall statement, the facilitator

can do so if he or she feels they can combine the threads of the discussion effectively.

Step 6. Consolidation

With the information gathered to this point, you should have enough material to create an identity statement. The task of synthesizing the input should be assigned to an individual or small team. The consolidated statement is not required to conform to any particular format. Rather it should be in a form the team will find comfortable to use during the remainder of the planning process. If there is no preferred method, breaking identity into standard identity elements works perfectly well:

- Mission
- Vision
- Philosophy
- Values
- Ethics

Step 7. Review and Edit

Once drafted, the team should review the statements and make changes as necessary. When complete, however, consolidated identity should fill the requirements of the *Identity Effectiveness Test.*

Agovia Consulting

Identity Effectiveness Test

In order for the identity statements of your organization to be effective, it must have certain characteristics and provide foundational information. Ask the below questions to test the strength of your identity:

1. Does it define the business effectively and clearly enough that it can be understood by employees, customers, and the market?
2. Does it provide enough information for you to identify your customers?
3. Does it provide enough information for you to understand your primary product, service, or deliverable?

4. Does it define your business philosophy and ethical standards?
5. Does it provide a high-level goal from a market perspective?
6. Is it detailed and specific enough to provide for creation of plans and effective decision making?
7. Is it clearly understood and used across the organization?
8. Is behavior based on identity? Can the actions and behaviors of the organization and the people within the organization be directly tied to elements of the identity?
9. Does the identity drive behavior? Is the identity used to generate actions, initiatives, and behaviors which define the organization?
10. Is the identity understood and visibly supported by the management team?

Agovia Consulting

Identity Worksheet

Date: _____

Organization Name: _____

Mission Statement: State your official organizational Mission Statement	
Mission: If the above cannot be given to a stranger and the stranger understand your primary business or mission, state, in a nutshell, the mission of your organization	
Anti-Mission: What do you not do? What things are off the table? This should include items that logically might be considered part of what you do but are deemed outside your identity.	
Vision Statement: State your official organizational Vision Statement? If the Vision Statement does not make it clear, what is the state your organization is trying to achieve?	
Values Statement: What are your key values and ethics, either officially stated as an organizational Values Statement or tacitly known? If tacit, please explain how it is communicated to the organization.	
Philosophy Statement: What is your philosophy, if known? This can be either officially stated as an organizational Philosophy Statement or tacitly known. If tacit, please explain how it is communicated to the organization.	
Elevator Description: What is your very brief description of your organization?	
To whom is your primary legal allegiance? Are you a stock company? A cooperative? A Privately held organization? A non-profit? State your ownership, and primary organizational obligations	
How would your respectful competitors describe you?	
How would your disrespectful competitors and enemies describe you?	
Describe your organization's regulatory obligation. Be specific if you are in an industry that is highly regulated and it impacts your identity or major organizational obligations (i.e. banking, insurance, airplane manufacturing, etc.)	

Agovia Consulting

Organization Bulleted Identity

Mission: What do we do?

-
-
-
-
-

Vision: Where are we going? *(Market or customer perspective)*

-
-
-
-
-

Philosophy: How do we choose to do business?

-
-
-
-
-

Ethics & Values: What is important to us? *(Moral, human, and integrity perspective)*

-
-
-
-
-

Foundation 2: Definition of Success

How will we know when to declare Victory?

AT SOME POINT, we need a clear and measurable definition of what it means to be successful. We all understand success in business is not the same thing as success in a war or graduating at the top of our class. Success in business is not a static goal which, once achieved is over. Organizations must be successful on a regular and repeating basis.

Definition of Success defined

The Definition of Success is the basic organizational result desired by the owners or, in the case of non-profits, by the organizational by-laws. This means the Definition of Success may or may not align with what the organization does. Organizations geared to produce value tend to have a Definition of Success grounded in value. These enterprises utilize their identity as a tool to produce value. Organizations geared to service tend to have a Definition of Success built on the ability to deliver that service. These enterprises use creation of financial value or margin as a tool to fund the delivery of service. For either type of organization, the Definition of Success provides an achievement objective for organizational planning. As with our identity statement, it gives us facts and criteria for making decisions about how and where we focus our energies and where we invest our resources.

Our identity tells us who we are and what we do. Our Definition of Success tells what the organization needs to achieve. As with organizational identity, it must have enough importance to the enterprise as well as clarity of definition to drive action and progress. To be effective a Definition of Success should:

- Define a result or outcome (as opposed to an activity or quality)
- Be measurable
- Reflect the requirements of the organization's owners
- If achieved:
  - Ensure the ongoing viability of the organization; or
  - Bring to a conclusion the need for the organization

The balancing act: goals, objectives, and success

Most organizations are run as ongoing concerns. This simply means there is an underlying assumption the business will stay in business and continue operating for the foreseeable future if it is successful. As a result of the need to continue as an ongoing and self-sustaining enterprise, the Definition of Success must be a renewable and continuing state of existence rather than a static goal or objective.

The ongoing nature of the Definition of Success can be a challenge for some organizations due to the human tendency to focus on a point of destination and put effort into reaching that destination. Think of it as publishing a book versus publishing a magazine. When bringing a book to market, the focus of the team is publication day and the run of sales for a period after publication. Success is tied to a point-in-time event. The success of a magazine is tied to the ability to repeatedly and predictably publish a periodical with a stable or growing circulation above a defined threshold. For a monthly publication, success must be repeated twelve times a year, year after year. By the time a monthly magazine hits the newsstands, the focus of the publisher has long since shifted to the issue planned six months from today.

The long term success of an organization depends on the capability of the management team in balancing specific goals and objectives with ongoing and repeated growth and results. Quarterly or annual goals and projects must be designed to fit into an overall pattern of success that moves the enterprise forward. Ongoing success requires before a specific achievement is made, the groundwork for the next one has begun. Organizational focus on a single achievement without a sequel queued up behind it leads to a loss of inertia and energy when the team relaxes and basks in the glow of triumph. Specific goals and objectives are stepping stones on the path rather than success in and of themselves. Celebrate them in context of the bigger picture.

Why a Definition of Success is Important

A solid Definition of Success provides clarity of purpose to the entire organization. It settles cultural and behavioral ambiguity. This would seem obvious but, much to the consternation of executives, there is frequently confusion about the reason we are in business – often among the executives themselves. As an example, if all the members of the team understand that, although we are fine craft brewing company, we are in business to increase the value of the our company as an asset of the owners, we gain a much better ability to align what we do with the outcomes the organization requires. If the dedication is to fine ales and beers as an end rather than a means to an end, behaviors and decisions will shift to that outcome rather than the organizational requirements for success.

Clarity in this area is important at all levels of the enterprise, not just the macro-level. The purpose of the Human Resources Department is not to develop people. The job of Human Resources is to facilitate and maintain the provisioning of a work force to adequately operate the business. The purpose of the Security Department is not to protect data or secure the premises. The job of the Security Department is to provide you with the necessary support to do business securely. Note the focus on business in the key phrases:

- . . .work force to adequately operate the *business*
- . . . do *business* securely

A good Definition of Success allows all of the contributors to the success of the enterprise to differentiate between the business we are in and why we are in business. Along with identity clarity it provides the two fundamental elements for decision-making and prioritization.

Killing the Goose – A Cautionary Tale

Be careful, however. Too much focus on the organizational Definition of Success can have the unintended consequence of killing the goose that lays the golden eggs. It is almost irresistible for executives, especially executives whose compensation is tied to financial results, to cut corners in a way that impacts the ability of the enterprise to achieve the very results they need. We have all seen examples of this.

Grocery giant Kroger has an eye for successful regional grocery chains which they buy and continue to operate under the original brand names. Stores purchased through this selection process have usually achieved success by carving a niche which differentiates them from their competitors. The differentiation usually turns on product or service, as the low price market space is saturated in most locations. However, the temptation of short-term gain from leveraging their massive buying and distribution systems soon eclipses the potential of owning a market segment. Stores that have drawn customers with their high quality fruits, vegetables, and meats find themselves unloading boxes of goods randomly chosen to fill an order sheet by warehouse workers at the Kroger Distribution Center. Kroger brand canned goods fill the shelves. Interestingly, in locations where Kroger purchases chains with overlapping territory, multiple stores in the same neighborhood can have exactly the same goods. Sometimes the same products will have significantly different prices due to holdover pricing model prior to the Kroger acquisition. Shopping around town begins to feel a little like going to a theme park. The same souvenirs line the shelves from the entrance to the far end of the park.

Remember: Achieving your organizational Definition of Success is driven by successful execution of your core business. If your core business is the creation of excellent cookies and you are well established with a loyal customer base, you better continue to execute with excellence and not take that business for granted. At some point the temptation to replace butter with margarine may seem like a good idea. After that, butter-flavored shortening might not seem too big a hit to quality. Regular shortening; why not? Lard might be okay. . . You get the idea.

Outcome

The outcome of this section of the framework should be a robust Definition of Success. As shown above, it should have the following characteristics:

- A clearly stated organization-based outcome
- Measurability
- Reflect the requirements of the organization's owners
- Incremental and long-term success definitions
- Sufficient specificity to allow the creation of plans and confident decisions
- If achieved:
  - Ensure the ongoing viability of the organization; or
  - Bring to a conclusion the need for the organization

Method

The methodology of the Definition of Success is the least describable in terms of repeatable process. This is because the Definition of Success is unique to each organization and can be created at the whim of an owner or by organizational charter. It can be as mundane and predictable as an ongoing return on investment of ten percent or as unfathomable as can be imagined. The Definition of Success originates in the head of a single person, a small group, or an organizational charter. A team of managers attempting to create a success definition therefore is problematic. The trait all acceptable definitions of success share, however, whether for a single department or a Fortune 500 company is connection to the organization as a whole. The Definition of Success is always driven from the organizational-level needs.

For planning purposes, the Definition of Success should be provided to the management team by an individual, such as an owner, or a body with authority over the entire organization such as the Board of Directors. Because of the potential for great diversity in a Definition of Success from organization to organization, there is no process universally applicable to its creation. There is, however, advice which can be profitably used when attempting to discover and articulate the Definition of Success in terms clear enough to create plans for achievement.

Getting to Definition

It is likely you will find yourself in one of two situations. Either the organizational powers-that-be provide you with a Definition of Success or they do not. How is that for simplicity? Within this, the scenarios you probably will encounter are shown below:

Scenario 1: Success definition provided – robust and detailed

If a Definition of Success is provided with enough detail to create and execute planning for achievement, excellent! You are done with this section and can move on.

Scenario 2: Success definition provided – generalized

Consider yourself fortunate if you are part of an organization with a clear Definition of Success. The owners, Board of Directors, or charter has provided the management team with an organizational focus for results. If this is the case, however, there is a good chance the requested results will be general in nature. Although you are a big step beyond the absence of a Definition of Success, there is still work to be done.

In this situation, it is in the best interest of the organization and the career paths of the management team to put flesh to the bones of the success definition. If the specifics of the required results are not at usable level of detail, the team should develop them and get them approved. This is important! If there is a common understanding of what you are expected to achieve, the conversation about whether you achieved it or not becomes much simpler. A lack of positive agreement around goals and results leads to various interpretations of the expected outcomes. This in turn can lead to unpleasant conversations at your end-of-year review. Remember: agreement on expectations is good for everyone. If you are creating plans for organizational success, you know what you must achieve. If you are managing others who are expected to achieve results, you have the ability to hold them accountable.

What should you do to get clarity? Below is a three-step model:

1. **Verify big picture:** Validate with the appropriate entities your understanding of the high-level requirements for success. Restate the overall Definition of Success. Obtain agreement from the owners or the Board or the executive team you have an accurate understanding of the requirements for your organization to be considered successful.

2. **Clarify:** Using your knowledge of the organization, create a rigorous Definition of Success with the elements we have previously listed. They are shown again below:
   - A clearly stated organization-focused outcome
   - Measurability:
     ○ How much?
     ○ How fast
     ○ How often
     ○ Agreed-upon metrics
   - Incremental and long-term success definitions
   - Sufficient specificity to allow the creation of plans and confident decisions
   - If achieved:
         ○ Ensure the ongoing viability of the organization; or
         ○ Bring to a conclusion the need for the organization

3. **Verify specifics:** Return to the organizational entity previously consulted; the group with the authority to approve a specific and detailed Definition of Success. Validate your understanding. Verify the success factors and speed of achievement you have proposed are acceptable. Get agreement they will be accepted as success for the organization and as well as success in terms of your performance and your career.

Scenario 3: Success definition has not been provided

Sadly, the lack of a Definition of Success happens fairly frequently. The situation and resolution share many of the characteristics of Scenario

2 but has a significant additional wrinkle. Unfortunate managers who find themselves in this situation are confronted with a need, not simply to clarify the elements of organizational success, but to read the minds of the Board of Directors or owners and, with that insight, manufacture the fundamental Definition of Success. As above, the management team is behooved to articulate a Definition of Success, quantify it, and get it approved. If you cannot agree on the reason you are in business and what you are expected to achieve, it is hard to have a rational discussion about whether you were successful or not. It is also a recipe for career disaster.

How do we do this? The process in this scenario is identical to Scenario 2 with one preceding step. The four steps to resolve this scenario are:

1. **Create:** This is a moment in your career when the art of management and insight into human psychology will trump repeatable technical process. Based on the type of organization and the personalities of the senior decision-makers, you will propose an organizational Definition of Success. Keep it as simple and high-level as possible. If the enterprise has a small ownership group, the success criteria may be cash spun off and asset value of the organization. If it is a publicly traded company, stock value and profitability may be the best Definition of Success. If the organization is a nonprofit, fulfillment of the mission may be the required outcome. Create and propose an organizational Definition of Success if the overarching leadership of the organization does not provide it.

2. **Verify:** Validate your high-level outline for the overall Definition of Success. Obtain agreement from the owners or the board or the executive team approving your understanding of what it means for your organization to be successful.

4. **Clarify:** Create a rigorous Definition of Success with the elements we have previously listed. They are shown again below:
    - A clearly stated organization-focused outcome
    - Measurability:
        - How much
            - What return on investment?
            - What valuation?
            - What number of dinner program clients served?

- ○ How fast?
  - ▪ How long do we have to achieve this?
- ○ How often
  - ▪ Annual growth?
  - ▪ Quarterly dividends?
- ○ Agreed-upon metrics
  - ▪ What measurement factors?
  - ▪ Accepted indicators of success?
- Incremental and long-term success definitions
- Sufficient specificity to allow the creation of plans and confident decisions
- If achieved:
  - ○ Ensure the ongoing viability of the organization; or
  - ○ Bring to a conclusion the need for the organization

3. **Verify:** Return to the organizational entity with the authority to approve your Definition of Success. Present your detailed and specific Definition of Success for validation. Verify the achievement of the success factors at the level and speed you have proposed will be accepted as success for the organization.

Got it! What now?

We now have our Definition of Success and our identity. That means we know who we are and where we are going. We have two of our essential points. We will need a third to triangulate and make a plan. Now it is time to find out where we are starting from.

Foundation 3: Current State

Where are we starting from?

IF WE HAVE done our work properly, we now have a pretty good idea of who we are and where we are going. There is one more piece of the puzzle we must discover in order to create a plan and manage to success. The remaining piece sounds simple to do and can prove to be dauntingly difficult. We must gain an understanding of the point from which we are starting the journey. If you plan to ride a bicycle across the United States, you need to know is where you will start from and the place you are aiming for. If you want to end up in Jamestown, Virginia, the journey is quite different if you start in Seattle, Portland, or Los Angeles. Your current state defines the amount and type of change you will need to undertake in order to reach your goal.

Current State defined

The current state of an organization cannot be understood by a simple review of our current financials and current operational results. Understanding the current state involves an awareness of a combination of elements about our capabilities, business success, trends over the recent past, and the things we know about our environment and what the future holds. Our ability to articulate and comprehend our true current state also requires us to have the ability to interpret the meaning of what we are seeing and imagine what it might mean to our future. The current state is viewed holistically in the context of the entire organization. Gaining an understanding the current state requires you have been paying attention to your business and using adequate management controls and reporting tools. Finally, in order to be usable, the team must be willing to be honest about what they are seeing.

Another Cautionary Tale

There once was a management team which was highly averse to admitting failures or discussing lack of performance. They were a prime example of executives who talked about performance culture and consistently failed to hold themselves accountable to any vestige of results or performance. This led to a repeated pattern of dodged accountability when bold plans failed to produce the hoped-for goals. About nine months into any given year, the goals posted on the walls and in company publications would mysteriously disappear. The subject was avoided in executive discussions. The inability to face the reality of their performance broadened into a general behavior pattern. They became more and more comfortable parsing words and concepts when talking to employees and the Board of Directors. It was common practice for the executive team to ignore their inability to reach sales goals, control excessive expense levels, stem the tide of the departing customers, and reverse declining revenue levels. Instead they consistently nattered about the strength of the company: the strongest it had ever been in the history of the company. This one statistic, their favorite, was indeed true. However, they were loath to remind people of the reason it was true. In this particular industry, strength is measured by a ratio of reserves to current business. An anomaly of the industry is this: as a company shrinks, strength improves. The reserves were built under a previous income stream. Paradoxically, as the business dwindled it became stronger. In this way they could become stronger and stronger as their business moved down a path toward failure.

The inability of this team to honestly look at their current state created a model in which they took refuge behind an anomaly. In fact, it was a dangerous fiction that allowed them to put off serious planning until the company was teetering on the edge of a cliff. Their staff and competitors certainly knew the true story. Market share continued to erode and erratic expense control efforts resulted in whiplash layoffs combined with increasingly risky corporate behavior. The team lost credibility with the staff and the competition. Competitors took advantage of the dilatory management. If the organization manages to survive, it will be at the cost of multiple missed opportunities an a host unnecessarily ruined lives. Lesson: Be honest with yourself about your current state and take your obligations seriously.

What you need to know to understand current state

Every system comprised of human beings is unique in terms of the things you need to know to understand it. The below discussion provides general guidance which can be used for most organizations. It is not, however, exhaustive and you will need to adapt it to fit the needs of your team and company.

The current state of an organization exists in two dimensions: competence areas and status. In any enterprise there are competency areas you must be able to execute with positive results. Within each of these areas it is important to gain an understanding of the status or state.

Competence Areas: Examples of competence areas include but may not be limited to:

- Business and Financials
- Service
- Regulatory and Legal
- Operations
- Projects and Portfolio
- Information Management
- Market/Marketing
- Product
- Organizational Management

Status: Example of measures that can provide insight into the state of our competence areas include:

- Snapshot:

- ○ Performance
- ○ Results
- ○ Skills
- ○ Capabilities
- ○ Current execution efficiency and quality
- • Committed plans and investments
- • Trends
- • Projections
- • Things we know that can impact the future such as:
  - ○ Expected retirements
  - ○ Competitors' expected behavior
  - ○ Supply chain fluctuations
  - ○ Pending legislation
  - ○ Guidelines and constraints
  - ○ Injunctions and consent agreements
  - ○ Board of Directors requirements
  - ○ Other pertinent information you know by paying attention

Why understanding the current state is important

An honest understanding of our current state and the context in which we operate is essential if we are to create and execute a plan to reach our desired future state. It gives us the knowledge to determine if the changes we are undertaking are big or small. Do we have the reserve cash and personnel bandwidth to make it happen? Are we already running lean and will need to create capacity or are we overstaffed and have excess capacity we can focus on bridging the gap? Are we tweaking or transforming?

Knowledge of the current state is required to create estimates and make informed decisions about how we will approach the work before us. Without this knowledge we are guessing or blindly groping forward.

Outcome

When we have gathered the pertinent information into a current state analysis, we should have a solid picture of the enterprise as it exists today.

There is no prescribed form the analysis must take. It should be holistic and provide an understandable baseline of the organization's current state of existence.

Method

There is some good news as you begin to think about putting together a reasonable current state analysis:

First, most good managers, especially in operational areas, already have most of the information you need. The truth is, it is almost impossible to effectively run an organization without it. If you look in the right places you will probably find most of what is needed. Second, the techniques used to collect the information are well defined and can be put into use quickly. They are repeatable and in most cases familiar to experienced managers.

There are two primary ways to capture the Current State, one objective and one subjective.

Objective Current State

Gather Data: The best method to capture a reasonably objective snapshot of your Current State is to use the information you already have. In each of the competence areas of interest, collect the known data about performance. A series of questions in the form of a data collection template provides structure for the functional leads to focus their information. A Current State Data Gathering Template can be created using the structure shown below and the tables at the end of this chapter. As always, the questions shown for use in the templates are not meant to be exhaustive. They require tailoring to the unique needs of your organization.

A cautionary note: When requesting current state information, remind all the participants about the desired outcome of the exercise. We are trying to get a handle on the state of our organization as it exists today. Hair splitting, debates about the meaning of industry-specific words, and partial truths are not acceptable behaviors. Information technology professionals must understand that questions about performance are not simply about mainframe MIPS and response-time. The team should be held accountable to cooperatively build a coherent picture and see beyond the horizon of their functional expertise.

List and Summarize: Once the basic information has been collected, the functional leads should compile the data to make it usable. A simple summary list works nicely for this. Whatever method is used, however, should be consistent across the various areas. It is important from this point forward that we do not waste time asking participants to relearn the presentation format of each unit. Consistency of format allows for rapid understanding by the rest of the team. A simple tool when summarizing is a four-column breakdown:

- **Column One – General Area**:
  - This is the high-level subject area.
  - It is possible for an entry in this column to be repeated. This is due to the need to use multiple characteristics required to describe the area.
  - Examples:
    - Revenue
    - Net Income
    - Business Volume
- **Column Two – Specific Characteristic:**
  - This column tells us the metric you are using to describe the general area current state
  - Examples:
    - Five year revenue trend
    - Units sold
    - Market penetration
    - Market growth
- **Column Three – Result:**
  - This is the column in which the performance metric you have described is shown.
- **Column Four – Action Rating:**
  - This column is used to indicate the need for action in this area.

- Rating = 1: In good shape; no action needed
- Rating = 2: Questionable; keep under observation
- Rating = 3: Unacceptable; action needed

Once the summarization of the data is complete, you will have the current state of the organization from the point of view of the functional leaders. You will know where we stand today and what the leaders feel needs to be done based on their understanding of the business today.

Subjective Current State

It is possible to get a less scientific but more often accurate look at the current state by asking for the participants' opinions. People are influenced by many subjective factors. They can be jealous and vindictive or overly optimistic and unwilling to face reality. We are creatures of emotion and are apt to display all the weaknesses and quirks of being human at any given moment. For all that, each of us still possesses the best computing mechanism and differential analysis engine on the planet. We walk around with an exquisite data management and computing tool resting between our ears. Miraculously, we all received one of these amazing tools free, simply by being born. A super-computer such as Watson from IBM can beat a human being at simple games. However, it requires thousands of people to spend tens of thousands of hours to get it to the point it can compete in a few very narrow categories. The human contestants who gave it a run for its money acquired their ability to compete by hanging around and paying attention. Humans can do amazing things with their brains when they decide to use them!

Getting information to assemble a subjective current state is a matter of fostering a conversation. If a way can be found to engage the brain-power around the table, the results can be startling in both quality and originality. There are many ways to do this. The key to effectively harnessing the creative energy of the room while simultaneously reducing emotional barriers is to divide and conquer. We must find methods to focus team and personal thought on problem solving rather than on themselves. One effective method is the use of a SWOT exercise.

SWOT

The Strengths Weaknesses Opportunities Threats Exercise (SWOT) is simple and effective. It engages the participants in a conversation about four characteristics of the organization:

1. **Strengths:** These are the things we are good at. The things we do well and are proud of. Strengths are usually internal; they come from within. They may be important or not. Although strength is usually considered a good thing, this is not always true. A strength area may be good for us or it may be detrimental. If we are really good at something that does not make a contribution to our success, that strength may actually be diverting resources and energy from other, more important things.

   - **Example:** If we have been successful at creating a recognizable brand which has strong people-appeal and gives us positive regional perception, we can say we have strength in that area. However, if that branding has not improved our market penetration or fostered a call to action among potential customers, we have developed strength in an irrelevant area. If the branding has not served its core purpose, it is a misdirection of corporate resource. Watch out for strengths not connected to the Definition of Success. They may more properly belong in the Weakness or Opportunities sections.

2. **Weaknesses:** These are the things we are not good at. They are the things that challenge us. Weaknesses are usually internal; they are about us. Similar to strengths but in the opposite direction, weaknesses are considered undesirable more often than not. In most cases, if an item shows up on the weakness list, it is not a good thing. People tend to self-edit weaknesses to a greater extent than strengths. If a weakness is mentioned by the team, it is probably related to something you need to do well in order to be successful. Weaknesses also tend to be high on the list of things people think about; it is human nature. Because of that, however, the weakness listing will often be the longest. That is okay – do not worry about it.

3. **Opportunities:** These are potential gains we see when we look around us. They tend to be external in nature although most teams automatically filter external situations for opportunities which can be exploited with an organizational strength. When looking for opportunities, remember improvement of an internal weakness can also allow you to take advantage of an external situation. Purely internal opportunities can also be found. The most common example of internal opportunity is seen in efficiency and expense management.

   • **Rule of thumb:** If you have not examined your operational efficiency and expense control in five years, there is probably 20% available for the taking.

4. **Threats:** These are almost always external although they tend to take advantage of your internal weaknesses. Examples of threats include:

   • Competition
   • Economic swings
   • Regulatory changes
   • Innovations such as:
     ○ Music industry and MP3 compression
     ○ Family automobile market and minivans
     ○ Data storage: Tape, disk, zip, flash
   • Changes in industry models
     ○ Newspaper classified advertising revenue vs. craigslist
     ○ Railroads vs. Interstate Highway System and cheap gasoline
     ○ Travel agents vs. web travel sites

A SWOT exercise is simple. Break your team into groups. Try to have no more than six in a group. Each group should have poster paper and markers. Have them divide a sheet of paper into four sections as shown below:

SWOT Diagram

Ask each group to brainstorm for a fixed period of time and list items in each of the four categories. The time allocated is up to you and the team but each section will not require a long period of time to adequately capture the information. It can, in fact, be counter-productive to allow too much time. Once the initial surge of thoughts is recorded, the productivity of the group will decrease and is likely to begin focusing on less important items or issues relevant to the individuals rather than the organization. You also stand the chance of losing the focus of the group members if they become bored. Each group should report once the entire team is reassembled.

The Time-to-Focus Relationship: There is an inverse relationship between the amount of time available for an activity and the amount of focus and energy it will receive. Tight deadlines encourage intense focus.

SWOT Consolidation

As an offline activity, the facilitator should consolidate the information gathered in the SWOT exercise. The consolidation is merely the grouping of like items to create a picture of the team's perception of the characteristics of the organization. A simple way to do this is with the use of a spreadsheet program. A spreadsheet allows the rapid rearrangement of individual items into groups. Mind mapping software applications can also work well.

It may take a few attempts to get a good consolidation. The best way to start is by eyeballing the lists for repeated items which may indicate areas of focus. Create a few preliminary headings and start moving boxes around. As you rearrange them, similar items will tend to fall together in natural groupings and those left behind will be easier to analyze. Remember, weaknesses and threats may contain overlapping items. Similarly, opportunities may be potential actions based on strengths or weaknesses. If there is an obvious connection, the groupings should be placed near one another.

SWOT Potential Action Items

Once the SWOT data has been consolidated, the team should be given a chance to identify action items and areas of potential change. If the participants are honest as they create the SWOT, it should generate items in need of action and attention. These items should be rated with the same scale used in the objective current state exercise:

- Rating = 1: In good shape or no action needed
- Rating = 2: Questionable; keep under observation
- Rating = 3: Unacceptable and action needed

The items with the rating of "3" will be candidates for action and resource investment in the plan we create to achieve our successful future state.

Current State Complete

If we have done our job well, we now have a reasonable current state picture of our organization. We should be in a position to articulate where we are starting from. Before we move on, however, the team should take a little time to review the data gathered and validate the accuracy of the picture presented. If there is information missing, this is the moment for people to speak up. Otherwise, we can now move on to our next major task: creating a picture of our future state.

Current State Template Examples

The below template examples can be used for the development of information gathering tools tailored to your organization. They are provided as a starting point for creation of your own templates and are unlikely to fill your need if used as is. Let them tweak your creativity but if you invest the time to produce your own tool you will get a better result.

	Business Current State	
	General Area	**Specific Characteristic**
1	Revenue	Primary source of revenue, income, or funding
2	Revenue	Revenue this year (estimated)
3	Revenue	Revenue last year
4	Revenue	Change in Revenue
5	Net Income	Net income this year (estimated)
6	Net Income	Net income last year
7	Net Income	Change in Net Income
8	Key specific ratios:	Expense ratio
9	Key specific ratios:	Cost of goods sold
10	Key specific ratios:	Other
11	Volume of business transactions this year (est):	Sales
12	Volume of business transactions this year (est):	Units Sold
13	Volume of business transactions this year (est):	Other
14	Volume of business transactions last year	Sales
15	Volume of business transactions last year	Units Sold
16	Volume of business transactions last year	Other

General Area	Specific Characteristic
Key service metrics: What are the key things you measure to determine if you are providing acceptable service?	Service Metric #1
Key service metrics: What are the key things you measure to determine if you are providing acceptable service?	Service Metric #2
Key service metrics: What are the key things you measure to determine if you are providing acceptable service?	Service Metric #3
Service objectives and results: Based on the above, what are your objectives and actual results? If trending information is available, attach charts showing results over time.	Objectives Results Comparison
Gap metrics: What gaps in the objectives vs. results are of concern and must be addressed in the coming year?	Key gap metrics
Root Causes	
Customer satisfaction	Customer Service Satisfaction
Tools used to measure service success What are the mechanisms used to understand the success or failure of service provisioning. Are they consistent with the customer perception and do they represent that perception?	Connection to customer perception and satisfaction
Complaint numbers and trends What types and how many complaints have we received in the past 24 months? Is there a pattern? Is it increasing or decreasing? Have we applied problem or incident management techniques to the complaints and crafted resolutions?	Specific Complaint Metrics
Service victories – last 24 months	
Service failures – last 24 months	
Efficiency and effectiveness: What are the efficiency indicators of the servicing areas? What is the range of service effectiveness of service representatives?	Efficiency Indicator #1
Efficiency and effectiveness: What are the efficiency indicators of the servicing areas? What is the range of service effectiveness of service representatives?	Efficiency Indicator #2
Efficiency and effectiveness: What are the efficiency indicators of the servicing areas? What is the range of service effectiveness of service representatives?	Efficiency Indicator #3

	Regulatory Current State	
	General Area	*Specific Characteristic*
1	Regulatory obligations currently requiring action	
2	Projected changes in regulatory or legal requirements	
3	Anticipated governmental, regulator, or governing body audits, examinations, or reviews.	
4	Regulatory preparatory action required	
5	Anticipated regulatory changes requiring action	
6	Proposed regulatory action requiring input, lobbying, and comment.	
7	Complaints filed with regulatory, or industry monitoring groups:	Numbers
8	Complaints filed with regulatory, or industry monitoring groups:	Trends
9	Complaints filed with regulatory, or industry monitoring groups:	Outcomes
10	Complaints filed with regulatory, or industry monitoring groups:	Indicators of required change?

	General Area	Specific Characteristic
	Operations Current State	
1	Operational results: What are our goals and how do our actual results compare to our goals	
2	Size and complexity:	What is the total size of our operational organization and by unit?
3	Growth:	How much (in terms of both head-count and complexity) has the organization grown in the past 24 months?
4	Supervisory ratios:	What is supervisor to employee ratio both overall and by unit?
5	Process:	Discuss the current state of documentation, repeatable processes, and training.
6	Operational Expense	What is our operational expense?
7	Operational Expense	How does that compare to benchmarked organizations?
8	Expense Breakdown:	What is the breakdown of operational expense by primary units?
9	What are our operational triumphs in the past 24 months?	
10	What are our operational failures in the past 24 months?	
11	Known issues:	List all known issues and challenges in the operational units
12	Primary root causes: Discuss the primary root causes of operational challenges. Possibilities: Management skill, Span of Control, IT problems, Complex product base, other	
13	Other: Discuss any other issues pertinent to the performance and needs of the Operations area.	

Market Current State		
	General Area	*Specific Characteristic*
1	Describe your marketing philosophy and effort currently expended	
2	Market segment, differentiation, niche, etc.	Describe the market segment you serve and how you differentiate your business to be successful in that market. Who are your primary customers and are they the same as the primary source of your income?
3	Outcome of Marketing objectives associated with branding;	Specific desired outcome
4	Describe the objectives of your marketing efforts designed to drive sales	Specific desired outcome
5	Describe the objectives of your marketing efforts - Other	Specific desired outcome
6	Marketing results metrics: How marketing success is measured and is it currently meeting results expectations? If not, what is the gap?	Results and Gap
7	Current known plans	What plans are currently known for future marketing efforts?
8	Long Term Market Goals	
9	Is there an ongoing marketing plan coordinated with long term business plans? If so, what is that plan and what support will be required from other parts of the organization?	Describe:
10	What are the major victories of the Marketing efforts in the past 24 months? Especially as related to measurable business success.	
11	What are the major failures of the Marketing efforts in the past 24 months? Especially as related to measurable business success	

Product Current State		
	General Area	**Specific Characteristic**
1	Product Mix:	How does current product mix meet the needs of customers
2	Success of current product mix - why and why not	Market Share / Penetration / Win-Loss positioning
3	Risks: Regulatory changes:	
4	Risks: Obsolescence	
5	Risks: Manufacturer discontinuance	
6	Risks: Component Costs / Supply chain	
7	Risks: Customer base	
8	Risks: Other	
9	Product Portfolio:	
10	Holes in your current product portfolio?	
11	Do your products meet the standards of:	Acquisition
12	Do your products meet the standards of:	Retention
13	Do your products meet the standards of:	Repeat Business
14	What plans are currently known for future product changes?	
15	Business plan support required	
16	Product mix support the future needs of your business?	Increased penetration
17	Product mix support the future needs of your business?	Customer affinity / need / desire
18	Product mix support the future needs of your business?	Long term relationships
19	Product mix support the future needs of your business?	Other

Information Technology Current State		
	General Area	**Specific Characteristic**
1	Is your technology support provided by an in-house team or through a 3rd party provider or a combination of both?	
2	What are the services you currently use and rate the adequacy of the service	Internet support / Desktop & mobile / Network / Telecom & VOIP / Mainframe / Data / etc. support
3	What are the services you currently use and rate the adequacy of the service	Other
4	Cost or expense ratio associated with information technology	Value received for dollar spent and comparison to industry benchmarks
5	Satisfaction with current technology model	Rate your satisfaction. (If switching costs were zero, would you keep the current provisioning model?)
6	Technology support areas currently in need of improvement or upgrade	Administration systems / Web presence / Productivity tools / Hardware / Data integrity /
7	Technology support areas currently in need of improvement or upgrade	Other
8	Business functions or business success dependent on changes in IT provisioning	
9	Business advantage currently provided by Information Technology	
10	Major IT failures in the past 24 months	
11	Major IT successes in the past 24 months	
12	What portion of your business is critically tied to working IT support?	
13	Security	Adequacy / Enabler of business / Robust advisory capabilities
14	Current State: business continuity, disaster recovery, and backup/recovery state.	

	Organizational Management Current State	
	General Area	**Specific Characteristic**
1	Known Management Challenges: Are there changes required or action that must be taken at the organizational management level that is currently known?	Changes in management personnel
2	Known Management Challenges: Are there changes required or action that must be taken at the organizational management level that is currently known?	Management or control failures
3	Known Management Challenges: Are there changes required or action that must be taken at the organizational management level that is currently known?	Other
4	Operational changes	
5	Changes to the operations model in the recent past that require changes to the management structure or model.	Increased use of 3rd party vendors for support or business processing
6	Changes to the operations model in the recent past that require changes to the management structure or model.	New and different products
7	Changes to the operations model in the recent past that require changes to the management structure or model.	IT systems changes
8	Changes to the operations model in the recent past that require changes to the management structure or model.	Other
9	Management event horizon: management changes planned or anticipated:	Retirements
10	Management event horizon: management changes planned or anticipated:	Decentralization of workforce
11	Management event horizon: management changes planned or anticipated:	Acquisition of business
12	Management event horizon: management changes planned or anticipated:	Other
13	Succession planning and management continuity plans	What is the state of management succession and continuity planning?

Projects Current State

	General Area	Specific Characteristic
1	Project #1	
2	Project #2	
3	Project #3	
4	Project #4	
5	Project #5	
6	Project #6	

Guidelines Current State

	General Area List Guidelines, Standards, Constraints	Specific Characteristic Describe Specific Nature of the Item
1	Technical Standards:	ITIL Framework
2	Technical Standards:	Microsoft products
3	Technical Standards:	Other
4	Expense Goals	
5	Product quality standards	
6	Limitations and Constraints	Geographic limitations
7	Limitations and Constraints	Acceptability of using various types of expense control mechanisms (e.g. reductions in force)
8	Limitations and Constraints	Requirement to utilize partners or subsidiaries
9	Limitations and Constraints	Investment limitations.
10	Limitations and Constraints	Other

	General Area *List Guidelines, Standards, Constraints*	Specific Characteristic *Describe Specific Nature of the Item*
	Guidelines Current State	
1	Technical Standards:	ITIL Framework
2	Technical Standards:	Microsoft products
3	Technical Standards:	Other
4	Expense Goals	
5	Product quality standards	
6	Limitations and Constraints	Geographic limitations
7	Limitations and Constraints	Acceptability of using various types of expense control mechanisms (i.e. reductions in force)
8	Limitations and Constraints	Requirement to utilize partners or subsidiaries
9	Limitations and Constraints	Investment limitations.
10	Limitations and Constraints	Other

The Future State

Design, Capabilities, Results, Organization

Future State Design

THE TEAM SHOULD now have a good understanding of three things about their organization:

1. Who they are;
2. Where they are going; and
3. Where they are starting from.

With the above information in hand it is possible to create a picture of what we will look like in the future.

Our framework uses three primary elements to create a picture of our future state:

- General future state description
- Requirements for achievement of our desired future state:
  - Competencies/capabilities
  - Results
- Operational/organizational model

The discussion below deals with each of these items.

General Future State Description

The high-level future state description is simply what it says it is. It is a narrative description of the state of the organization at some point in the future. It should be primarily a description of results, outcomes, and major capabilities. It is based on two of the three foundational elements previously created: Identity and Definition of Success. It should address both of these. The future state description adds substance and form to the meaning of success. The third element necessary for the future state description is a timeframe. By what date does your organization intend to achieve this state?

The creation of the future state description can be accomplished as a team or by breaking into small groups. If breakouts are used, the descriptions devised by the various sub-teams will be merged into a single version. Items to consider when framing your future state are:

- Size
- Volumes:
  - Revenue
  - Transactions
  - Units sold
- Organizational Focus:
  - Product
  - Price
  - Service
  - Relationship
- Geography
- Market
  - Perception
  - Penetration
  - Rank
  - Brand
- Operational model
- Organizational model
- People and human resources model
- Cultural state
- Profitability / Margin
- Valuation
- Strength

- Static vs. transforming
- Stability vs. growth
- Single corporation vs. multiple corporate entities

The future state of some of the above items will be known as the exercise begins. These may be mandates or firmly fixed tribal knowledge. Each team should immediately document these elements. If you are breaking into groups, however, it is preferable not to discuss these items prior to the break-out session. The listing of predetermined elements of your future state is a valuable indication of the underlying assumptions of team members. Frequently, when the given elements of the future state are reviewed, it becomes clear the management team is not operating from the same set of assumptions.

Each breakout team should create a description of the future state of the organization. The description can be in narrative form, a bullet list, or any format the team wishes. The only requirement is the ability to paint a picture of the future state that has enough specificity to be used as a horizon goal for planning. At this point we do not need a specific metric in each area. The description must simply be clear enough to build metrics around it.

Allow the breakout to proceed for a limited period. Again, do not allow too long. A goal of this exercise is to force team focus with the knowledge we will address the concepts several times in the planning process. Half an hour is usually enough.

Once the breakout teams have completed their future state descriptions each group should present their ideas to the full group. Scan and analyze the concepts presented as a whole. If a reasonably congruent picture has emerged, it is time to move on and allow an individual or small team to merge and consolidate the ideas. At this point, the only concepts which should be debated or heavily analyzed are those which clearly stand out from the main body of thought in basic and fundamental ways. Look for conceptual outliers rather than degrees of difference. A mid-market hardware chain entering the big-box market space is a fundamental change that deserves additional vetting. Increasing profits by fifty percent is not a fundamental change.

If a single breakout team returns with the idea for a fundamental change to the organization, discussion is needed at two levels. Vetting will be required in terms of consistency of thought with the consolidated planning team (why did none of the other break-out teams mention it?) and an understanding of the basic changes being proposed. If multiple break-out teams describe a similar future fundamentally different than today, the concept should be discussed to validate there is a basic understanding of the magnitude of change being proposed.

A Note on Underlying Assumptions

At this point in the planning process we are making a fundamental assumption. We have assumed that one of two things is true:

1. The basic identity of the organization will not change; or
2. A new or altered identity has been mandated by the powers-that-be in your organization.

If one of those assumptions is not true, return to the identity exercise and rerun the discussion to create an identity in alignment with the place your organization is now and the place it is going.

Consolidation and Validation

The information gathered in the previous session should now be consolidated by a small team or an individual. This is simply a matter of merging the data into a coherent statement. If the team has agreed on a conceptual picture of the future state, it will be a matter of aligning similar concepts and reducing them to as few elements as possible.

It is likely you will get descriptions of the future that include specific items. Common examples include things like up-to-date systems or facilities upgrades. Make an effort to avoid these types of statements. In general, the future state description should fit into statements that begin, "We will be. . ." or "We will be able to. . ." If a statement begins with, "We will have. . ." it is usually an enabler of the future state rather than an element of the future state itself. As always, however, this rule of thumb is not absolute.   Some enablers are big enough and important enough to qualify as part of the future state picture. It is also likely you will be unable to convince the participants to let go of the idea that some of their cherished enablers are actually fundamental elements of the organizational future state. In that situation, discretion may be the better part of valor. Do not fight useless battles which, even if won, have marginal return. Include the item in your future state and move on. It is more important to have the required items recorded in the plan somewhere rather than wrangle over the proper label.

The standard against which you should measure the future state description is the ability to build a plan to achieve it. This means it is okay if the description of the future does not have specific numeric objectives. The description must, however, have enough specificity to allow measurable objectives to be derived. We do not need to know at this point if we will plan to attain a ten percent year over year growth in sales. We do need to know that year-over-year growth in sales is a required element of our future state. Absolute measurability is desirable at this point but not essential.

Once the team is satisfied with the Future State Description, it should be validated with the appropriate organizational authority. If the planning team has that authority, the task is already complete. In many organizations, the core executive team or the Board of Directors is the correct source of approval. It is important to get the Future State Description validated and accepted at the enterprise level. From this point forward, the planning for organizational objectives, capabilities, and operations, as well as the organizational model will be built to attain the future state. This controls where and how money is spent and resources used. Careers can be impacted if reorganization is necessary in order to best support our future success. If there is not agreement on this, at a minimum it is an invitation to waste energy and time. In more severe situations, lack of clarity on where you are going can lead to turf battles and dysfunctional behavior. Save yourself heartache: get everyone on the same page about where the organization is going.

Future State Breakdown

Once the overall future state has been agreed upon, it is time to break it down to manageable pieces. The breakdown of the future state creates areas of focus each with their own future state. The areas of focus are buckets for components which will combine to form the overall picture. The areas of focus can be results-driven and outward facing, such as market, product, or customer. They can, alternately, be support or inward facing, such as administration, technology, or facilities.

The breakdown will be different depending on the industry, organization type, and culture. The current organizational structure is likely to form the way the future state breakdown is crafted. This is the default path planning teams naturally follow. There is logic and comfort in turning to the current owners of the various departments of the organization. These are leaders who have traditionally accepted responsibility and whose capabilities are known. This is perfectly fine with one caveat: in an upcoming step of the planning process, we will be determining the optimal organizational structure. This may create the need for a change to our current structure.

Areas of Focus: Capability and Competence

In order maximize our chances of achieving the desired future state, all the parts of our organization should contribute. The various components of the enterprise, from accounting to product to information technology provide a piece of the puzzle. This means there will be several areas in which we must focus our energy to attain a future state that will support organizational success.

The overall organizational future state is driven by the results required of the entire enterprise. The future state of each area of focus is more often about development of capabilities to support overall results. Although they should be crafted in terms of outcomes, they are usually supportive in nature rather than ends in themselves. Examples of Areas of Focus include:

- Permanent and Ongoing:
  - Marketing
  - Product
  - Operational efficiency
  - Technology

   ○ Personnel
- Achievement Oriented and Temporary:
  - ○ Territorial expansion
  - ○ Mergers and acquisitions
  - ○ Major systems or supply chain changes (i.e. ERP)

There are a few ways to approach the selection of the areas of focus. The simplest and easiest is an exercise in which a question is posed along the lines of:

In order to achieve our desired future state we must. . .

The team should then develop areas within the organization's inventory of competency which must reach a specific level in order to achieve success. These can then be grouped into buckets which will become the major areas of focus.

Assign, Design, Validate

Assign: Each area of focus should get an owner. The owner is responsible for the development of their focus area.

Design: The owner of each area should be given the opportunity to design the future state of their focus area. There are three primary hallmarks to look for in the focus area future state:

1. **Inventory**: An inventory of the capabilities and competencies that define the desired future state of their focus area. Much of the work for this should be complete, based on the elements created in the exercise that identified the various focus areas. However, a similar question should be asked for each area: *In order to achieve our desired future state we must . . .* The team expectation of the owner is they use their expertise to further define what is needed in their area. The inventory should be qualitative and quantitative to define both what we must be competent at and what level of competency we need to attain.
2. **Priority**: The owner should provide a prioritization of the competencies and capabilities they have proposed. The priority rating

312 IT COMES DOWN TO THIS

should reflect the importance to the future state as well as the culture of your organization but should make clear two things:

    a. Threshold: Is this a threshold item? Is it critical to achieve a certain level of competence in order to succeed? Is it defined as a "no choice" element of our future state?

    b. Advantage: If this is an element of our future state that confers a level of advantage? If so, how much?

3. **Contribution**: What is the line of sight contribution the focus area future state contributes to the organizational future state? Why would we do this and what does it give us?

Validate: The full complement focus areas and future state descriptions should be validated with the appropriate decision-making bodies in your organization. If the appropriate group is the team who developed the enterprise future state description, that is perfectly fine. The objective of this step is not to ask permission like a teenager borrowing the family car. It is to validate the commitment of the organization to the investment and effort required to attain it.

Operational and Organizational Model

If we have done our job right, we have a handle on:

1. Who we are;
2. What it means to be successful;
3. Where we are starting from;
4. What the future looks like; and
5. What we need to be good at to go there.

Now it is time to make preliminary decisions about how we want to operate and what kind of organization we will need to support that operation. We will be looking at our operational and organizational models.

Ops and Org: What is the Difference?

The difference between an operational model and an organizational model can be confusing. Here are some rough and ready definitions to help keep them straight:

- **Operations:** The operational model is how we get things done. If we have decided to hire and manage our own janitorial and facilities maintenance staff, it is an operational decision. If we decide to contract with a vendor for janitorial and facilities services, it is a different operational decision. In this case, from an operational perspective, we choose whether we should develop, own, and manage a competence in a given area. There are many reasons an organization may make one or the other operational decision and there is no right or wrong model. Operational decisions, however, drive organizational decisions.

- **Organization:** The organizational model is the structure and the staff required to support your operational model. In the example above, if the operational decision is to manage your own building services, you will need management expertise and capability around custodial services and facilities management. You will require people who understand building management, janitorial staffing, and engineering. If, on the other hand, the decision is to contract for those services, a different corporate expertise will be needed. You will require people who have skills in contracts, vendor management, negotiation, and delivery control. Organizational structure and requirements are driven by operational decisions.

Ops/Org Decisions and Guidance

At this point in the planning process, decisions are philosophical in nature and intended to provide guidance for planning. Most of the decisions will be around operational parameters as these drive the organizational needs. The decisions should be made with the idea they will give the team the ability to make decisions about the best and most acceptable way to achieve our desired future state. As specific plans are created, these guiding principles will be used. Questions to ask yourself and the team:

- What are the driving factors in making operational decisions? Is there a concept or a driver that trumps other items? If the driving need is operational efficiency and expense control, does that take precedence over customer service or employee-provided services (as opposed to outsourced services)?

- Are there philosophical decisions that have already been made? Has a decision been made to farm out non-core support activities such as information technology support? Do we buy market ready software applications rather build them ourselves?
- What is allowable by the organizational senior management and the organizational culture?
- What are the organizational core competencies? If the organization's business model is build on relationship, it is probably not a good idea to have an outsourced call center as the first point of contact with the customer. Are there market differentiators that depend on specific operational execution?
- Are there operational activities the organization feels are so important they must be done in a certain way? This might include the ownership of certain pieces of technology infrastructure in order to assure control over the quality and delivery.
- Is there an overriding operational philosophy such as: We only do things directly related to our core business – everything else we farm out?

The direction provided by operational decisions at this stage will have impacts at the next stage of planning and in the creation of the organizational structure required by those plans.

What will it take?

Map the Gap, Imperatives, and Initiatives

How Big a Leap is it?

THERE IS GOOD news. The further the team progresses down the planning path, the less complex the process gets. Much of the work from this point forward is nuts-and-bolts estimating and selection combined with project, and portfolio management. The creative work has been mostly completed and now we just need to figure out how to turn the gears to get us from here to there.

There is also bad news. It is still pretty hard; it is just a different kind of hard. We now know where we are going and, at least at a basic level, what we need to be able to do to get there. There will be one or more points in the next few steps when we will be tempted to relax and feel like we have made it. It will feel like it is time to take a deep breath and settle back with a beer. Sadly, this often happens. The "plan" is printed, put in a shiny binder, and slid onto the shelf until next year.

This part of the planning framework is designed to get a handle on what will be required of the organization in order to achieve our future state. To do this we will need to understand three things:

- Current state of the specific capabilities and competencies identified by the owners of the focus areas;
- The gap between where we are and the state defined by the focus area owners; and

- The changes we must make in terms of initiatives, imperatives, and investments.

It is important at this point to instruct the focus area owners to avoid self-editing. Encourage them to create a true picture of what needs to happen, not what they think we are capable of. Try to get them to leave behind comments like: "We really need to do that but we can't afford it." This step is about understanding what it will take to achieve our desired future state. If the ideas are not mentioned, it is extremely difficult to discuss and consider them. Likewise, the team should keep an awareness of the purpose of this step. Free and far-ranging dialogue is a key to success. If the ideas raised are subjected to excessive or derisive criticism, especially from the senior members of the team, it is unlikely the conversation will remain open and productive. Keep reminding them:

> *Say what you need to say. Listen attentively. Debate with passion and respect.*
> *Don't say no to yourself. We'll have plenty of time for that later.*

The Gap

Understanding the gap involves two pieces of information: The current state and the future state specific to the capability at hand. In the previous exercise we defined the future state. We now need to understand the current state (where we are starting from) and something about the nature of the gap between them.

The best and most intuitive way to understand our starting point is simply to think about it and get advice from those who are most familiar with the area. In the future state exercise we asked ourselves this question:

> *In order to achieve our desired future state we must. . .*

We answered the question by creating an inventory of capabilities and competencies. The inventory was both qualitative and quantitative in nature and defined what we need to be good at and what how good we need to be. It is now time to take the same inventory and tease out the next level of information.

The owner of the focus area should get answers to the following questions:

- How close are we to the desired state?
- Is the ability to have this capability a matter of improvement or development of an entirely new competence?
- What is the reason we do not have this capability already? Is this something we have tried before and failed? Is it a performance question? Is it simply something we have never considered in the past? Are we in a position of being required to fix a problem or starting with a green field?
- What would need to change in order to achieve the desired state?
- How big is the change we will need to make?

A Cautionary Note: The focus area owner is unlikely to be able to answer the above questions. He or she will need to get help. However, when the owner is gathering data about our current abilities, the concept of the Fix Threshold should be kept in mind. The Fix Threshold simply states:

- The longer a person or group has been associated with a problem, the less likely they are to be able to fix it. At some threshold point, the odds the current owner can fix it become so small the options for resolution are:
  - Transfer the problem to some other person or group for resolution.
  - Replace the person in charge
  - Forget it; live with the problem

Focus area owners should keep their ears open for indicators the individuals or groups in charge of critical capabilities are approaching the Fix Threshold. There is no single flag to tell you this is happening; you will need to use your intuition and experience to spot it. Common indicators include slow, carefully crafted answers to questions, highly technical analyses (often including bell-curves and statistics), and activity-based explanations. If the answers to your inquiries cannot be phrased in a simple, common-sense, and results-focused way, keep digging.

Assemble the Information

You have now gathered most of the information necessary to make a plan. Each focus area owner should begin assembling their section in a way which will be useful to the team. Documentation from different focus areas should follow a consistent format. This will not always be possible due to the varying nature of the subject matter. However, to the extent this can be done, it facilitates the task of comparing opportunities and making decisions. Using a consistent template, each focus area should document the future state proposals they are recommending. The items required to understand the effort required to achieve the desired future state are listed below. It should be noted that the template we are creating is an initiative proposal document.

Future State Initiative Template

Background:

Focus Area:

Proposed Future State:

Contribution to Organizational Future State:

Priority:

Current State Description:

Required Change:

Magnitude of Required Change:

Additional Information:

Proposed Initiative

Initiative Name:

Initiative Description:

Describe the New Capabilities the Initiative will Deliver:

Describe the Results the Organization will Harvest and When:

Timeframe

Estimated Cost (People, Investment, Other):

Other Information for Consideration

The Gap is Mapped

We have acquired an understanding of the effort and cost required to achieve our desired future state. Sadly, however, simply because we know what it will take to get there does not mean we have the wherewithal to make it happen. We have identified a destination and informed ourselves on a possible route. So far, we have been careful to work in the realm of what needs to happen. Now it is time to bring reality back into our calculations.

The Journey: Making it Happen

Alignment, the Plan, Execution, Governance

Alignment: Are our eyes bigger than our stomach?

UNTIL THIS POINT we have carefully avoided bringing in the reality of what we can afford to do. It was important to do this. By avoiding random self-editing we can now approach crafting a plan that falls within our tolerance for change and investment with all the necessary pieces visible. We can trim, move, and tweak the elements of our future state to align them with our capabilities and resources with confidence we will not accidentally leave a gaping hole in our future.

The first step in creating a plan for a realistic journey is to make sure our desire to achieve our desired future state does not lead us to significantly over estimate what we can pull off. In other words, we need to make sure our eyes are not bigger than our stomachs. No organization has an unlimited amount of surplus money and human resource. We must align our desires and needs with our ability to make it happen.

Keep it Simple

The best way to create a realistic plan is to keep it simple. There are three elements you will need in order to conduct a simple alignment exercise: staging, cost, and confidence.

Staging: This is the order and timing of the things you need to do. What must come before what? What must one thing deliver

322   IT COMES DOWN TO THIS

before another thing can take off? Some questions you should ask yourself:

- What is the timeframe within which all this must be completed?
- How long will the initiative take to complete? What is the duration?
- Which initiative is dependent on which other initiative?
- Does a previous initiative need to produce a capability or an actual result in order to move on to the next thing?
- Can things happen simultaneously?
- Can initiatives overlap or must they happen end to end?
- Which initiatives can float? Which are not dependent on others or others are not dependent on them?
- What organizational preparation or communication must be created and managed?
- What is the lead time for contracts, vendors, hiring, etc?

Cost: This is pretty self-explanatory. What will you need to invest in order to make an initiative happen? Some questions you should ask yourself:

- What is the monthly out of pocket cost of the initiative?
- What is the spend profile? High front-end? Low back-end?
- Is the cost profile flexible?
- How and when will the funding be acquired?
- How many and what types of people will be required?

Confidence: You must estimate the likelihood you can actually do the things you say you can do. Confidence in delivery becomes very important if you have several initiatives or activities dependent on one another. Remember, when you layer activities that are dependent on one another, the decrease in confidence and increase in risk is multiplicative. If you have a 90% confidence in ten dependent tasks, the overall confidence level is 35%. If you have a 90% confidence in twenty dependent tasks, the overall confidence level is about 12%.

- What is the confidence in delivery?
- What is the confidence in achieving the projected result?
- What should be done to increase the confidence or add contingency?

Chart It

Use a simple charting tool to create a timeline for the activities and initiatives forecasted. The timeline should show the major tasks and milestones in a monthly or quarterly format. Each initiative should have data points showing resource utilization in terms of cost and people both for the individual increment (month or quarter) and as a cumulative total. Spreadsheets such as Microsoft Excel work well for capturing the information. Now, just plug and chug.

The focus area owners should provide an estimate by month or quarter for each of their proposed initiatives. If it is possible to break out the investment or personnel requirements to a more granular level, it can be useful. This is especially true for initiatives or projects which utilize specific limited resources. Resource contention is one of the most common risks organizations encounter when managing multiple projects in a coordinated fashion. It happens when several initiatives need the same people or skill sets at the same time. Subject matter experts, technical resources (database analysts, network technicians, programmers, etc.), and decision-capable management personnel are often areas of highest risk. Conflicts in these areas should be planned for and watched closely.

The initiatives are charted according to the best-guess staging and dependency from the initiative owners.

Initiatives and activities closest to the present will have the highest confidence levels. In general, if an initiative has a confidence level below 100%, you should add time and cost in an amount equal to the difference. If a confidence level is 90%, your contingency should be about 10% in both time and cost. If the confidence level is 80%, the contingency should be 20%. If the confidence level is below 80%, you should go back to the drawing board. At less than 80%, you should not be basing your plans on the outcome of that initiative.

Adjust It

We are ready to step back and take a look. By adding up each month, we should have a good rough-and-ready visual representation of the path to our desired future state. At this point, most planning teams take a deep breath and say, "Huh!" Even with the high level estimates (aka: guesses) used to make the timeline, most organizations come to the realization they must adjust their plans. Be clear, however, it is not time to panic or change where we are going. It is simply time to adjust our plans in such a way as to match up our capability and capacity with our desires. It is similar to planning a home remodel. Once we see the estimate we may realize we can have the new hard-wood floors or we can have the new master bath with the Italian tile and the dual shower heads. But we can't have both right now. We don't give up, we adjust.

It is likely you will find sections of the timeline with unacceptable resource or funding requirements. You are also likely to find points where limited personnel and skills are in contention across activities.

Using staging and dependency information, you can start moving the pieces on the chess board. If there is an excessive level of spend within a specific timeframe, you can adjust activities to smooth and extend the required investment. During this exercise you may discover the need to approach your desired future state in an incremental fashion. You may discover the need for additional funding or the need to raise capital.

If the team discovers its desire was greater than its capacity, there are a number of ways to craft an answer. Here are a few:

1. Stretch the timeline
2. Adjust your sights to an achievable outcome
3. Find additional funds
4. Find a new approach

Regardless of the types of adjustment, the team must create an approach that matches the available resources with the required investment. If this is not done, it is unlikely the organization will achieve the hoped-for future state. If, by some chance, the desired future state is achieved, it is likely the road will be unpleasant and full of nasty surprises. If that happens do not expect many thanks for it. It is a near certainty an executive team that takes an organization down a painful and rocky road will not endear itself to the Board of Directors or the remainder of the company, even if the eventual outcome is the hoped for future state. If a rough road is absolutely necessary, so be it. If however, it is in any way avoidable, make the effort to manage and control the journey rather than ride along as a passenger. The increased stability and organizational tolerance for the journey will be well worth the effort. Bottom line: in business planning, surprises are not a good thing.

The Plan

After all this time we have arrived at the moment of "Plan Creation." We have all of the pieces available and it is time to put together a tool to help us manage the journey. There are many ways to make a plan document and it is not within the scope of this book to present a technical how-to about project or portfolio planning. However, there are some concepts you should keep in mind as you create the mechanism that will take you into a successful future.

When Changing for Tomorrow don't Forget about Today

As you prepare to create your forward-moving plan, remember you must pay attention to both the processes of change and the adequacy of operations. All organizations do two things: operate and change. In order to survive, even in the medium term, they must not forget both are necessary. Without the ability to change and grow, organizations stagnate, dwindle, and become irrelevant. Without the ability to operate effectively and efficiently, they will not have the opportunity to change for the future. If they can do neither, they are probably being run by a relative.

When creating your plans for change, keep operations on an equal and parallel footing. Project and portfolio governance should be approached in partnership with current operations. Your organization may be a well-oiled machine. But you will be amazed how fast the gears start to grind and shudder if you take your eye off the ball.

Again: you must manage current operations in tandem with organizational change. There is no tomorrow without a today.

Portfolio

In order to achieve the desired future state, the organization should approach its initiatives and projects as a managed portfolio of investments. An organization is a unified entity that survives and grows based on the coordinated contribution of all of its parts. It puts energy and funding where they will do the most good. You should optimize the use of scarce resources and avoid contention and bickering.

An effective portfolio of change activities is a deliberately crafted and managed tool. The portfolio is made up of the required initiatives, programs, projects and other items in which the organization will invest. The portfolio approach provides a bird's-eye view, not only of the activities of change, but also the logistics necessary to be successful.

The portfolio is like the big floor map you used to see in World War Two movies. The entire Pacific or European theater or whatever was represented on a huge flat surface. The generals and admirals stand around with arms akimbo while a well-groomed lackey pushed models of ships and submarines and army groups around the world. The overarching picture made it easier to coordinate strategies and logistics. If an army was sent in one direction and a naval task force in another, a visual representation of the action made it much less likely resources would get double allocated or supply lines forgotten. Amateur military historians talk about battles. Professionals talk about supply lines and logistics. The portfolio helps you think like a professional planner rather than an amateur. Remember: When projects fail, it is usually not the core concept that killed them. Technology projects seldom fail because of technology. Mergers and acquisitions seldom fail because the original concept was faulty. Failure nearly always happens because of poor management surrounding the MacGuffin at the middle. Bad management kills projects, not bad concepts.

If you effectively use the portfolio as a tool for managing your progress, you can anticipate and assure the proper resources are in the proper place at the proper time and the preparations for organizational changes are started with the correct lead time. A visual portfolio approach makes it easier to see slippages and understand their impact on your business plan.

Portfolio management is the key to moving your organization to your desired future and avoiding unpleasant surprises.

Milestones

At an organizational level, manage to milestones rather than activities. This pushes your team to a place where they talk, report, and take accountability for outcomes rather than actions. Each initiative, program, and project should be built around and discussed in terms of milestones. The milestones should be on the critical path. This means if they move, the timeline of the project is impacted.

> **Red Alert Warning:** Do not allow reporting on activities outside the context of milestones. One of the favorite tactics of project and program managers is the progress report stuffed with activities and actions which may or may not be impactful. Do not accept activity reports. Require impact and outcome driven reporting. Actions and activities may serve to explain the reasons for a timeline change but outside their impact on the timeline they are, at a minimum useless, and can actually cause damage by laying a smoke screen which hides what is really going on. As rude as it may feel, your best weapon in the battle for outcome-based reporting may be the two words: "So what?" If someone reports about programming quality or the number of meetings held to solve a problem, or how late the team worked, look at them and say, "So what?" Eventually your team will learn reports on the types of activities listed above without results or impacts are unacceptable.

Capability, Outcome, and Harvest

Be clear on what you are trying to achieve and who is accountable for achieving it. Most projects are designed to improve a capability or create a new capability for an organization. They are geared to an endpoint of operational hand-off. Only after they have been accepted by the operational departments and are in use will we see if they are achieving the outcome we had intended. Over a period of time the new capability should produce a benefits harvest that will pay back the original investment and improve the organization in general. As you create your plan, remember the original development project is simply the first step and does nothing for you if outcome and harvest are not managed well and produce benefit. The technology group may create a perfectly peachy e-commerce site. If it doesn't create sales due to product, pricing, or marketing issues, you have a boat anchor on your hands. Don't forget:

Capability: The original activity or project that gives us the ability to do something.

Outcome: Once the capability is in production or being used on an operational basis, is it doing what we thought it was supposed to do? Are we getting the results we predicted?

Harvest: Over time, what was our return on the investment we made in acquiring the capability? If we develop the capability to spin awareness in the social media sphere, is it actually producing results? If we create a new pricing model or product, did we actually acquire new customers or increase our retention and penetration? If not, someone must be held accountable.

Line-of-Sight

This is simple. Your projects, programs, and initiatives should have a line-of-sight to your future state and your Definition of Success. All your activities should be conducted in the context of how they contribute to the desired outcome of your organization. Make it your business to hold the focus area initiative owners accountable to a projected level of contribution to the success of the organization. Initiatives and projects are sold and approved on the basis of their anticipated contribution. If your teenager committed to mowing the lawn in exchange for using the car on Friday night, you would require delivery. If the Marketing Vice President asks for $500,000 for an advertising campaign and promises $1,000,000 in sales, you should hold that executive accountable for delivery. Consistent accountability trains your team to be serious about both the ideas they pitch as well as executing to outcomes.

During the execution of initiatives, in addition to milestone reporting, you should receive line of sight reports. This is simply a way to assure that, as we move forward, we are regularly reviewing our actions in terms of where we want to go. If an initiative was expected to deliver a 10% increase in sales, we should know if we are on target, falling below the expectations, or getting better than planned results. Regular monitoring of our line-of-sight projections allows you to make decisions on the ongoing value of various activities. If an investment is underperforming or performing better than expected, it is possible to act appropriately in a relatively short timeframe as opposed to after the fact.

A note on informed decision-making: Line-of-sight is a tool that helps you understand the contribution of your various undertakings. It should be approached as one piece of information. It is always the right of the management team to choose to pursue an activity regardless of its impact on the achievement of the organization's desired future state. However, if that is the choice, it should be made deliberately, not by accident.

Governance and Accountability

The plan has been created. We have put together a reasonable path to a successful future. It feels like we are done. Not to be trite but now the work begins. This is the point where many organizations assemble the documentation, proof-read it, bind it and give it a place of honor on the bookshelf. The "plan" takes its place next to identical binders from previous years; the result of uncounted executive retreats in unnamed, but usually luxurious, resorts. If you are truly interested in achieving a successful future, you need to grab hold of the plan and give it life.

The managing and executing your plan is about two things. They are shown below in order of importance:

1. Discipline and accountability
2. Repeatable and predictable process

In the past few years, there has been a great awakening on the part of the consulting industry about the importance of portfolio management.

This rather belated focus on overriding governance has come about due a couple of factors:

1. An overwhelming percentage of projects in which these consultants have been involved either failed or achieved unsatisfactory results – often after paying a huge tab to those same consultants. There has been a recognition that a scattershot approach to portfolio management is not working.
2. There is money to be made from the uncertainty, fear, and doubt around the complexity of project and program management.

The upshot of this has been the creation of consulting practices built around Project Management Offices and Program Management Offices, generically called "PMOs." The concepts are being presented as esoteric and new. In reality, successful organizations have used the PMO principles from as far back as you can imagine. Companies have always had the need to manage projects and balance priorities with available resources. They have purchased fleets, created new products, and installed new technology systems. The key is to find the right level of portfolio management for your organization.

PMO – The Concept

For those interested, a brief discussion of the PMO is included. This section and the following section titled: *PMO - The Four Challenges* are quoted from: A Project Management Framework for Successful Implementation of Information Technology Projects, Chris Kaufman and Raghu B. Korrapati, Proceedings of the Academy of Information and Management Sciences, Volume 11, Number 1. Used by permission:

> The concept of a distinct organizational entity within an enterprise dedicated to project, program, and portfolio management has gained a vogue and momentum in the past several years. In common parlance, these entities are referred to generically as "PMOs".
>
> Business trends cast shadows in terms of discussion in industry literature. An illustration of this trend is provided by a search for articles generated by the research and consulting firm Gartner for the

past five years. A search of the Gartner research database using the criteria "PMO" reveals

- In 2002: Article count = 1
- In 2006: Article count = 50
- In 2011: Article count = 388

The increasing interest in PMOs is indicative of the value businesses are placing on the management, control, and business results expected from the projects and programs intended to bring about necessary business change. This interest may be driven from the low success rates of information technology projects ($\sim 30 - 35$ %) or from the increasing press and "buzz" associated with the PMO concept.

PMO – The Four Challenges

What is clear, however, is the increasing acceptance of the need for mechanisms to increase the chances of success of IT and enterprise projects and programs as indicated by the willingness to provide funding for such "overhead-heavy" entities. This places PMOs in the "triple threat" position of:

1. High Expectations. It is hoped and expected the PMO will solve the decades-long enduring challenge of high project failure rates;
2. Flavor of the Month: The PMO is the latest "airline magazine buzz" from which consultants can expect to derive significant income, and with which internal enterprise sources have significant experience and which deservedly have achieved a Dilbert-ish aura (i.e. BPR, TQM, ITIL, MBO, Workflow Management, etc.)
3. Enterprise Critical Path: The PMO has been placed in the pivotal role of facilitator of the success of the business.

As with most of the previous programs mentioned above, (BPR, TQM, etc.), the PMO is a strong and valid concept and can provide value to the enterprise if created and managed correctly. Additionally, the success or failure of the PMO (and the changes it is mandated with providing) will be driven and determined by the strength and success of the organizational management of the concept rather than the strength of the concept itself or the internal management of the PMO.

332   IT COMES DOWN TO THIS

In addition to the three challenges shown above, a fourth and over-arching cultural challenge must be acknowledged. Although the PMO as an articulated concept is relatively recent, all of the activities associated with it have been occurring in all companies that incur any level of change (read: all companies). These functions may have been more or less formalized in one or more places, from various committees to the back side of envelopes to a tattered sheet of notebook paper in the CEO's desk drawer. The act of creating a PMO, however, transfers some or all of this control to a bureaucratic entity and inevitably creates (at a minimum) the perception of loss of power. Even if, intellectually, the executives chartering the PMO understand the need and the benefits, the gut-level loss of control can lead to cultural resistance, "under-the-radar" projects and an eroding lack of effectiveness. This cultural reaction must be dealt with by exchanging value and success for the perceived loss or the PMO is at risk.

Governance for Your Organization

The above discussion about the PMO concept is for your information only. Don't get wrapped around your axle trying to create ultimate governance mechanisms for your organization. As we have said before, don't let the perfect be the enemy of the good. There are many ways to establish adequate management for your portfolio. Depending on the complexity of the enterprise and the changes you are contemplating, it can vary from a simple list to a full-blown software application suite. The key is to keep it simple while maintaining the ability to adequately manage. It is likely, regardless of what vendors tell you, you do not need a portfolio management toolkit created for NASA or General Electric. The specific framework best suited to your organization is a function of the culture and capability of your company. There are, however, some universal concepts to remember:

- **Decision and Commitment**: The most important element needed for the successful management of your portfolio is the real decision and commitment to make it happen. This does not mean standing in front of an all-hands meeting or the Board of Directors and telling them you are *COMMITTED TO SUCCESS*. It means active leadership and management; doing what is necessary to achieve success. The essence of commitment is not the moment of decision or announcement; it is the consistent and disciplined action and the impacts that flow from it. If you have made the decision to do what is necessary, there are some behaviors you will need to hold your team accountable for and model yourself. Some of them are listed below:

○ **Accountability**: This number one on the hit parade if you plan to be successful. If you are interested in a performance-driven organization and individuals taking accountability at all levels, you must be accountable yourself and hold your team accountable for both their actions and the results they produce. This means that business projections for increased sales or profits cannot simply disappear during the year. It means that if the organization has expense control problems or is losing money, the executive team should have the common sense not to take bonus payments. It means if an executive is not producing results, there is a consequence. It's pretty basic; think back to what you learned in the second grade.

○ **Public and visible support**: As leaders, you must show you have an interest and investment in the success of your plan. People, in general, are pretty smart. They will figure out very quickly if you don't care about your plans for success and they will behave accordingly. The only way your team and the enterprise know if you care about something is by observing your behavior. If your organization is not succeeding or achieving the plans you approved and you spend a month in Hawaii or on a cruise, the message is pretty clear: you are not that worked up about it.

○ **Transparency**: Sometimes you must keep things behind closed doors. It is simply a fact of life. However, to the extent possible, let the sun shine in. If you are open and honest about your reasoning and how you manage, you will educate and train the people of your organization to the logic and grounding of your management philosophy. Trust is built and, when you must close the curtain, there will be a depth of integrity people can comfortably rely on. There is trust you are doing the right thing, even when you are out of sight. If you parse words, only talk about part of the story, or shut down conversations (i.e. "that's an unsanctioned discussion") you will be suspected of hiding something. And, sadly, history shows that, in most cases, the suspicion is justified.

○ **Participation**: If you are there, be there. If you are on the management team, manage the business, including the project portfolio. Executives who spend most of their time at conventions or board meetings of other companies, or participating in governmental advisory boards, especially if their organizations are not performing adequately, are derelict and are unlikely to succeed. Participate and be proactive.

○ **Play by the rules:** This could also be called "Completeness." Like the others, it is pretty simple but hard to enforce. The value of a managed portfolio of projects goes down rapidly if there is a shadow-portfolio of projects off-book. If the CIO or the marketing executive or other potentate can divert resources to pet projects, not subject to portfolio review, it doesn't take a genius to see what is likely to happen. Suddenly the organization is not acting as a team; rather, it resembles a grouping of fiefdoms, each with its own parochial interests. Instead of synergy, you see under-the-table dysfunction. And just to complicate matters, because individuals are aware they are skirting the rules, they will often make an effort to disguise what they are doing. So. . . not only is it damaging, it is hard to find. It's simple: play by the rules and we will be better off.

○ **Pay Attention:** Keep your eyes and ears open. Listen to conversations. Watch for anomalies. Watch for operational and project-related patterns that might indicate a need to ask questions. Does twenty percent of your sales force make eighty percent of the sales? Check it out. I have worked with executive teams that denied, to a person, they should be aware of a systems problem causing them to spend over 25% of their annual income on mitigation efforts. All the flags were up to indicate problems but not one thought to ask a question about it. They managed to work their way through an entire planning cycle without noticing a pattern of failure right in front of their eyes. They were asleep at the wheel. Wake up! Look around! There is almost always enough chatter and kafuffle on the breeze to give you a heads-up if you are listening.

- **Processes of Governance:** Best advice for the process of portfolio governance: keep it simple. High-level visual timelines and streams of activity are your best tools.

  o **Portfolio Management Applications:** Chances are you do not need a sophisticated portfolio management application. There are many on the market and most of them work pretty well – to a degree. However, when the sales person is in your office showing you the slickest toolset on the planet, keep two thoughts in your mind:

    ▪ **Midway Barkers:** Remember when you were a little kid and went to the state fair? On the midway there were guys selling all kinds of miracle gadgets. I bought a little tin gadget that the barker made sound like forest full of birds. But when I tried it all I heard was air. He wasn't lying, it could work the way he played it. But I didn't have the time or interest to develop the skill. Fifty cents wasted. Some sales people are really good at making sows' ears look like silk purses.

    ▪ **Workflow Systems:** Another blast from the past. In the wake of imaging systems of the eighties, workflow engines were going to be the killer app. Map the process in an IDEF tool and viola! No more nasty paper or lost work. The work practically does itself! Again, at some level it was true. What they didn't tell you was the reality of creating a system version of a complex workflow (humongous) and that work flows and work processes change all the time. Is was painful to get set up and once done, the tools were so inflexible as to make updating them way more work than it was worth. The pending and notification mechanics were overwhelming. When people quit or moved to another department, their work often disappeared into a black hole. The systems quickly became white elephants and, as a defensive measure to preserve the sanity of all involved, they were allowed to fade quietly into the night.

The lesson to learn from all this is: A spreadsheet and a simple visual timeline work pretty well as the basic management tools for most companies' project portfolios.

○ **Regular Review:** This is one of the most obvious and most overlooked. You need to have regular governance meetings and, as a group, review your portfolio for progress and needed adjustments. Use basic concepts in evaluating your project portfolio:

  ▪ **Investment Thinking:** Projects are investments. What is the projected return? As we move forward does it hold true? If an investment is losing value, deal with it. If it looks like it will pay off higher than anticipated, think about investing more.

  ▪ **Line of Sight:** What is the projected impact on our future state? What is the direct connection? How will we harvest the benefit?

  ▪ **Sunk Cost:** With the exception of lessons-learned, it makes no difference how much money or time or human resources we have spent on a project or program if it is no longer the best route to the future. That time is gone and that money is spent. If we see the cost to reach our desired goal by continuing the current path is $1,000 and the cost of killing the current project and starting on a different path is $500. Kill it and start over. It happens. Throwing good money after bad is stupid.

  ▪ **Milestones:** Require milestone and overall reporting. Are we on track? Have we managed to scope? Remember, activity reporting outside the framework of milestones, cost, delivery, and duration, is meaningless.

Conclusion

Keep your portfolio governance simple and pay attention. How's that for a succinct wrap up?

To Sum Up

Made it!

IF YOU MADE it to this point and you have read this entire book, I congratulate you on your perseverance and discipline. I also thank you for sticking with it and for putting up with my idiosyncratic approach to leadership, management, and organizational success. I certainly hope the advice and methods you found here are useful. When you put this book back on the shelf or send it to the thrift store, I hope you will take away some helpful concepts and ideas. If nothing else, try to remember that puffery and technical management theories are not half as important as paying attention, using your common sense, and doing what is necessary.

The Key Concepts

In case you didn't get to read the entire book (and who could blame you?) or you would like to see a recap, below are the key concepts for managing to success.

- **Make the Decision:** The most important factor in success or failure is your decision to succeed. This means you have decided to consistently do what is necessary to assure your success.
- **Do What is Necessary:** The decision to succeed is meaningless without the consistent discipline and action built on the line of sight to where you want to be. Managing for success can make you a good competitor and one of many. Managing *to* success ties all of your energy to becoming successful.

- **The Three Keys:** There are three foundational elements you need to have in order to manage to success:
  - ○ **Identity:** Who are you? What do you do?
  - ○ **Definition of Success:** What is the measurable outcome that, if achieved, qualifies as success?
  - ○ **Current State:** What is the current state of our business? Where are we starting from? Honesty is crucial.
- **Leadership:** You must have the ability to inspire and motivate people to follow you and support you without coercion or bribery.
- **Management:** You must have the ability to implement and run the systems and organizational mechanics that allow a group of people to become a corporate entity.
- **Change and Operations:** These are the two things you need to do. In order to survive, all organizations must have the ability to operate effectively in the present as well as anticipate and make the changes that will allow them to grow into the future.
- **Results:** Successful organizations work to outcomes. You must commit to getting results. Activity without progress, no matter how good it feels, is just churn.

That's it

You are as capable as anyone of crafting success for your organization. The reality about highly paid executives is this: An executive making $25 million a year is no more talented than an executive making 99% less. They are simply members of the same club. They can be as spectacularly wrong or as right as you can. Don't be intimidated by the esoterica of management systems or cliquish overbearing executives. Pay attention, be accountable, do what makes sense and do it well. That's it.

Now, go!

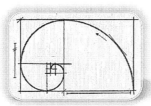

About Agovia

AT AGOVIA CONSULTING we work with leadership teams who have made the decision to do what is necessary to succeed. Our focus is the whole business and the organization rather than any single element. In order to succeed, it is necessary to have results in all the areas of your business, not only your area of core expertise. We help organizations take control and manage their path to the future with common-sense planning and governance mechanisms that work. We help you focus on the three primary leverage points of all successful organizations:

Identity

Definition of Success

Current State

Using the fundamentals of management, planning, execution, and leadership, we work together to design the path to success. We work with you to decide what it will take to succeed *and* how to do it.

Failure in business (whether for-profit or nonprofit) almost always occurs outside the core and essence of the enterprise. Most businesses have a high degree of core competence. They are pretty good at what they do, whether it is making bread, issuing insurance policies, or manufacturing computers. Most failures occur in the management structures surrounding the core business.

Agovia Consulting works primarily with the leadership teams of organizations, from the enterprise-level to the department level. If the leadership team can gather around a table, we can hammer out who we are, where we are going, and how to get there. If you feel caught in the grip of inertia and are having trouble breaking out, we can help you get perspective, establish structure, and get moving again.

A firm decision to succeed is the most important ingredient.Once you have the commitment, together we can find a way to make it happen. Let's talk!

We listen.

We pay attention.

We work with you.

We can help.

www.agovia.com

CPSIA information can be obtained at www.ICGtesting.com
Printed in the USA
BVOW052102181011

273966BV00004B/139/P